P9-DWC-386

FLIRTING
WITH
DISASTER

FLIRTING
WITH
DISASTER

WHY ACCIDENTS ARE
RARELY ACCIDENTAL

MARC GERSTEIN

with MICHAEL ELLSBERG

Foreword and Afterword by DANIEL ELLSBERG

UNION SQUARE PRESS
An imprint of Sterling Publishing Co., Inc.

New York / London
www.sterlingpublishing.com

*For Judi and Jamie—my reasons for
trying to make the world a little safer.*

STERLING and the distinctive Sterling logo are
registered trademarks of Sterling Publishing Co., Inc.

Library of Congress Cataloging-in-Publication Data Available

10   9   8   7   6   5   4   3   2   1

Published by Sterling Publishing Co., Inc.
387 Park Avenue South, New York, NY 10016
© 2008 by Marc Gerstein
Foreword and Afterword © 2008 by Daniel Ellsberg
Distributed in Canada by Sterling Publishing
^{C}/o Canadian Manda Group, 165 Dufferin Street
Toronto, Ontario, Canada M6K 3H6
Distributed in the United Kingdom by GMC Distribution Services
Castle Place, 166 High Street, Lewes, East Sussex, England BN7 1XU
Distributed in Australia by Capricorn Link (Australia) Pty. Ltd.
P.O. Box 704, Windsor, NSW 2756, Australia

Book design and layout: Scott Meola

Manufactured in the United States of America.
All rights reserved.

Sterling ISBN-13: 978-1-4027-5303-9
          ISBN-10: 1-4027-5303-9

For information about custom editions, special sales, premium
and corporate purchases, please contact Sterling Special Sales
Department at 800-805-5489 or specialsales@sterlingpublishing.com.

CONTENTS

FOREWORD

Learning from Past Disasters, Preventing Future Ones

I have participated in several major organizational catastrophes. The most well known of them is the Vietnam War. I was aware on my first visit to Vietnam in 1961 that the situation there—a failing neocolonial regime we had installed as a successor to French rule—was a sure loser in which we should not become further involved. Yet a few years later, I found myself participating as a high-level staffer in a policy process that lied both the public and Congress into a war that, unbeknownst to me at the time, experts inside the government accurately predicted would lead to catastrophe.

The very word *catastrophe*, almost unknown in the dry language of bureaucracy, was uttered directly to the president. Clark Clifford, longtime and highly trusted adviser to U.S. presidents, told President Lyndon Johnson in July 1965: "If we lose fifty thousand men there, it will be catastrophic in this country. Five years, billions of dollars, hundreds of thousands of men—this is not for us. . . ."

But it was for us, casualties included, after Johnson launched an open-ended escalation just three days later. In time, Clifford's estimates were all exceeded: Before our ground war was ended in eight years (not five), the cost in dollars was in hundreds of billions, over five hundred thousand men served in Vietnam in a single year (1968) out of three million altogether, and—uncannily close to his predicted figure—more than fifty-eight thousand soldiers had died. Clifford's prophecy in his face-to-face session with the president at Camp David—"I can't see anything but catastrophe for our nation in this area"—could not have been more urgent in tone or, tragically, more prescient.

And Clifford's was not a lone voice. Johnson's vice president, Hubert H. Humphrey, had used almost the same words with him five months earlier; others, including Johnson's career-long mentor Senator Richard Russell, had also made the same argument. Yet Johnson went ahead regardless.

Why? I have pondered and researched that question for forty years. (The documentation in the Pentagon Papers provides no adequate answer.) But one seemingly plausible and still widely believed answer can be ruled out. The escalation in Vietnam was not the result of a universal failure of foresight among the president's advisers, or to a lack of authoritative, precise, and urgently expressed warnings against his choice of policy.

The nuclear arms race, in which I was intimately involved between 1958 and 1964 as a RAND Corporation analyst serving the executive branch, is a moral catastrophe on a scale without precedent in human history, even though its full tragic potential has not yet occurred. The arms race involved—under both Democratic and Republican administrations, soon joined by the USSR—the mutual construction of a physical and organizational capability for destruction of most of the world's population within a matter of hours. That project—building two matched and opposed "doomsday machines" and keeping them on hair-trigger alert—is the most irresponsible policy in human experience, involving as it does a genuine possibility of creating an irreversible catastrophe for humanity and most other living species on a scale that the world has not seen since the dinosaurs perished sixty million years ago. Even if the system were decommissioned totally—and it is not yet remotely close to being dismantled—such a course of action would not cancel out the fact that over the past sixty years, a moral cataclysm has already occurred, with ominous implications for the future of life on earth.

I have been trying since 1967—when I realized that the Vietnam War must end—to understand how we got into that war, and why it was so hard to end it. Since 1961, even earlier, I have viewed the nuclear arms race as an ongoing catastrophe that has to be reversed, and a situation that has to be understood. I assumed then, and still believe, that understanding the past and present of these realities is essential to changing them. In my life and work, I have tried to do what Dr. Gerstein's book is trying to help us do: to understand these processes in a way that will help us avert them in the future.

A major theme to be gained from this important book is that organizations do not routinely and systematically learn from past errors and disasters—in fact, they *rarely ever do.* This intentional lack of oversight can partly explain why our predicament in Iraq is so precisely close to the Vietnam experience, both in the way that we got into the war, deceptively and unconstitutionally, and in the way the war is being conducted and prolonged.

It might not seem surprising that after thirty years, a generation of decision-makers and voters would have come along that knew little about the past experience in Vietnam. What is more dismaying is to realize that much the same processes—the same foolish and disastrous decision-making, the same misleading rationales for aggression—are going on right now with respect to Iran, with little political opposition, just *three years* after the invasion of Iraq, and while the brutal and tragic consequences of that occupation are still in front of our eyes every day.

One reason for this folly is that many aspects of disasters in decision-making are known only within the organization, and not even by many insiders at that. The organizations involved tend not to make relevant and detailed studies of past errors, let alone reveal them outside the organization. In fact, the risk that such a study or investigation might leak to the outside is a factor sufficient to keep inquiries from being made in the first place. Making or keeping possibly incriminating documentation earlier, at the time of the decision, or later is similarly sidestepped.

This deliberate decision within organizations not to try to learn internally what has gone wrong constitutes what I have called, with respect to Vietnam, an *anti-learning mechanism*. Avoiding improved performance is not the point of the mechanism. But because studying present and past faulty decision-making risks may invite blame and organizational, political, perhaps even legal penalties, those outcomes "outweigh" the benefits of clearly understanding what needs to be changed within the organization.

The valuable cases studies, analyses, and information in the pages of this book were not provided by the organizations involved. This compendium arose from the accounts of individual whistle-blowers, journalistic investigations, and in some cases congressional action—and from Dr. Gerstein's own initiative in collecting and analyzing the data. Did any one of the organizations detailed herein conduct a comparable study? Quite possibly not a single one. And even if they did, they certainly didn't publish the results in a way that would allow other organizations and individuals to learn from their mistakes.

Societally, then, we don't have an easy way to learn from organizational mistakes of the past. That's one reason that disasters are so likely, and why comparable disasters occur again and again, across organizations and even within the same organizations. In the case of Vietnam, Americans did not learn from the French or Japanese occupations before ours. Nor did Republicans under Nixon manage to learn from Democratic missteps before theirs. Specifically, there was no systematic study of the Pentagon Papers, which were available within the Defense Department to the Nixon administration, but no one ever admitted to having read them or even to directing their staff to analyze possible lessons from them. (I personally urged Henry

Kissinger, in a discussion at the Western White House in 1970, to do both of these, or at least the latter, but he later claimed he had never read anything of them or about them, though he had a copy available to him.) As far as we know, Secretary of Defense Laird, Henry Kissinger, and others had no interest in the documentary record and analysis of twenty-three years of decision-making in the same geographic area, against precisely the same adversaries. And so they ended up committing many of the mistakes made by those who'd gone before, with the same results.

This "anti-learning" phenomenon also explains why it is possible to reproduce our experience in Vietnam years later in Iraq, and now, from Iraq to Iran. In sum, there is strong and successful resistance within many organizations to studying or recording past actions leading to catastrophe—because doing so would reveal errors, lies, or even crimes.

There is no substitute for the kind of comparative study analysis Dr. Gerstein shares on these pages. I hope this book is read widely; if we are to avoid the kinds of disasters and catastrophes described, we first need to understand them. *Flirting with Disaster* is a pathbreaking, indispensable step toward such a goal.

Daniel Ellsberg
Berkeley, California
July 2007

INTRODUCTION

This book is about disasters. From Chernobyl to Katrina, *Challenger* to *Columbia*, BP to Vioxx, and the Iraq War. Were these—and practically every major catastrophe that has befallen us in the past twenty-five years—unforeseen, unavoidable misfortunes that no one could possibly have imagined? No. All of them, it turns out, were accidents waiting to happen, and many influential people on the inside saw them as such. The events were not really "accidental" at all.

These disasters were not merely imagined, but they were often accurately predicted as well, sometimes forewarned in strident tones. However, the alarms were ignored by those who had the power to disregard them. Why? How do smart, high-powered people, leaders of global corporations, national institutions, and even nations, get it so wrong?

I was never interested in accidents—that is, until they happened to me. The first accident involved my career; the second landed my son in the hospital. I'll tell you the first story here and save the second for later in the book.

It was a drizzly morning in the fall of 2001. A group of us—my firm's senior management team—sat in the high-tech boardroom of our spectacular new Manhattan skyscraper. Though everyone had already received my memo by e-mail, I handed out hard copies and quickly summarized its contents: an in-depth analysis of the conditions that might lead to our firm's demise. For the most part, the memo contained detailed market share data and the results of simulation studies akin to those used by hurricane forecasters. Most of the scenarios were distressingly gloomy.

My description of possible futures was not intended to be an exact prediction. It represented "possibilities," as forecasters like to call them, and in this case the stories were intended to stimulate the team sitting around the table to steer us out of harm's way. In effect, my presentation was about industry climate change rather than about tomorrow's weather forecast. But few of my peers were listening.

One of the team members pressed me hard: "Are you *sure*?" he asked in a tone that conveyed his obvious skepticism. "No," I confessed, "the warnings seem clear, but this is about the future, so it's impossible to be 100 percent certain."

From the collective exhalation of breath and almost everyone's body language, I knew I had just invalidated my own argument. If I couldn't be sure, then why should they believe me? After all, from their perspective, things were going okay, even though our market share had been eroding at a worrisome rate for some time. (There were lots of inventive reasons offered up for that trend.) I had a few people on my side, but somehow, most of the group at the table had convinced themselves that, despite the rough seas, our ship was on course and more or less unsinkable.

To bolster my case, I proposed a more thorough study. But that suggestion was roundly rejected as a waste of money. Unsubstantiated intuition had just trumped inconclusive analysis for most people around the table, so there was really no reason to go any further. Things would proceed as before.

Nevertheless, over the next few months I continued to voice my growing alarm at the direction I thought we were headed, to little effect beyond riling up the group that was already won over. In the meantime, the skeptics—including the board's leadership—waited for the storm to pass and the good times to return.

Fast-forward eighteen months: Radical downsizing in which hundreds lost their jobs was followed by a humiliating merger with a competitor. It was, sadly, one of the scenarios that I had outlined in my analysis on that dismal autumn morning, but in my positive version, we would have taken the initiative and ended up in charge, not the other way around.

In the end, this corporate mishap resulted in the loss of a great deal of shareholder money as well as a substantial number of jobs, including my own and those of many others who had sat around the conference table in 2001. As reflected in so many cases in this book, there had been plenty of warning, and no small amount of data to support the view that things were going downhill in a hurry. Nevertheless, many high-powered people had remained unconvinced that we were at risk, so nothing was done—until it was too late for anything but damage control.

I have since discovered that my Cassandra-like experience is far from unique. With corporate fiascos, of course, the stakes aren't life and death, but "only" people's money and livelihood. However, I have found the same distorted thinking, errors in decision-making, and self-serving politics at the root of the many industrial accidents, product-liability recalls, dangerous drugs, natural disasters, economic catastrophes, and national security blunders that we read about on the front pages of newspapers or watch with morbid fascination as events unfold on twenty-four-hour global news networks. It's hard to grasp the scale of the suffering such mistakes can create.

Today, after several years of research and the review of dozens of disaster case histories, I have learned that virtually all these "accidents" were not what we normally mean when we use that term—that is, unpreventable random occurrences. In Chernobyl, Hurricane Katrina, both space shuttle incidents, the Asian tsunami, and the monetary crises of East Asia, these disasters had long buildups and numerous warning signs. What's more, they display a startling number of common causes, and the same triumph of misguided intuition over analysis that I saw firsthand that fateful day. This book tells the story of the underlying causes of those disasters, and what we can all do to reduce the chances that anything similar will happen again.

In chapter 1, we begin with the *Columbia* space shuttle and the tale of one Rodney Rocha, a thirty-year veteran and NASA's man in charge of figuring out whether the large piece of insulating foam that hit the spacecraft during liftoff did any real damage.

Rodney was a very worried man, and said as much. His engineering associates were worried, too, but their concerns were not voiced in such a way, or to the relevant people, as to galvanize NASA's top brass into action. The *Columbia* case is the story of how organizational pressures, public relations concerns, and wishful thinking contributed to a phenomenon known as bystander behavior—the tendency of people to stand on the sidelines and watch while things go from bad to worse.

After the *Columbia* tragedy, chapter 2 explores the human biases and distortions in thinking that affect each of us in a way that contributes to risk. Many accidents are natural outgrowths of these quintessentially human characteristics, but that does not mean they are inevitable. After all, we seek to control many aspects of natural but otherwise undesirable human behavior—such as war-making and thievery—through the tools of civilization, and dangerous decision-making is just one more domain that requires us to protect ourselves from ourselves.

Understanding why we do what we do when it comes to risk is vital, although it can be a bit of work to get one's head around some of these ideas. Be patient, especially with my discussion of probability, a subject many people find challenging if not downright confusing, yet one that is essential to understanding the true nature of risk. I have tried to make that discussion as accessible as possible.

Chapters 3 through 10 discuss a series of accident and disaster cases, using them to demonstrate the forces that give rise to catastrophe.

We begin with Hurricane Katrina, arguably the best-predicted accident in American history. The central question is why more wasn't done before, during, and after a storm that so many saw coming. Katrina is also the story of irrationality in financial decision-making, since it will be made clear that preventing the flooding of New Orleans was far less expensive than rebuilding the city. Unfortunately, short-term thinking about money is a factor in many accidents. In Katrina, we will see that not protecting New Orleans was, among the many errors associated with it, financially irresponsible.

The space shuttle *Challenger* is one of the most well-known disasters of all time. Most people know that the *Challenger* blew up because of faulty O-rings, the rubber seals that prevent dangerous leaks between the sections of the massive booster rockets that help get the space shuttle off its launchpad. The mystery of *Challenger* is why it was launched in extremely cold weather over many objections, and particularly why it was launched on that day and at that time before the sun could melt the ice on the gantry and warm the spacecraft. Even if you are familiar with the *Challenger* case, the answers in chapter 4 may surprise you.

The Chernobyl meltdown, examined in chapter 5, has the terrible distinction of rendering vast tracts of land in Ukraine and Belarus uninhabitable for six hundred years because of radiation, and it has created a legacy of medical problems that persist to this day, more than twenty years later. The nuclear incident at Chernobyl is our gateway to the exploration of faulty design as the source of many disasters, and chapter 5 discusses a number of those errors from around the world.

Merck & Company's Vioxx is also, in no small way, a design mistake, although the emphasis of chapter 6 is how the lure of profits and compromised regulation inhibited the company and the U.S. Food and Drug Administration from needed action, despite considerable evidence that Vioxx might well be a dangerous drug. According to

Vioxx's many critics within and outside of government, tens of thousands of people have died unnecessarily because of the drug. In that chapter, we explore the moral culpability of both Merck and the FDA, especially the worrisome problems that arise when regulators are too cozy with those whom they are supposed to regulate.

Chapter 6 also discusses the BP Texas City refinery explosion that killed fifteen and injured 180 in 2005. It is considered the past decade's most serious industrial accident in the United States. The Texas City refinery had a long history of accidents and deaths, including several after BP acquired it in 1998. As in many other stories chronicled here, there were many warning signs. The barriers to taking action at Texas City were cultural and, just as important, financial. BP management believed that investing in better and safer equipment and practices was unjustified. In light of more recent events, especially the shortage of refinery capacity in the U.S. and windfall profits, that contention strikes a hollow note in an industry renowned for its long-term planning capabilities.

In contrast with all the well-known accidents reviewed thus far, chapter 7 discusses one that most people have never heard about. In 1994, in the aftermath of the first Gulf War, two patrolling American F-15 fighter jets shot down two American Black Hawk helicopters. The big choppers were carrying a multinational VIP contingent of Operation Provide Comfort peacekeeping officials on a tour of the no-fly zone in northern Iraq. Here is the unimaginable story of the failure of a safety system consisting of multiple checks and balances including a large number of people, explicit rules of engagement, electronic friend-or-foe detection, state-of-the-art communications, and extensive training. That catastrophe—the worst friendly fire episode in the modern U.S. military—occurred over just eight minutes.

As you will have discovered from my earlier discussion of design, the essence of creating safe systems is multiple layers of protection, or redundancy. The Black Hawk shoot-down reveals that without understanding the ways in which these safety systems themselves can fail—particularly the failure of redundancy itself—we cannot truly hope to protect ourselves.

Chapter 8 deepens our understanding of failure in such complex real-world systems by introducing systemic effects to our explanations of accidents and disasters. While some of the disasters examined earlier were certainly complicated, in the two cases in this chapter the concept of *interdependence* plays a starring role. The first case, in which Texas legislators inadvertently destroyed a vast amount of their citizens' wealth in the pursuit of the worthy cause of public education, is a modern-day version of the tale of the Sorcerer's Apprentice. Why did it happen? The experts say it's because "lawyers, not economists, designed the system." The system they created, ironically named Robin Hood, is an object lesson in the difficulties of applying naive commonsense logic to a complex dynamic system.

The second case is the collapse of the vibrant thousand-year-old Polynesian culture on Easter Island. Easter was destroyed by its leaders' relentless societal obsession to build *moai*, the giant stone statues that still grace the perimeter of the island, and whose carving and transport baffled the European explorers who arrived in 1722. The civilization eroded from within, and its ruin serves as a cautionary tale applicable to our modern-day challenges of climate change and the environment.

In contrast with that tale from long ago, chapters 9 and 10 are contemporary disaster stories of business and finance. The collapse of Arthur Andersen in the wake of the Enron scandal is primarily the story of the ethical erosion of what was once the most straitlaced of the global accounting firms. Many of the biggest corporate bankruptcies in U.S. history were Andersen clients, and the firm's collapse was a result of the corrosive effects of envy, greed, and divided loyalties, combined with the deeper issue of organizational culture and its role in the fostering of disaster. Andersen's fate (like the FDA's in the Vioxx case) also carries a warning of the possible consequences when watchdogs become consultants.

The backdrop for chapter 10 is the "roaring nineties," a heady, sky's-the-limit period for global business. As the decade began to close in on the millennium, however, the world economy was marked by a series of economic shocks: The Asian tigers, along with Russia and Brazil, became infected in quick succession by financial and foreign exchange crises. Our global economy, now tightly coupled through banking and trade, convulsed repeatedly as country after country went bankrupt.

That story begins with Mexico's 1994 peso crisis and charts a course through East Asia, Russia, and beyond, ending with the collapse of Long-Term Capital Management, a huge global hedge fund that grew overnight to dwarf many traditional investment banks and corporations. That chapter tells the story of how the world's financial system came perilously close to freezing up, and how the pursuit of free trade and self-interest, the ideological cornerstones of modern global capitalism, runs risks that few understood, risks that are still with us today.

Finally, chapters 11 and 12 consider what we might all learn from the foregoing disasters, and what we can do to prevent similar mistakes in our personal lives, at work, and as leaders in business and government. While the main thrust of this book is the understanding of large-scale incidents, let us not assume that organizations are the only venues in which we can reduce risk. There is plenty we can do as individuals to diminish risks at home and at work, so please do not infer that this book's lessons apply only to the top brass of big companies, the military, and government agencies.

That said, a major dilemma in the final part of this book is the apparent simplicity of some of the ideas for reducing the risk of accidents, be they at home or in the boardroom. I offer these tactics without apology, however, for superficial simplicity often belies enormous difficulty in implementation. Many solutions involve going against the very reasoning biases described in chapter 2, and exemplified in the book's many case analyses. Just because a suggestion is obvious, that does not make it less relevant or necessary. When ignored, most risks do not somehow take care of themselves, or simply cease to be an issue. Each uncorrected risk is one more accident waiting to happen, and the last chapters chart a course toward solutions.

Beyond what we might do as individuals, the suggestions in those final two chapters also confront the darker side of institutional life, a world in which production, financial results, politics, and loyalty are often more important than ethics and safety. The good news is that the creation of dysfunctional incentives is often unintentional and, in fact, runs *counter* to leadership's intent. Chapter 12 deals with what willing leaders can do about making their enterprises better and safer for their customers, employees, and partners. That chapter contains optimistic, change-oriented material, and I believe that the engaged reader can make enormous progress by heeding its advice.

On the other hand, in some organizations, the disclosure of unpopular or embarrassing facts is deliberately suppressed, and going against the grain often precipitates ruthless, vindictive retaliation that punishes the "offenders" and sends a chilling warning to would-be truth-tellers. In such punitive organizations, leadership is the problem. In his afterword, Daniel Ellsberg addresses what to do when leadership itself is broken. The mechanisms he suggests are an unfortunate but necessary element of the architecture of effective governance, a need that was foreseen by the U.S. founding fathers when they created the balance of constitutional powers. We are all obliged to take Dr. Ellsberg's ideas seriously despite the obvious difficulties involved in bringing powerful people in government and industry to task.

The lesson of this book is that while not all disasters are preventable, a surprising number of them are. In virtually all cases, the damaging aftermath can be substantially reduced by better planning, hard work, and most of all, a mind open to the nature of risk. As with all such difficult and persistent human problems, the question is whether we have the wisdom and the will to change. I invite you to join me in the quest to find out.

CHAPTER 1

THE BYSTANDERS AMONG US

Alan R. "Rodney" Rocha was deeply worried. As he played and replayed the films of space shuttle *Columbia*'s launch on January 16, 2003, he saw a large piece of white foam fly off the spacecraft's external tank and slam into its left wing, creating a shower of particles, a dreaded phenomenon known as a debris field. When Rocha's NASA colleagues saw the same dramatic footage the day after the launch, the room was filled with exclamations of "Oh, my God!" and "Holy shit!"

While foam strikes like that one had plagued launches from the beginning of the Space Shuttle Program in 1981, no catastrophic damage had occurred. Nonetheless, two launches prior to *Columbia*'s, NASA experienced a close call. Rocha, who was responsible for structural engineering at NASA and was head of the Columbia mission's Debris Assessment Team, feared that this strike might be different: Nothing he had ever seen was so extreme as the incident he and his colleagues were watching.

Despite his intuition, Rocha knew that he needed more data to determine what might happen when *Columbia* was scheduled to reenter the earth's atmosphere in two weeks. The tiles on the space shuttle's heat-absorbing underside had always been fragile, and Rocha was worried that the foam strike he observed on the launch films might have damaged them to the point that a catastrophic "burn-through" might occur. For now, Columbia was safe in orbit, so Rocha's team had some time to figure out what to do. Unfortunately, Rocha didn't have many options for getting the necessary data about what, if anything, might have gone wrong. While in orbit, only a robot camera or an EVA—extravehicular activity, or a space walk—could conclusively determine the extent of the damage to the spacecraft from the foam strike. But *Columbia* had no camera, and sending an astronaut on an unscheduled EVA was not a step to be taken lightly. Nevertheless, on Sunday, January 19, the fourth day of *Columbia*'s mission, Rocha e-mailed his boss, Paul E. Shack, manager of the shuttle engineering office at Johnson Space Center, to request that an astronaut visually inspect the shuttle's underside. To Rocha's surprise, Shack never answered.

Undeterred, two days later Rocha again e-mailed Shack and also David A. Hamilton, chief of the Shuttle and International Space Station Engineering Office, conveying the Debris Assessment Team's unanimous desire to use the Department of Defense's high-resolution ground-based or orbital cameras to take pictures of *Columbia*. Using boldface for emphasis, he wrote, **"Can we petition (beg), for outside agency assistance?"** Long-range images might not be as good as a physical inspection, but they would be a lot better than what they now had.

Linda Ham, the Mission Management Team chair responsible for the *Columbia* mission, was a fast-rising NASA star, married to an astronaut. Like everyone in the Space Shuttle Program, she viewed foam debris as a potential risk, but did not think it constituted a "safety-of-flight issue." Without compelling evidence that would raise the Debris Assessment Team's imagery request to "mandatory" (in NASA's jargon), there was no reason to ask for outside assistance. Besides, Ham stated in a memo, "It's not really a factor during the flight, because there isn't much we can do about it." *Columbia* lacked any onboard means to repair damage to the shuttle's fragile thermal protection system.

Outraged at being turned down by Shack, who said that he was not going to be Chicken Little and elevate Rocha's request when Rocha confronted him on the phone, and by Ham, who put him in a position of proving the need for imagery that was itself the key to additional proof, Rodney wrote the following blistering e-mail on January 22:

> *In my humble technical opinion, this is the wrong (and bordering on irresponsible) answer from the [Space Shuttle Program] and Orbiter not to request additional imaging help from any outside source. . . . The engineering team will admit it might not achieve definitive high confidence answers without additional images, but without action to request help to clarify the damage visually, we will guarantee it will not. . . . Remember the NASA safety posters everywhere around stating, "If it's not safe, say so"? Yes, it's that serious.*

Despite his frustration, Rocha never sent his e-mail up the chain of command—or to anyone else in NASA—although he did print out a copy and show it to a colleague, Carlisle Campbell. From his long tenure, Rocha knew that it was better to avoid appearing too emotional. Instead, he decided to work through channels by using the Debris Assessment Team to analyze the existing data to assess the risk that the mission and crew would face upon reentry.

When the Mission Management Team meeting started on day eight of Columbia's sixteen-day flight, there were twelve senior managers sitting at the long black conference table and more than twenty others around the periphery or on the speakerphone. Colorful logos of former missions covered the walls of the large gray conference room at Kennedy Space Center, reminders of NASA's past achievements.

The meeting started promptly, and Linda Ham moved things along in her characteristically efficient manner. Don McCormack, manager of the Mission Evaluation Room that supplies engineering support for missions in progress, offered a summary of the Debris Assessment Team's damage scenarios and conclusions based on a briefing he had received from Rocha's team earlier that morning. Even though the team admitted that its analysis was incomplete, McCormack unambiguously concluded during his briefing that there was no risk of structural failure. At worst, he said, the resultant heat damage to some of the tiles would mean delays for subsequent missions in order to refit the tiles that may have been damaged.

During the brief discussion that followed McCormack's summary, one of NASA's most highly regarded tile experts, Calvin Schomburg, concurred that any damage done by the foam strike presented no risk to *Columbia*'s flight. Surprisingly, no one even mentioned the possible damage to the orbiter's wing—into which the flying foam had slammed—focusing instead on the thermal tiles on the spacecraft's underside. Based on previous analysis, RCC—the high-tech material from which the wing's leading edge was made—was considered highly durable, although it might be damaged if hit head-on with enough force. But based on the initial film footage, ambiguous though it was, no one thought that was likely to have happened, so the potential risks of RCC damage were not aggressively pursued.

Seemingly impatient to move on to other business, Ham wrapped up the assessment of the foam strike for those who were having trouble hearing all the conversation over the speakerphone: ". . . he doesn't believe that there is any burn-through. So no safety-of-flight kind of issue, it's more of a turnaround issue similar to what we've had on other flights. That's it?" Turning to those seated around the room—senior NASA officials, astronauts, engineers, scientists, and contractors—Ham queried, "All right, any questions on that?" No one responded, including Rocha, who sat quietly in the second row of seats surrounding the conference table. The shuttle would reenter the earth's atmosphere as scheduled in a little over a week.

On February 1, 2003—eight days after that last-chance meeting—*Columbia* broke apart and incinerated as it descended at a rate of five miles per second over California, Arizona, New Mexico, and Texas. The gaping hole punched by the foam into the edge of the shuttle's left wing allowed superheated gases to enter. First, temperature sensors went haywire, then wiring fused and short-circuited, tires exploded, and, finally, the wing's structural supports melted. The space shuttle *Columbia*'s automated flight controls compensated as best they could, but when the wing lost its structural integrity, the spacecraft went out of control and disintegrated into a meteor shower in the bright blue morning sky.

Many disasters, such as this one, have the distinction that some people clearly foresee the crisis before it happens. For instance, we know from the Pentagon Papers that many high-level officials within the U.S. government accurately predicted the catastrophic events that would unfold in Vietnam. In more recent years, reports coming out on a nearly monthly basis show the same predictable catastrophe was true before the United States launched the war in Iraq in March 2003.

Examples are not limited to national security matters. Similar stories can be found about natural disasters (the vulnerability of the New Orleans flood-control systems and risks of an Asian tsunami); major industrial disasters (the explosions at the Chernobyl nuclear power plant and BP's Texas City refinery); product safety disasters (Merck & Company's Vioxx); and large-scale accounting frauds (Barings, Arthur Andersen, and Enron). Since people in the responsible organizations clearly knew of the potential doom, why was nothing done about it? If we're ever to understand why catastrophes occur and how to prevent them, we must probe that central question. Indeed, we must also ask if in our sophisticated society, we can learn to stop routinely flirting with disaster.

We will examine the destruction of the space shuttle *Columbia*, a case in which we know that a well-respected and responsible person on the inside believed there was a good chance that the spacecraft was damaged, putting its crew at serious risk.

Although Rodney Rocha initially acted on his concerns with his colleagues and local management, he eventually became a passive observer to a tragic set of decisions. He failed to emphasize to NASA's top management the danger he foresaw, and did not speak up during critical meetings when he had an opportunity to do so. Rocha was an *organizational bystander*.

WHAT IS AN ORGANIZATIONAL BYSTANDER?

Organizational bystanders are individuals who fail to take necessary action even when important threats or opportunities arise. They often have crucial information or a valuable point of view that would improve an organization's decision-making, but for a variety of psychological and institutional reasons, they do not intervene. Understanding why they become and remain bystanders is crucial to grasping how disasters arise. Coming to grips with that knowledge is a central theme of this book.

Rocha was, of course, not alone. In situations like the one at NASA, many individuals subjectively employ what might be called "bystander calculus." They consider what will happen if they are right, what will happen if they are wrong, and what will happen if they simply do nothing at all.

Since predictions can only be right or wrong, and the person may either escalate his concerns or remain passive, there are four possible situations we must consider when deciding what to do:

- First—and clearly best from the institution's point of view— would be if one's concerns come to naught, and one has not pressed them up the line. That outcome allows for displaying prudent care about risk while demonstrating savvy professional judgment by not allowing one's concerns to escalate into unnecessary public alarm. Not overreacting is much admired in many organizations.

- Second, the opposite case occurs when concerns are aggressively advocated up the line and the threat is real. Importantly, how this plays out depends on other people's reactions. On the one hand, the advocate may be hailed as a hero for saving the day. Far more often, however, the person is condemned—perhaps even ostracized—despite the accuracy of his warning. Correct predictions may offer scant protection if a whistleblower has encountered hostile resistance along the way, and if people didn't take his warnings seriously.

- Third, the advocate presses her case aggressively, but the threat turns out to be false. For this, she is labeled an alarmist: someone who presses the panic button for no reason. Curiously, alarmism is often the label applied even when one is just seeking more information, as Rocha did. Paul Shack, Rocha's boss, who obviously knew NASA well, was likely wary of being perceived as an alarmist himself by supporting Rocha's potentially overwrought concerns.

- Fourth, one can be a bystander, a passive observer to tragic harm.

STORIES WE TELL OURSELVES

Remaining silent in the face of serious risks is selfish behavior; it places our own need to avoid embarrassment and damage to our reputation above the safety of others. Yet, as common as ordinary selfishness is, conscious selfishness that will almost certainly harm others is rare.

In fact, most of us don't like how it feels to think of ourselves—or to have others think of us—as willfully self-interested. So we explain away our behavior with rationalizations, stories we tell ourselves to protect our egos from self-criticism. Common ones include the following: "I'm sure it's nothing serious," "Somebody else has probably already reported it," and "My actions wouldn't have made any difference." Here are some others:

> *"It's none of my business, not my area of authority."*
> *"I don't want to get into trouble."*
> *"I don't want to take sides."*
> *"I don't have all the information/proof, so I can't take any action."*
> *"Others must know more than I do."*
> *"The situation is more complex than it seems."*
> *"I'm only following orders, so it's not my fault."*
> *"My efforts won't make any difference."*
> *"I tried, but no one listened."*
> *"I don't want to rock the boat."*
> *"Nothing could have been done."*
> *"I don't want to get burned again."*

Rationalizations have a mantralike quality—the ability to shut down external debate as well as to quiet the inner arguments we might otherwise have with ourselves.

As the *Columbia* accident investigation unfolded, a number of these rationalizations surfaced, along with clear signs of outright psychological denial. While Rocha was recognized as an expert, and most observers portrayed him as a well-intentioned engineer who sounded an alarm that others ignored, several critics suggested that he should have spoken up more forcefully.

When questioned about why he hadn't sent his strident e-mail to top management, Rocha replied that he hadn't wanted to appear overly emotional or go outside the chain of command. About his silence during the critical MMT meeting, Rocha appeared to have been awed by the circumstances: "I remember a pause and [Linda Ham] looking around the room like it's okay to say something now. But no one did. I just couldn't do it. I was too low down here in the organization and she's way up here."

On the day the *Columbia* was destroyed, a colleague said consolingly: "Oh, Rodney, we lost people, and there's probably nothing we could have done." While that conclusion is emotionally appealing, it's a flawed after-the-fact argument that justifies inaction. In fact, the *Columbia* Accident Investigation Board documented many things that could have been done.

Even as the investigation unfolded, rationalizations continued. Rocha defended the Debris Assessment Team's conclusions of no risk to flight because he'd had no additional photographs and no compelling analysis to substantiate his initial fears. While recognizing that he had been explicitly denied access to the proof he needed, he explained away the fact that he abandoned his own advocacy. Other rationalizations abounded, but in the end each one was invalidated by the accident investigation board's analysis. That reflects the essential nature of rationalization: It provides its own justifications and shuns contrary evidence.

WHY DO PEOPLE BECOME BYSTANDERS?

The research on the bystander phenomenon suggests that certain specific characteristics of the situation—especially the presence of others and their behavior—strongly affect whether or not people will take action in situations with potential risk to others, and to themselves. The former often affects people's health and safety, the latter impacts one's livelihood, reputation, and ego. Other characteristics include the following:

- *Ambiguous precipitating events.* When it is not clear whether one is observing a potentially dangerous event, the likelihood of passivity increases. In the case of *Columbia*, images of the foam strike were suggestive but inconclusive, and the crew reported no problems in flight.

- *A large number of people observe the event.* When many people observe an event, there is a diffusion of individual responsibility as well as a widespread belief that "somebody" will take action. In *Columbia*, hundreds of people viewed the film of the debris field created by the foam strike, yet no one came any closer to taking action than Rocha.

- *Failure of others to act.* When most observers of a particular event take no action, it is more likely that others will do the same. Only Rocha and his team seemed concerned about the foam strike, and while there were others who were equally concerned, they were located in different NASA groups and did not communicate with Rocha and his team.

- *Uncertainty regarding one's ability to help.* In situations that appear to require special skills, unique abilities, unambiguous proof, or formal authority, the likelihood of observer passivity is increased. Rocha believed he lacked the conclusive data and formal power needed to alter the views of NASA's decision-makers.

- *Presence of formal authorities or "experts."* Observers are not likely to act if "better-qualified" authorities or experts are present or nearby. A host of senior NASA officials reviewed the results of analysis performed at lower levels, concluding that there was no risk to flight.

Additional pressures arise in highly cohesive groups: People may unconsciously strive for unanimity, a phenomenon known as *groupthink*. By intuitively shunning alternative points of view and radical courses of action, insiders may cause dissent to evaporate before it can even be expressed.

Strong pressures to conform also mean that one can be right but still be rejected by one's own group as well as by the larger organization. Such is the common fate of whistle-blowers, who are often ostracized or persecuted. Those who protested BP's lax safety standards at the Texas City refinery that exploded in March 2005—killing fifteen people—as well as Vioxx's external critics, suffered relentless persecution. In government, retaliation can be particularly vindictive. For example, as revealed in the I. Lewis "Scooter" Libby trial, those who raise embarrassing questions or express opinions counter to the stated policy invite a vicious response.

It is believed that the identity of covert CIA employee Valerie Plame Wilson was leaked to the media to punish her husband, Joseph C. Wilson IV. He had published an op-ed column in the *New York Times* that accused the Bush administration of manipulating intelligence about purported uranium purchases in Africa, described by the president as part of the administration's justification for the invasion of Iraq. In the process, Plame's CIA career was ruined, and the lives of the Wilsons and of many of the operatives with whom Plame worked were arguably imperiled. For actions related to that brazen act, Libby was convicted, sentenced to thirty months in prison, but then had the term of incarceration commuted by President Bush. Later, the Wilsons' civil suit against Vice President Cheney and Libby was dismissed because the judge stated that there was no basis in law for damages. As a result, Libby, one of the culprits, was nominally punished but allowed to go free while the Wilsons paid a heavy price. Such is, sadly, often the fate of those engaged in truth-telling when an institution, be it a government, a university, or a corporation, chooses not to heed a warning message.

Factors promoting bystander behavior work in concert to maintain the status quo—preserving people's jobs and the relationships among them, the status and rewards of higher-ups, and the social patterns within and among groups. Strong pressures to conform—as well as the many other factors that we will examine in the chapters that follow—operate to maintain the status quo, even as a situation is headed for disaster. As in the *Columbia* incident, and many others we will examine, not "rocking the boat" often becomes a way of life—even while that boat is going right over Niagara Falls.

CHAPTER 2

HUMAN BIASES AND DISTORTIONS

A famous psychological experiment first performed in the 1980s asked participants to assess the likelihood of a number of possible conclusions about someone based on a description such as the following:

Linda is thirty-one years old, single, outspoken, and very bright. She majored in philosophy. As a student she was deeply concerned with issues of discrimination and social justice and she also participated in anti-nuclear demonstrations. How likely is each of the following?

1. *Linda is a bank teller.*
2. *Linda is a bank teller and is active in the feminist movement.*

Draw your own conclusions before reading on.

Overwhelmingly (by 85 percent in some tests), participants felt it is more likely that Linda is a feminist bank teller than just a plain bank teller. And yet, this opinion runs contrary to logic because the inclusion of the additional requirement of feminist reduces the likelihood, adding a specific restriction to a more general case.

Despite that input of logic, and even after learning the technically correct answer (that Linda is more likely to be a bank teller), many people still feel a strong preference for the feminist bank teller scenario. Why should that be? The explanation offers a key to many aspects of human reasoning, particularly the steps we are willing to take, or not take, when dealing with risk.

The logical error revealed by Linda-the-feminist-bank-teller may be explained by the term *reasoning illusion*, which is like the familiar visual illusions most of us enjoyed as children. A common visual illusion shows two lines of the same length in which one appears longer than the other because of the shapes of other lines added to their ends. This and several other common illusions reveal how easily our visual system can be fooled. (See figures 2.1.)

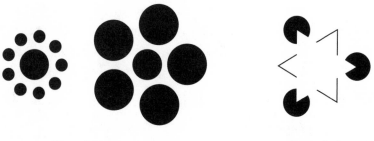

Figure 2.1a   *Figure 2.1b*

Visual illusions: the power of context. Note here, referencing Amos Tversky and Daniel Kahneman, "Extensional Versus Intuitive Reasoning: The Conjunction Fallacy in Probability Judgment," Psychological Review *90, no. 4 (October 1983).*

These two visual illusions demonstrate the role of context in influencing perceptions. In figure 2.1a, the apparent size of the circles in the center is strongly related to the relative size of those that surround them. Most people like to think of themselves as objective, but this simple illusion makes it clear that our visual perceptions are strongly influenced by comparisons. This distortion is also true for other types of judgments.

Most of us, for instance, consider cost savings in relative rather than absolute terms. When buying a car, we might consider a fifty-dollar price difference inconsequential, yet we will make a fuss to negotiate a similar discount on a lesser-priced object, such as a camera or an iPod. Evidence suggests that for most of us such mental accounting is contextual despite the fact that all our money flows through the same pocket. Fifty dollars should always be fifty dollars—but it isn't.

Figure 2.1b demonstrates a very different effect: our capacity to literally "invent" a perception out of whole cloth. The visually top-most all-white triangle appears quite distinct to most viewers in spite of the fact that it is not there—merely implied by the gaps in the other shapes. Curiously, many people also have a strong sense that this white triangle is lighter in color than the field behind it. (The image contains only pure white and pure black.)

Most people also describe this illustration as three circles and two triangles—whole shapes—rather than as the three Pac-Man objects and the three V-shaped lines that actually compose it. Similarly, the human capacity to discern patterns in everyday life sometimes leads us to see patterns in behavior (as well as to attribute causes to them) when that behavior is, in fact, purely random.

As the illusions above illustrate, context makes a big difference in drawing conclusions. In the case of Linda-the-feminist-bank-teller, the inclusion of more information about Linda makes for a more credible story. Careful studies show that when we are asked to assess likelihood, we often answer with a subjective assessment of how well the story fits with our expectations. The degree of narrative fit rather than our objective assessment of the actual likelihood determines our ultimate probability judgment.

If you are one of the many who feel that Linda is more likely to be a feminist bank teller than a plain bank teller, you might wonder whether how well a story plays is just a scientific curiosity. It is not.

A substantial body of research supports the power of a good story—even one created out of whole cloth—to sway the outcomes of jury trials, even ones involving murder. In mock juries—the source of a great deal of our in-depth information about how people reach conclusions—when identical evidence is presented in story order rather than witness order, it proves to be far more convincing to jurors, whether employed by the prosecution or the defense.

In the infamous O. J. Simpson murder trial, defense attorney Johnnie Cochran successfully convinced the jury of the validity of the framed black man story, one with many historical precedents and great emotional appeal. In court, it appears that the best story—not necessarily just the best facts—wins the case.

This chapter examines how recollected incidents, personal experiences, and credible but misleading stories strongly influence how people perceive the world and make decisions about risk. Like visual perception, reasoning can be biased, causing people to make mistaken judgments. We are prone to reason by example, invent details that go beyond the evidence, and place more trust in our direct experience than in statistics. While there are many areas of life in which our intuitive judgment is reliable, we often get into trouble in the complex and low-probability situations that set the stage for accidents and disasters.

For example, the dominant story leading up to the *Columbia* space shuttle disaster was that the foam strike was a "turnaround issue," similar to other flights, possibly affecting the launch date of the next mission, but with no safety implications. Likewise, as we'll examine in the next chapter, during the long lead-up to Hurricane Katrina, key decision-makers believed that New Orleans was safe because they believed the story that the city had "two hundred to three hundred years of flood protection." Each disaster in this book has its own credible but misleading story. These stories more often than not encouraged people to take catastrophic risks.

EASE OF RECALL VERSUS RELEVANCE

People are pretty good at assessing risks that they encounter regularly in their own lives, such as common household injuries and illnesses.

However, when events occur so often that they are no longer news, or when they occur so rarely as to create news if they do occur, our accuracy at estimating risks plummets. That is to say, people overestimate rare but memorable events (especially if they make the news) and underestimate the more frequent but forgettable incidents. Both mistakes appear to be a product of two mutually reinforcing phenomena, one cognitive and the other social.

Most of us are predisposed to start our risk estimates from recalled incidents and then adjust our estimates from there. This behavior pattern introduces three potential sources of bias: the relevance of one's experiences, their emotional potency, and the nearly universal tendency to inadequately adjust from the remembered reference case to the actual situation at hand.

For instance, a doctor might be inclined to overestimate the risk of contracting certain diseases in her community since she sees an inherently biased sample of the population—those people with illnesses. And a mother whose child was approached by an online pedophile is likely to overestimate the likelihood of such danger based on the emotional power of her personal experience. Many other professionals, including policemen and school guidance counselors, are subject to the same types of biased experience errors.

The bias from top-of-mind data is so strong, research shows that even irrelevant data can shift judgments in its direction. For instance, in psychological experiments asking participants to focus on their Social Security numbers—which are essentially a random set of numbers—any numerical estimates that they make immediately afterwards, such as guessing prices, are biased by this random data. Even professionals who are familiar with real-life data, such as real estate agents, can be influenced by similar arbitrary facts, such as artificially high or low house asking prices. Such agents naturally claim that they would notice and disregard those prices that are out of line, but that isn't really the case. They may adjust, but not enough. Based upon this result, it should not be surprising that making irrationally extreme demands in lawsuits increases court settlements. Indeed, starting a negotiation from an outrageous position is a tried-and-true tactic because it often works—even when the other side knows exactly what you're doing.

THE EFFECT OF THE NEWS

The media is a powerful force that can cloud our perceptions of risk. Since the news media and social gossip tend to promote stories that are unusual and emotionally intense, most of us are likely to have better access to our memories of the collapse of the World Trade Center that killed approximately three thousand people than to statistics about the ordinary automobile accidents that kill over forty thousand people each year in the United States. If asked, we might subjectively overrate the likelihood of being hurt in a terrorist attack and underrate the probability of a car crash. You might wonder whether that matters. It does, and it has a direct and fatal correlation.

After 9/11, many people were terrified to fly, and they took to the roads instead. According to David Ropeik of the Harvard School of Public Health, the shift of people from commercial airlines (which are extremely safe) to cars (which are less safe when measured on a comparable basis) meant that one thousand more people died in the three months after 9/11 than would have if people had traveled as they usually do. This added one-third more fatalities to the 9/11 death toll. The fear of terrorists actually killed a third as many people as did the terrorists themselves.

Stories and generalizations are applied not only to people, objects, and events, but also to time-series phenomena, such as accidents, company growth rates, and athletic performance. For instance, the "hot hand" in basketball is a persistent sports illusion. Although the hot hand is an appealing notion that fits many people's experience of being "in the zone" while engaging in strenuous physical activity, there is no evidence that streak shooting that defies probability actually exists. It's not that performance clusters don't exist—they do—but rather that simple random patterns can explain them.

The stereotype of random-looking time series has other implications as well. For instance, observers of company performance might be prone to believe that a few months of consistent improvement indicates a business turnaround rather than simply a completely random sequence.

We will see this type of mistake in the space shuttle *Challenger* case of 1986—examined in chapter 4—in which the O-ring sealing problem was considered "captured" (solved) with a single trouble-free flight. More broadly, people tend to discount purely statistical evidence, preferring proof that has plausible explanatory stories attached to it. Juries are often not swayed by statistical evidence alone (even DNA fingerprinting), yet they can be strongly influenced by eyewitness testimony in spite of its notorious and well-documented unreliability. Again, it is apparent that people love stories.

Even experts prefer to apply the human touch to statistical relationships, often at the expense of the reliability of their predictions. It seems that we humans fervently want to believe in our ability to divine patterns and outguess statistics, although there is little evidence that such a thing is possible and much evidence that it is not. Ironically, since people are often unconvinced by purely statistical proof, we should expect the experts to continue to believe that they can outguess statistics, even if there is statistical proof to the contrary.

Many people—not just experts—prefer to trust their instincts rather than rely on statistics, often employing individual case examples to invalidate a more general pattern so that they can believe what they want to believe.

VALUING GAINS VERSUS DEVALUING LOSSES

It goes without saying that people have different attitudes toward risk. Some people are adventurous while others tend toward caution. What is less well known is that within groups that are more or less open to risk, people's attitudes toward gains and losses form a characteristic pattern that is predictable.

The primary—and nonintuitive—finding is that people are risk-averse when anticipating a gain but risk-seeking when anticipating a loss. In other words, when people feel confident that they are going to be successful in some venture or investment, they will forgo the uncertain possibility of additional gains in exchange for greater certainty. On the other hand, if they anticipate a loss, they will often double down their bets in the hope of getting even.

Another important observation is that people are twice as sensitive to losses as they are to gains. That is, losses create a lot more pain than comparable gains create pleasure. If you reflect upon how you feel when reviewing the changing value of your home or the ups and downs of your stock portfolio, I think you will find that this sensitivity is true.

It is also surprising how people's definition of gain and loss is relative, and changes easily with their point of view and various forms of mental positioning. These shifts are known as *framing effects*. If framed positively, the outcome is likely to be evaluated in the domain of gains, but if framed negatively, it may well be evaluated quite differently. Here is a famous problem from Daniel Kahneman and Amos Tversky, the pioneers in the field of behavioral economics that applies research on human and emotional biases to better understand economic and risk-related decisions:

> *Imagine that the United States is preparing for an outbreak of an unusual Asian disease that is expected to kill 600 people. Two*

alternative programs to combat the disease have been proposed. Scientific estimates of the consequences of the programs are as follows:

* *If Program A is adopted, 200 people will be saved.*
* *If Program B is adopted, there is a 1 in 3 probability that 600 people will be saved and a 2 in 3 probability that no people will be saved.*

Which solution would you recommend?

In the original sample of college students responding to the problem, 72 percent chose program A, which is framed positively in terms of lives saved.

What would be your answer to the following two variations of the choices?

* *If Program C is adopted, 400 people will die.*
* *If Program D is adopted, there is a 1 in 3 probability that nobody will die and a 2 in 3 probability that 600 will die.*

A second group of respondents answered in the opposite way by preferring option D when presented with the same problem statement—with its identical numerical outcomes—except for the negative framing of the alternative decisions in terms of deaths rather than lives saved.

You may be thinking that people can't be so easily influenced in real-life, high-stakes situations. Surely people are more rational than that! Yet in choosing between radiation therapy or surgery in cancer treatment, when the facts of the choices are framed in terms of risks of death from each procedure, doctors, medical students, and patients choose radiation; when they are framed in terms of overall life expectancy, surgery is preferred.

In that example, the facts alone do not permit a clear medical decision, hence the need for choice. The research was undertaken because of the legitimate concern that subtleties in the presentation of the alternative treatments might bias the decisions that patients would make. Indeed, they clearly would have. One solution has been to present the information both in words and graphics, using both framings and, thus, giving the patient a wider view.

This is good advice for all sorts of choices.

In our everyday lives, we are just as vulnerable to framing biases, and in similar ways. If the default scenario is presented optimistically, it is likely that that our answer will be risk averse and cautious. On the other hand, if the likely future is characterized in negative terms, then the stage is set for more aggressive and riskier solutions in an attempt to avoid losses.

In today's world, with its seemingly imminent prospects of avian flu and terrorist attacks, public policy alternatives are ripe for framing manipulations. Such tricks are not secrets to spin doctors and pitch-men, who are more than willing to use them to try to convince you of their point of view. If you listen carefully to political debates, you can often recognize these manipulative methods at work.

The larger phenomenon all these examples illustrate is called a *failure of invariance*. Invariance would exist if people made the same decisions irrespective of how the relevant information is presented. People enthusiastically want to do so. In experimental situations, respondents express a strong desire to obey invariance by giving logical, consistent answers. Unfortunately, most of the time they can't help themselves from emotional and inconsistent ones. Human beings have such a strong desire to avoid losses that changes in framing easily shift their responses, even in high-stakes, real-life circumstances such as cancer treatment.

The oddities about how humans perceive risk do not stop there. For very low-probability events, the general tendencies described above to avoid risks for gains and seek them for losses are reversed.

People seek risk when they buy lottery tickets because they subjectively overestimate the chances of winning in comparison with the actual slim statistical likelihood. At the same time, they often exaggerate low-probability health risks, exhibiting unusually strong risk aversion considering the low actual likelihood. This phenomenon compounds people's tendency to overassess the low likelihoods themselves due to selective memory and media effects, as already mentioned.

In the environmental arena, for instance, people strongly overestimate being harmed by low concentrations of certain pollutants. Their bias may cause them to demand disproportionate resources from the government to try to reduce the risk to zero from what already may be safely low values. If successful, such demands might well shift scarce resources away from other situations in which additional spending would produce greater benefit, with the reapportionment putting larger numbers of people in harm's way.

The tendency to distort probabilities at the extremes also encourages a different way of coping with risk. Rather than living with the heightened anxiety created by low-probability risk, people simply write off the residual risk to zero. Most of us deal with many ordinary risks in our daily lives in that way by simply assuming all will be well: We will not fall down the stairs going to breakfast, we will not be involved in a traffic accident on the way to work, we will not suffer a heart attack while jogging. Those possibilities exist, but most of us choose to ignore them and just get on with our day.

If you'd like to explore your own feelings about very high and very low personal risks, take a look at the "Buying Bullets" problem (originally created by Richard Zeckhauser) in figure 2.2.

FIGURE 2.2. BUYING BULLETS: EXPLORING THE "CERTAINTY EFFECT"

Imagine that you believe that "dying rich is the same as dying poor," and are forced to play a special game of Russian Roulette with a gun that holds six bullets. In this version of the game you can pay for a single bullet to be removed from the gun. You are willing to pay $10 million to remove the one and only bullet.

What would you be willing to pay to go from four bullets to three bullets? How about from a fully loaded six bullets to five? Think about your answers before proceeding.

Removal of the fourth bullet improves the odds of survival from one-third to one-half, but still leaves a fifty–fifty chance that one will not be able to spend one's money. From an economic perspective, why should one limit one's payment? Nevertheless, many people feel compelled to pay more to remove the one and only bullet—the value of certainty of life—than to remove the other bullets, the rational arguments notwithstanding.

Removing the first of six bullets—and thus having a one-sixth chance at life—also appears to have strong emotional appeal.

How much were you willing to pay?

In the context of professional risk assessment, of course, the implications of ignoring small residual risks are somewhat different. The *Columbia* Accident Investigation Board characterized NASA management as being "in denial" when dealing with foam strikes.

Many other examples of ignoring residual risks are found in this book. A fascinating real-life case is described in figure 2.3.

FIGURE 2.3. NO APPARENT DANGER

A graphic example of real risk being denied by a person in charge took place in January 1993 when, as part of a conference field trip, a group of volcanologists went into the crater of Galeras—an active volcano in the northern Andes near Pasto, Colombia—largely without safety equipment. The group was led by Professor Stanley Williams, a specialist in volcanic gases from Arizona State University. Williams was convinced by his own theories that the volcano was safe because its output of sulfur dioxide was low despite contrary seismic evidence which suggested that Galeras was becoming unstable.

During the visit to the crater by the scientific party, two journalists, and three tourists, Galeras erupted, killing nine people. Miraculously, the critically injured Williams was saved by the heroic efforts of one of his graduate students, another scientist, and a team of rescue workers.

While Williams' reckless self-confidence was undeniably foolish, it is less clear why other volcanologists would follow him into an active volcano without hard hats and other protections, especially since theories about the safety of Galeras contrary to Williams' had been available at the conference they were all attending.

PROBABILITIES AND ANCIENT MAN

Human beings have been making judgments about probabilities since long before they had the language or the mathematics to analytically examine their risks. While walking through a forest, a hunter-gatherer might well have had to assess the likelihood of finding a particular edible fruit. When he approached a water hole, he had to figure the benefits of hunting game in that locale versus the risks from dangerous predators that also sought out this source of water. The ability to solve these common probability problems was a life-and-death issue, and those who could do so successfully were much more likely to pass on their genes than those who could not.

It should come as no surprise, then, that when people today are given probability problems phrased in an evolutionarily sensible way (framed in commonsense terms, such as the life-and-death example above), they perform better than when given the same problem phrased in percentages, the language of mathematical probability. The former is the way our ancestors learned to encounter the world; the latter is a product of modern life.

Even so, compared with our prodigious talents to learn languages, recognize faces, and sense others' emotional states, the ability to figure likelihoods, no matter how they are phrased, is a skill many people lack. Notwithstanding the potential advantage, many scientists think that human evolution did not demand that we solve particularly challenging probability problems to survive, just as it did not require us to see well in the dark like a cat, or follow a subtle scent through the woods like a bloodhound.

Ironically, humankind's long-term drive to put probability on a firm footing was not derived from our power to solve lofty or even useful problems, but from the desire to win at gambling. Various forms of dice and games of chance have been played for thousands of years, and humans have always wanted to gain some advantage in such contests. The formal mathematics of probability is a much more recent phenomenon, 350 years old at most. While that may seem like a long time, a few hundred years is just an eyeblink in evolutionary time, and not nearly long enough to have an impact on the human gene pool, even if a facility for probabilities has become important to survival and procreation in modern times.

A GIVEN B IS NOT NECESSARILY B GIVEN A

One story that illustrates why understanding probabilities is important in the modern world involves a common medical procedure, mastectomy.

In the late 1970s, in Bay City, Michigan, Charles S. Rogers, M.D., developed a procedure he called "prophylactic mastectomy" as a way to deal with patients he considered at high risk of breast cancer. Rogers's definition of high risk was based on research by radiologist John Wolfe, who found that 92 percent of breast cancers occur in the 57 percent of the population that could be identified by his specialized mammography criteria.

The question is whether Rogers's radical procedure was advisable for people clearly identified as high risk by Wolfe's method.

Figuring the answer requires what are called inverse probabilities. Of all the probability-related confusions, that is one of the most troubling. As you might have guessed, Dr. Rogers reasoned incorrectly about Wolfe's findings. While it is true that the vast majority of the breast cancers are to be found in an identifiable subset of the population, the risk of actually having breast cancer as a member of that high-risk group is only 14 percent. In other words, if high-risk women were to universally choose Rogers's preventive surgical procedure, they would be wrong to have done so roughly six times more often than they would be right. Can you imagine the harm done? How could Dr. Rogers have made such a grievous error?

Reasoning mistakes about such inverse probabilities run rampant because the probability of A given B—the probability of being identified as high risk, given having cancer (92 percent)—is not the same as the probability of B given A—the probability of having cancer, given being high risk (14 percent).

The following is an updated version of another famous, and surprising, example that involves similar reasoning:

Two racial groups form the population of River City: blacks and whites. Ninety percent of the people are white and the remaining 10 percent are black.

A fatal hit-and-run accident occurs at night. An eyewitness later identifies the driver as black. The court tested the witness's ability to distinguish between black and white drivers under nighttime visibility conditions. It found that the witness was able to identify each group correctly about 90 percent of the time, but he confused each with the other about 10 percent of the time.

What do you think is the probability that the driver in the accident was black, as the witness claimed?

It turns out that even though the identification rates for black and white drivers are the same, the relative sizes of the subpopulations of blacks and whites (known as *base rates*) produce very different results. Specifically, a 90 percent reliable witness saying that a driver is black is likely to be correct only 50 percent of the time, whereas a witness reporting a white driver is likely to be correct 99 percent of the time.

Many people find that this fact violates their sense of accuracy. How can a 90 percent reliable witness be right only half the time—no better than the flip of a coin? And yet, that is one of the most important counterintuitive results in probability theory.

Is it possible to come to the correct answer intuitively? Not really. The problem is that the imbalance of proportion of blacks and whites affects both the number of correct assessments and the mistakes made by the witness. On average, half of those identified as black will be whites who are mistakenly identified because the white population is so much larger. Put another way, a 10 percent rate of mistakes within the larger white population creates just as many false identifications as the correct ones from the smaller black population. A similar issue arises with medical tests and all other assessments that are less than perfect when dealing with skewed population sizes.

Let's say, for example, that you test positive using a 98 percent accurate test for a form of cancer that occurs in five hundred of every one hundred thousand people of a certain age group. Given the test's results, how worried should you be? While you have every reason to be concerned, the likelihood you actually have cancer based on the test is actually just one in five. Four out of five of the people who test positive are errors—known as *false positives*—from the much larger subpopulation that does not have cancer. (That's just an example. Tests vary widely in reliability, and doctors use multiple ways of making disease assessments. The book's Web site, www.flirtingwithdisaster.net, contains all the calculations as well as several more examples.)

Armed with a better understanding of inverse probability issues, one often finds that some critical information is missing from reported statistics that tell only half the story. These omissions encourage some misleading conclusions. In the O. J. Simpson trial, Harvard law professor Alan Dershowitz, a member of the defense dream team, stated in a television interview that among men who batter their wives, only a tiny fraction—one-tenth of 1 percent—go on to murder them.

Statistician I. J. Good pointed out in a 1995 letter to *Nature* that Dershowitz paints an incomplete and misleading picture. Using

Dershowitz's assumptions, Good calculated that of the husbands who batter their wives and whose wives are subsequently murdered, the husband is the murderer in over half the cases. Other estimates by statisticians using a different but equally plausible set of assumptions place the estimate even higher. Here we have a dramatic example of the value of a proper probability analysis—and the pitfalls of a wrong one. The statistic Dershowitz cited was meant to convey the likelihood of Simpson's innocence; in fact, the proper calculation of probabilities lent support to the likelihood of his guilt.

RISK VERSUS UNCERTAINTY

When we think about the words *risk* and *uncertainty*, they seem almost the same. Risk, however, is often associated with something going badly wrong, whereas uncertainty involves outcomes of any kind. It turns out that the ideas behind these words are more different than you might think.

Let's start with two basic and known probabilities of the sort often used by gamblers and mathematicians: the likelihood of rolling an even number with a single die (3 in 6, or 1 out of 2), or that of being dealt a full house in poker in the first five cards (3,744 in 2,598,960, or approximately 1 in 700). To turn each such probability into a risk, we simply ask you to state how much you would be willing to bet for the chance to win a certain amount of money (let's say a hundred dollars, fifty pounds, a hundred euros, or ten thousand yen) on each of these outcomes. Most of us would bet a lot more on rolling the die than on the full house because the likelihood is so much higher.

But what happens to betting when you don't know the probability?

This is a type of gamble that is more uncertain than a known risk. Let's say that I ask you how much you will pay for the chance to win the same amount of money as above if you can pull a red ball from a closed bag containing a hundred balls of an *unknown mixture* of red and white balls. In other words, the bag could contain any number of red balls from zero to one hundred. How much would you be willing to pay for a chance to win the money?

Before you protest that this is an unfair question because you don't know what the odds are, I would point out that a lot of real-life bets have this same characteristic. For example, most business ventures have payoffs that are probabilistically vague in the sense that we don't really know the odds that the venture will succeed. Nevertheless, we take such chances all the time. The same is true when we take a case to court, apply to college or graduate school, or undertake a medical treatment. (It's not that we might not know the statistics in general, but we usually don't know the odds for our specific situation, which is the one that really matters.)

It turns out that when people compare bets of known probability (let's call them "clear bets") with those of unknown probability ("vague bets"), they consistently see the vague bets as less attractive. Effectively, they are saying that *unknown probabilities are riskier.* This behavior demonstrates ambiguity avoidance, a phenomenon recognized by Daniel Ellsberg in 1961.

In the case of the red and white balls, the expected value of choosing a red ball is actually one out of two, a result that is plain if you imagine a two-step process. First, choose a random number from zero to one hundred, and use that result as the number of red balls in the bag. Since the likelihood of choosing a red ball is proportional to their number in the bag, this experiment produces a result that is the same as the drawings from a single bag that has fifty red balls and fifty white ones. Of course, it doesn't seem that way, and that's precisely why people avoid ambiguous probabilities if given a direct choice.

Work by researchers Craig Fox, Amos Tversky, and other psychologists reveals that the additional perceived risk of vague probabilities seems to arise from the *comparison* people make between known and unknown situations, and it tends to disappear when people assess vague probabilities on their own. This may seem an odd result in light of the earlier one, but people seem quite content to bet on matters of unknown probability in real life as well as in psychology experiments. The experiments show that these vague bets are close in size to those they place on events of known probability as long as a comparison is not evident.

Not surprisingly, people experience less ambiguity avoidance in familiar versus unfamiliar situations. For instance, people knowledgeable about sports but not about politics will prefer to bet on the outcome of a football game or soccer match rather than on a chance event of equal probability. However, they will prefer betting on a clear chance event to betting on a political outcome. These results extend to situations involving personal skill. In fact, people far prefer to bet on their own skills, such as in darts, rather than on a purely chance outcome with the same likelihood of success.

Experiments also show that when people believe that others with more expertise will be making similar bets to the ones they are making, they tend to lower their bets as a sign of increased caution. Essentially, they are saying that they perceive greater risk when the performance of experts forms a basis for comparison even though the objective situation is the same.

In general, these results suggest that people see greater risk when making decisions about which they feel comparatively ignorant. This anxiety can arise from a direct comparison of two events in which it is clear that they know more about one than the other, or via an indirect comparison with someone they believe knows more. The preference for situations in which people feel they have some direct control (dart throwing) recalls experts who believe they can outguess statistical methods. Even though their greater confidence is not justified, people's overconfidence in their own abilities is surprisingly unshakable.

What does all of that have to do with disasters? First, and perhaps foremost, people's decisions about uncertain situations are neither strictly logical nor consistent. However, objectively analyzing probabilities is not the only standard by which to judge human decision-making, and it pays to examine an alternative point of view.

As mentioned above, mankind evolved to survive and reproduce in the ancient world, a hostile and dangerous place quite different from our own. Survival meant developing many skills, including making decisions about uncertain events related to food, the weather, and safety. In such a world, one might expect humans to value direct experience, prefer hard facts to soft knowledge, and put their trust in their own abilities rather than in abstractions while, at the same time, reserving respect for people they might encounter from whom they might acquire knowledge and new skills.

Each of those characteristics would add to the chances of survival of one's offspring, the ultimate evolutionary payoff.

The anomalies of decision-making and the relative ease with which people can be swayed by comparison sheds some light on the dangers revealed by many of the disasters examined in this book. As we shall see in the *Challenger* tragedy and Merck's Vioxx debacle, people often show a preference for hiding or ignoring new data that might compromise institutional decisions already made. In the modern world, new data can be disruptive if one is committed to a course of action. And also in the modern world, many of the unfortunate outcomes occur to other people, not to the decision-maker and his kin.

THE "MONTY HALL" PROBLEM

As a final illustration of probability-related reasoning difficulties, here is a notorious brainteaser. It is a genuine seeing-in-the-dark problem because so few people get the answer correct, even statisticians.

When first publicized in her syndicated "Ask Marilyn" column in *Parade* magazine, Marilyn vos Savant received ten thousand letters, many arguing that her analysis was incorrect. (Except for a minor ambiguity in the wording of the problem, it was not.) The problem is named after Monty Hall, the American game show host who presided over the popular television show *Let's Make a Deal* for fifteen years.

The problem:

Imagine you are a game show contestant who must choose from one of three doors. Behind one is a valuable prize—a car—and behind the other two doors are goats. The probability of choosing the car is one in three. There are no tricks.

After you have chosen a door, the host—who knows where the car is hidden—points to a different door and opens it to show that there is a goat behind it. (He can always do this, of course, because there is one car, two goats, and three doors.)

The host then offers you a choice: You can stay with your original choice or switch doors to the other one remaining. What do you choose?

There are obviously two choices, but the challenge of this problem is not just getting the right answer, but explaining why it is correct.

The answer:

One's intuition says that the host's offer to switch is worthless. There are now only two doors (after the third door has been shown to hide a goat), so one's odds are fifty–fifty. It shouldn't make any difference which door one chooses. And the vast majority of people say that it doesn't. Ah, but it does!

If you decide to stay with your original choice, you face two possibilities. One is that the car is behind the door you originally chose, which it will be one-third of the time. So, if you stick with your original choice, you will win the car one-third of the time.

The other possibility is that the car is behind the door the host didn't reveal. Here's the secret: The car will be behind this door two out of three times. Why? When you made your original choice, the car was behind the door you chose one out of three times, and it was behind one of the two doors you didn't choose two out of three times. Yet, in these two out of three times when it's behind one of the two doors you didn't choose, the host is essentially telling you (by revealing the goat) precisely which of the two it's likely to be behind! Thus, by always switching to the door the host didn't reveal, you will win the car two out of three times (since you will lose the one-third of the time you had chosen correctly at the start).

Despite such irrefutable logic, most people find this result surprising. Again, it is something that violates their sense of what would seem to be accurate. However, the sum of the probabilities must be one, and the probability of the car being behind the door you originally chose is still one in three, the same as it was before, since you made your choice when there were three doors from which to choose. Now, as then, the remaining probability must reside in the choice or choices that are left. Once the goat has been revealed, the one remaining door's probability of hiding the car has to be two out of three. It can't be anything else since the door with the goat that has just been opened has a probability of hiding a car of zero, and the door you first chose has a probability of one in three.

Don't be disturbed if this problem continues to bother you. It bothers most people. It is a favorite problem in courses on probability precisely because it is so strongly counterintuitive. Persi Diaconis, a former professional magician who is now a mathematics and statistics professor at Stanford University, has said that there is no disgrace in getting this one wrong.

"I can't remember what my first reaction to it was," he said, "because I've known about it for so many years. I'm one of the many people who have written papers about it. But I do know that my first reaction has been wrong time after time on similar problems. Our brains are just not wired to do probability problems very well, so I'm not surprised there were mistakes."

HUMANS AS "PARANOID OPTIMISTS"

Like most people, you are probably tired of reading about the things at which humans are not good. If probability reasoning is important, and we're so lousy at it, how have we survived and prospered these many millennia?

Actually, ancient humans were good at making decisions that were critical to their survival. Their strategy was to avoid making the worse mistake, rather than necessarily making the best decision. We humans are certainly biased in our reasoning—that much is clear and exhaustively documented as seen in this chapter—but it turns out that our biases have a deeper pattern, sometimes overly optimistic, sometimes obsessively cautious.

In the context of a medical test, for example, a false positive says that you have a disease when you do not, while a false negative fails to detect the presence of the disease when it is actually present. Clearly, it would be better if both types of mistakes were eliminated, but this is often impossible, especially since reducing one error tends to increase the other. Which type of error is better? It depends.

With a medical test it would seem better to suffer the anxiety of a mistaken false positive rather than miss a deadly disease that might be cured by early intervention. The same applies to most warning systems, such as smoke alarms, which are calibrated to prevent false negative errors—failing to detect a fire when there is one. The cost, as we all know, is that they produce many false positives, such as screaming blue murder when you burn the toast.

Forensic DNA evidence methods, in contrast, are designed to avoid false positives—that is, not to falsely conclude that an innocent person is guilty. In our legal system, it is preferable to allow a guilty party to go free than to imprison an innocent one. Fortunately, the risks of DNA mistakes are low, especially since one would have to be a suspect for other reasons to be considered for a DNA match.

Rather than being generally cautious or risk-seeking, human beings appear to have been programmed by evolution to live with false positives to avoid a disadvantageous false negative, and sometimes the reverse. For example, men have been found to consistently overestimate their sexual attractiveness to potential mates. Women, in contrast, do not make this mistake, but are prone to underestimate the willingness of men to make long-term commitments. What might account for this difference? Why don't both men and women over- or underestimate their attractiveness as mates?

Psychologists believe that both biases seek to minimize the more costly error. Since natural selection rewards the spreading of genes, men have been encouraged by evolution not to miss any opportunity for procreation (of high value in evolutionary terms) even at the risk of many rejections (of low cost in evolutionary terms). Women, on the other hand, must cope with the potentially serious consequences of being abandoned. If a woman becomes pregnant but is left by her mate, she will be less able to care for her child, as well as become less attractive to other men as a potential partner since she will inevitably divide her attention among her children, at least one of whom shares no genes with the new mate. Since both problems reduce the likely spread of her genes, evolution would have selected women for caution.

The same logic helps explain people's greater fear of out-group members than of people similar to themselves. From the inverse probability analysis above, it is evident that the presence of a much larger in-group population means that people have numerically more to fear from a small percentage of their own kind who might harm them than from a modest number of strangers. Ancient man, however, was justified in his concern about the aggressive intentions of outsiders, a large number of whom were hostile. Since there was also little downside to assuming hostile intent when encountering a stranger, paranoia about out-groups minimized the risk that trusting strangers represented. Supporting this tendency is the greater unconscious attention people pay to angry faces than to happy or neutral ones. In large and small ways, evolution has blessed us with many such instincts to ensure our survival.

Of course, the modern world is not the ancient one, and biases that developed to cope in that world don't necessarily work in this one. As we have already seen in the *Columbia* space shuttle story, perfectly rational but self-interested behavior contributed to the tragedy. Objectively, it is hard to argue that the cost of a few people getting into trouble for speaking out was more important than the lives of the astronauts, the cost of the spacecraft, NASA's reputation, and American prestige. For ancient man, in contrast, there were far more serious consequences to angering the local elite, since ostracism from one's group was equivalent to a death sentence. Evolution would have selected for keeping your own counsel.

While some of the self-protective biases developed over countless evolutionary generations are not always functional in today's society, the principle of avoiding the greater mistake still works. In the Hurricane Katrina case examined in chapter 3, for instance, it will be clear that the costs of a devastating storm in lives, hardship, and property were far greater than the costs of strengthening the levee system. It would have been logical to make the protective investment.

Unfortunately, as people run such trade-offs through those parts of their brain wired with ancient programming, the greater mistake appears to be the one that affects them personally rather than the one that produces the greater good. Unchecked intuition, therefore, may not necessarily be the best guide when deciding how to avoid catastrophic mistakes in the modern world, especially when judgment is clouded by a plethora of natural biases, the influence of framing, and the intuitive limitations of computing probability.

Nevertheless, people trust their instincts. They, in fact, treasure them. One of the main lessons of this book is that our instincts do not always recommend the best course of action when it comes to avoiding disaster.

CHAPTER 3

UNDERSTANDING UNCERTAINTY: WHY DID SO MANY PEOPLE BET AGAINST KATRINA?

The storm hit Breton Sound with the fury of a nuclear warhead, pushing a deadly storm surge into Lake Pontchartrain. The water crept to the top of the massive berm that holds back the lake and then spilled over. Nearly 80 percent of New Orleans lies below sea level— more than eight feet below in places—so the water poured in. A liquid brown wall washed over the brick ranch homes of Gentilly, over the clapboard houses of the Ninth Ward, over the white-columned porches of the Garden District, until it raced through the bars and strip joints on Bourbon Street like the pale rider of the Apocalypse. As it reached 25 feet (eight meters) over parts of the city, people climbed onto roofs to escape it.

Thousands drowned in the murky brew that was soon contaminated by sewage and industrial waste. Thousands more who survived the flood later perished from dehydration and disease as they waited to be rescued. It took two months to pump the city dry, and by then the Big Easy was buried under a blanket of putrid sediment, a million people were homeless, and 50,000 were dead. It was the worst natural disaster in the history of the United States.

—A hypothetical scenario from "Gone with the Water" by Joel K. Bourne Jr., *National Geographic*, October 2004. Published ten months before Katrina.

If ever there was "an accident waiting to happen," it was the cataclysmic flooding of New Orleans. Many had predicted it, including Joel K. Bourne in his chillingly accurate prophecy above. In October 2001, *Scientific American* published "Drowning New Orleans," an article by Mark Fischetti that warned "a major hurricane could swamp New Orleans under 20 feet of water, killing thousands." Less than one year later, the *New Orleans Times-Picayune* ran a series of articles over five days analyzing the flooding risk. This seventy-five-page chronicle—replete with vivid illustrations—left no doubt that New Orleans was in danger, and that things were getting worse.

A few months later, PBS *Frontline* aired the broadcast "The City in a Bowl." And in 2003, Mike Tidwell's impassioned book, *Bayou Farewell: The Rich Life and Tragic Death of Louisiana's Cajun Coast*—part travelogue, part environmental plea—described a storm flattening Louisiana's cities like a "liquid bulldozer."

One year before Hurricane Katrina made meteorological history, in the summer of 2004, the Federal Emergency Management Agency (FEMA) conducted a preparedness exercise called "Hurricane Pam" that was based on a slow-moving Category 3 storm—considered the most likely disaster scenario for New Orleans. Tragically, the planning was never completed because of budget cuts, even though Hurricane Pam revealed the risks and preparedness needs such a disaster would engender should it ever come to pass.

The people who predicted the devastation in New Orleans were not wild-eyed hysterics. Rather, they were reputable journalists, scientists, and government engineers who had examined historical facts, previous studies, computer simulations, land-development patterns and human activities along the Mississippi River, and expert opinions to arrive at the unavoidable conclusion that the city of New Orleans would almost certainly one day drown unless vigorous precautionary measures were taken.

Given that so many knowledgeable and reputable people foresaw the disaster in New Orleans, why did it actually happen? Shouldn't solid foreknowledge spark efforts at preparedness? Why was the city—and the state and federal response systems—so ill prepared to deal with a storm of Katrina's magnitude?

The simplest answer to those questions is that officials inside the agencies responsible for protecting New Orleans did not see the risks clearly. In chapter 2, we examined the kinds of biases to which humans are prone in assessing potential risk; in chapter 1, we focused on the ways in which humans in organizations face even more pressures to assess or ignore risk in often irrational ways.

To begin to see how these factors play into the Katrina disaster, it is useful to reflect on a statement made by Carl Strock, commander of the U.S. Army Corps of Engineers at the time of the hurricane. A few days after Katrina hit, General Strock told reporters, "We figured we had a two-hundred- or three-hundred-year level of protection. That means that an event that we were protecting from might be exceeded every two hundred or three hundred years. So we had an assurance that, 99.5 percent, this would be okay. We, unfortunately, have had that 0.5 percent activity here."

The general's statement makes it sound as if the U.S. Army Corps of Engineers was acting prudently. Who could be blamed for failing to offer protection from an event that had only a 0.5 percent chance of occurring, an event that might not even occur once in the span of time between the signing of the Declaration of Independence and the present day?

The trouble with Strock's statement is that his reasoning is glaringly wrong. In fact, we can easily see that for any given ten-year period, the risk the Corps of Engineers failed to protect against was closer to one in six.

One in six—the very same odds as Russian roulette.

THE MEANING OF PROTECTION

To begin to unravel the extent of General Strock's miscalculation, a few things need to be clarified. First, the figure he cited, two hundred to three hundred years, is even less frequent than the most rare and severe storms, the so-called Category 5 hurricanes. The New Orleans official I-49 evacuation Web site estimates the interval between such storms at 180 years, not 200 to 300. While that does not on the face of it appear to be a significant difference, the discrepancy is emblematic of officialdom's faulty reasoning.

The truth is that New Orleans was vulnerable to storms less intense—and therefore far more probable—than Category 5s. Since the early 1990s, the U.S. Army Corps of Engineers had been working to create, but had yet to complete, the New Orleans hurricane-protection system. That system was based on a target storm intensity known as the Standard Project Hurricane, or SPH, that was approximately equal to a strong Category 3 storm. Even when, or if, its flood-protection project was completed, therefore, New Orleans would likely still be vulnerable to hurricanes of any greater intensity—Category 4 or 5 storms—as well as any slow-moving Category 3 storm, capable of more damage than a storm of equal intensity that sweeps through quickly.

Since less intense storms are more frequent than more intense ones, General Strock's comforting two hundred to three hundred years of "protection" is dangerously misleading. The key problem with his conclusion originates in the meaning of the interval between storm events used by Strock to define "flood protection."

In contrast to hurricanes and other random occurrences, most humans experience events that have more predictable averages. Oak trees, people, and basketball players all have average heights, and babies are born an average of nine months after conception. Generalizing from such averages will usually not lead anyone too far astray.

On the other hand, the most frequent intervals between hurricanes are short, and they do not cluster around a common value but spread out from very small intervals to very large ones. The often quoted average interval used to define flood protection is actually the result of combining the large number of short intervals with a small number of very long ones. Unfortunately, that type of average does not tell us what we really want to know: How long will we have to wait before the next "big one"?

One of the most common reasoning mind bugs is that randomness possesses its own form of uniformity. Many people believe that random events, such as sequences of heads and tails in coin tosses or winning lotto numbers, have to "look random" to be random. That is, they must not contain obvious sequences or repeating patterns. Although lotto numbers are, in fact, perfectly random, people's guesses conspicuously avoid obvious sequences like the sequential numbers one through seven, despite the fact that such patterns are just as likely to arise as choices that are varied.

For example, Steve Jobs, the head of Apple Computer, introduced the tiny iPod Nano in September 2005. At the same time, he announced that users would henceforth have a choice to make the iPod's song shuffle feature "less random." Some users were apparently annoyed that the iPod's random shuffle algorithm sometimes chose sequential songs from the same artist or album. Jobs announced, with some amusement, that by providing an override to such natural occurrences, randomness was now under user control. Thus, users who opted to use this feature were in essence making the playlist less random in reality in order to make it appear more random according to their preferred notion of what randomness should look like.

Although the arrival of storms is random, many people erroneously but instinctively expect the average frequency of storms to translate into a predictable periodic interval—not unlike the gaps they desire between Frank Sinatra songs or Beethoven concertos on their iPods. Nature doesn't work that way. Independent random events like hurricanes can occur anytime, and the intervals between them can be of any length. Hurricane Rita, which arrived less than one month after Hurricane Katrina, was not surprising to those who understood how probabilities actually operate.

It should be obvious then that any definition of protection based on the average years between storms will be misleading. People appear to mentally transform any average into the ordinary type in which values cluster around the mean. That is a mind bug, one that is apparently wired into our genetic code: An average nine-month pregnancy makes sense to people, while this second kind of average, made up of many short intervals combined with a few long ones, does not. It would be as if the average pregnancy of nine months came about from many healthy births occurring only weeks after conception, with a few occurring years after conception. That's not the way things work, at least not for most of our experience. For precisely that reason, our experience can often lead us astray.

To see how this distinction played out in the case of Hurricane Katrina, let's ignore the known design limitations of the New Orleans levee system, its unfinished state, and its uneven maintenance, all factors that complicate any analysis, even though they contributed to the actual risk of flooding. Furthermore, let's restrict our definition of a dangerous storm to a Category 4 or Category 5 hurricane even though the city was vulnerable to storms like Katrina that had eased to Category 3 as they passed through the city. Without those factors, the analysis below may well understate the actual risk. Yet, as we will see, even this best case is far riskier than was officially acknowledged.

We need to answer two related questions: (1) How often, in general, does a Category 4 or 5 storm occur? and (2) What is the expected interval between such severe storms? While these questions seem almost identical, they're actually not. The difference hinges on the varying averages we've been examining.

The answer to the first question is available from the I-49 evacuation Web site data. The average interval between Category 4 storms listed there is 70 years, and between Category 5 storms it's 180 years. Combining those averages to predict a Category 4 or 5 storm results in a fifty-year interval between storms—four times the frequency Strock quoted. (Whenever you add separate probabilities, the combined likelihood is higher than either of the separate ones, and the interval between reoccurrences is shorter.)

Still, fifty years of so-called flood protection seems like a long time. It would certainly be enough time to upgrade the levees, assuming the money and political will to do so were there. Unfortunately, "fifty years" does not necessarily mean what you think—half a century—because this type of average is not a typical value. It is not, in other words, the "nine-month pregnancy" type average.

As for the second question, let's assume that the New Orleans flood-control system had to be completed to protect against Category 4 and 5 storms rather than the weaker SPH specification actually used by the Corps of Engineers. The critical question would then be, "What are the chances that such a storm would flood the city before the levees were completed?" To get the answer, we calculate the probability that there will be zero dangerous storms over the period of interest, and then subtract it from 100 percent. We then repeat this calculation for any interval we choose.

If you run the numbers over a reasonable set of intervals—let's say one hundred years—the results may surprise you.

FIGURE 3.1. PROBABILITY OF ONE OR MORE STORMS OVER VARIOUS TIME FRAMES

Years	Probability	Years	Probability
05	9.6%	55	67.0%
10	18.2%	60	70.2%
15	26.1%	65	73.1%
20	33.2%	70	75.6%
25	39.6%	75	78.0%
30	45.4%	80	80.1%
35	50.6%	85	82.0%
40	55.4%	90	83.7%
45	59.7%	95	85.3%
50	63.5%	100	86.7%

The average interval between storms is 50 years.

The probability of one or more storms rises quickly. For the first ten years—the time frame over which many Corps of Engineers projects are planned and the time between the city's most recent flood from a devastating 1995 rainstorm and the arrival of Katrina—the chances are one in six (18 percent) that one or more major storms will occur. One in six: We're back to the familiar odds of Russian roulette. With odds like that, alarm bells should have been ringing throughout the New Orleans area and within the Army Corps of Engineers. The city, situated below sea level, would flood catastrophically if the levees were incomplete or weak when such a storm arrived. A major storm was a revolver with a single bullet, cocked and held to the heart of an entire city.

The second surprise in the table is that by the time the interval grows to the average of fifty years, the probability of one or more storms rises to 64 percent. That is the nub of the issue: "Fifty years of protection" does not mean fifty years without a storm. In fact, for any low-probability disaster such as a hurricane, when the chosen interval is equal to the average interval, there is more than a 60 percent chance that one or more adverse events will occur and only about a 30 percent chance that no adverse events will occur in that period. For most people, the period of "protection" does not mean a 60 percent chance of a loss!

RETURN ON INVESTMENT

A more realistic calculation of the risks involved allows us to answer another question: Would fixing the levee system have been a good investment? Let's begin to answer this question by assuming that the costs of levee construction and upgrading, as well as other necessary flood-control projects, would have been $2 billion (to be expended uniformly over ten years) and that a reasonable interest rate for U.S. long-term debt was 5.5 percent. Two billion dollars is just a guess, since estimates vary widely, but it's a good place to start. We can always vary it later to see if it changes the decision we would make, a process called *sensitivity analysis.*

Standard financial discounting creates a "present value" of the cost of fixing the levee system of about $1.5 billion. That number is equivalent to ten years of $200 million expenditures—its value as if all the funds were expended at the outset of the rebuilding period when the impact of interest is included.

If we further assume that the cost of rebuilding New Orleans is $200 billion (a figure that was, in fact, often cited), and that these funds are also expended uniformly over a decade, the discounted value of such expenditures at the start of the first year would be $151 billion. We can use that number as a single period stand-in for the ten-year rebuilding outlay of $20 billion per year just as we can use $1.5 billion as the cost of the flood-control system were it built all at once at the start.

Of course, the actual present value of the rebuilding expenditure stream (now encapsulated in a single present-value number of $151 billion) would have depended on when a crisis-level storm hit. The longer the delay, the less expensive it would have been to rebuild when viewed in present-value terms. If the storm never arrived, then rebuilding costs nothing. To get a feel for this relationship, we calculate the present values if the storm were to arrive at different points in time over a long period. Several hundred years will suffice.

In this calculation, the numbers show that the cost of rebuilding is higher than the $1.5 billion present-value cost of prevention if a major storm hits New Orleans at any time less than about 85 years from the time that the flood-control upgrade funds have to be expended. The calculation also shows that a misunderstanding of the likelihood of a major storm produces an incorrect perception of the financial trade-offs of protecting versus rebuilding. For instance, if we apply Strock's stated belief that New Orleans actually had two hundred to three hundred years of "protection," we would have falsely concluded that it is less expensive not to fix the levees because the present value of rebuilding two hundred to three hundred years down the road is lower than spending for prevention today. Of course, as we have seen, Strock's estimate of the risks were way off because New Orleans has had to worry about more commonplace storms than the less likely Category 5s his risk estimates included.

Combining the calculation above—which tells us the net present value of rebuilding for each time in the future that a disaster would occur—with the true probabilities for each year when such a disaster might occur, gives us a "probability-weighted" figure for the net present value of rebuilding. That figure is $40 billion. *Since the net present value of protection is $1.5 billion, this means that it is more than twenty-five times more expensive to rebuild New Orleans than to protect it from a Category 4 or 5 storm.* (Vulnerability to less intense storms makes the case even stronger.)

Turning this statement around, upgrading the flood-control system would have required a present-value cost of $40 billion or more for it to be a good decision to leave flooding to chance using these probabilities and cost figures.

To test the mettle of this conclusion in another way, we can examine what the probability of a severe storm would have to be to reverse our position that preventing flooding is less expensive than rebuilding in its aftermath. If it would take a large reduction in the storm-risk probability from our assumption of one in fifty, we can be confident that prevention was the preferred policy decision, at least within the assumptions of this simplified model.

Solving for the probability of storms that will produce a break-even between prevention and rebuilding, one finds that the required single-year probability is about 1 in 1,800. That is a huge change: thirty-six times smaller than one in fifty, and six to nine times smaller than the two-hundred- to three-hundred-year estimate used by Strock.

Let's put such a rare possibility in perspective: For rebuilding rather than prevention from Category 4 and 5 storms to have been a wiser financial choice using the costs and interest rates above, New Orleans would only have to be concerned about the arrival of a storm so violent that it is unlikely ever to have been seen. A 1-in-1,800-year storm has a 92 percent chance of never occurring during the entire 154-year period we have kept hurricane records. It has only about a 25 percent chance of having happened since Christopher Columbus reached the Americas in 1492, and only about a fifty–fifty chance of occurring from the crowning of Charlemagne as Holy Roman

Emperor in A.D. 800 to the present day. *On purely financial grounds, the decision not to protect New Orleans was indefensible,* since the intensely violent kind of storm described above would have been even worse than Katrina, the more frequent strong Category 3 storm that did actually swamp New Orleans.

Officials who should have known better seemed to fall prey to unrealistically optimistic calculations of the risks facing New Orleans. Those calculations might be more understandable if the preceding period had not offered plenty of warnings. As it turns out, however, the forty years before Katrina were a veritable shooting gallery of warnings.

Unlike many of the disasters examined in this book, such as Chernobyl and the space shuttles *Challenger* and *Columbia,* all of which never had major accidents to offer undeniable advance warnings, New Orleans was no stranger to damaging storms.

The first major modern-day alarm came in the form of Hurricane Betsy in 1965. Betsy was not a particularly strong storm, as we have now come to know them, but it set a new standard for destruction as far as New Orleans was concerned. Eighty-one people died and $1 billion in damage was done ($6.23 billion in current dollars).

Soon after the disaster, Congress passed the Flood Control Act of 1965, authorizing the use of federal funds for the U.S. Army Corps of Engineers to build a levee system to protect the city from an SPH hurricane.

Congress's apparent generosity was not just pork barrel politics—it made good economic sense. The Port of New Orleans was critical to commerce to and from the thirty-one states that share the Mississippi River, as well as an important base for Louisiana's fast-growing oil and gas industry.

A second warning shot came in August 1969 when Hurricane Camille, at that point the most intense storm ever to make U.S.

landfall and one of only three Category 5 storms ever to hit the United States since record-keeping began in 1851, came alarmingly close to swamping the city. A third warning shot came courtesy of Hurricane Andrew in 1992. Andrew caused the most damage of any natural disaster in American history, despite the fact that it didn't strike a major city. Although Louisiana experienced Andrew only as a Category 3 storm, people began—in light of Andrew's prodigious devastation—to worry what would happen if a Category 5 storm were to hit New Orleans at full force.

The final warning shot came not in the form of a hurricane, but as a massive rainstorm in May 1995 that dumped twenty inches of rain in twelve hours and left six New Orleans residents dead. It was now clear that New Orleans either had to protect itself more effectively or surrender to the inevitability that one day a major storm would kill thousands and possibly render the city uninhabitable.

Over the next decade, the newly created Southeastern Louisiana Urban Flood Control Project (SELA), under the direction of the Corps of Engineers, spent $430 million in federally and locally provided funds to reinforce the levee system and its associated flood-control mechanisms to protect against SPH-intensity storms. Unfortunately, by May 2005—just three months before Hurricane Katrina—the levee projects around massive Lake Pontchartrain were only 60 percent completed in some places due to lack of funding. Although Katrina's winds would weaken over Lake Pontchartrain to only Category 3 strength as the storm moved inland (therefore making the storm just within the levee's design capabilities), the incomplete, technically inconsistent, and ill-maintained levee system was unable to cope. The city flooded as some of its levees breached and collapsed under a storm surge that reached only 10.5 feet, 3.5 feet below the levees' 14-foot design specification.

Various journalistic accounts have chronicled the erosion of the funding for the New Orleans region levee and flood-control projects that led to this tragedy. There seems little doubt that funding was systematically reduced, despite considerable agitated concern on behalf of local officials about the vulnerability of New Orleans to the upcoming 2005 hurricane season. (Some say this funding was reduced to pay for the war in Iraq, Homeland Security, and other Bush administration priorities, although some funding shortfalls also predate his administration.) Money had grown so tight in 2005 that the U.S. Army Corps of Engineers was forced to institute an unprecedented hiring freeze despite all the work yet to be done.

RISK BLINDNESS

Katrina's flooding of New Orleans was a disaster largely of mankind's own making. The hurricane itself was, of course, a natural occurrence (unless you believe, perhaps justifiably, that mankind's contributions to climate change may have intensified and exacerbated the storm). The direct role of humankind can be observed in other aspects of Katrina. That is, we had all the information we needed to see that this event was coming; we had the knowledge, the time, and the resources to mitigate the worst impact of the disaster; and we had many concerned individuals who worked tirelessly to ensure that decision-makers knew the risks and what urgently needed to be done. In spite of all of this, the disaster happened anyway.

Were decision-makers truly aware of the objective risks being taken? In other words, were they intentionally negligent? Or just blind?

As we will see often repeated, those distinctions are sometimes hard to make. There are several reasons why decision-makers might not have taken the necessary steps to minimize the damage to New Orleans and its people:

> 1. *They might not have had the information they needed to reach the proper conclusion that the risk was serious and imminent.*

At a minimum, such knowledge needed to be available and fully understood by them for it to be a foundation of action.

2. Even if decision-makers had the information they needed, they may have discounted it because of their worldview and political ideology. The issue here is whether decision-makers truly believed what they were told.

3. Even if people are aware of a problem, accept its potential harm, and are cognizant of what needs to be done to correct it, they may not be willing to support a solution inconsistent with their own self-interests, be they financial, political, or organizational.

Though listed sequentially, these three factors do not operate in isolation. Rather, they are linked in complex and subtle ways. For instance, vested interests and ideology are not separate from information, but they affect people's search for and perceptions of the truth. Facts and analysis that lead to undesirable or anxiety-producing conclusions may be undeservedly dismissed, whatever their intrinsic merit. Furthermore, since people may generate new information and knowledge for self-interested as well for as altruistic reasons, decision-makers often reflexively discount every pitch they hear in an attempt to correct for latent bias. Sometimes, of course, they overcorrect.

The question of whether all the parties were aware of the risks to New Orleans is better left for journalists, trial lawyers, and historians. Our analysis in this chapter suggests a different yet equally disturbing possibility: Despite having been told otherwise by credible sources, it's possible that decision-makers at many levels did not actually believe the risk assessment, particularly the implications of delays in levee upgrading, correcting engineering deficiencies, and so on. As we will see, being "risk-blind" underlies most tragedies.

It also seems likely that decision-makers were locked into the short-term constraints of annual budget cycles and the inevitable horse-trading that results. We will see that tragic pattern repeated in coming chapters.

In hindsight—with vivid pictures in our minds of the water lapping at the rooflines of New Orleans houses—it is hard to imagine that decision-makers didn't perceive the flooding as the proverbial accident waiting to happen. However, as General Strock said, the official view was that the corps had centuries to prepare. It seems likely that urgently expressed fears of imminent risk were strongly attenuated, if not dismissed out of hand by people whose loved ones and interests were located far from the Big Easy.

Katrina cost the nation 1,800 lives, incalculable hardship, $200 billion or more that federal, state, and local governments can ill afford, and compromises to many future programs that will now have to be cut back or delayed to pay for this error in judgment. If we are to avoid such colossal mistakes in the future, we must learn to face the probabilities and likely consequences squarely, and be less sanguine that everything will work out okay if we merely follow our instincts.

CHAPTER 4

SPACE SHUTTLE *CHALLENGER*: COLD, WARM, AND HOT CAUSES OF DISASTERS

On January 28, 1986, at 11:38 A.M. on an unusually cold Florida morning, the space shuttle *Challenger* lifted off from Pad 39B, Kennedy Space Center, Florida. The launch, broadcast on all three major television networks, was a special moment for Americans. Among the crew of seven was Sharon Christa McAuliffe, a high school teacher from New Hampshire who was to be the first civilian in space. She carried the hopes and dreams of millions of young people and spaceflight enthusiasts.

Seventy-three seconds later, the unimaginable happened. The *Challenger* was transformed into a smoking fireball as fuel from its ruptured external fuel tanks ignited, leaving a national audience stunned and horrified. Exacerbating the viewers' collective anguish was the news that the crew module separated intact during the explosion, careened into a two-minute free fall from fifty thousand feet, and plunged into the sea at two hundred miles per hour. The crew had no parachutes or means of escape, and all seven perished.

Even as Americans mourned the loss of these heroes, the difficult question remained: How could such a disaster have occurred when NASA had developed elaborate procedures for identifying, classifying, and remedying the myriad potential risks to crew, spacecraft, and mission? NASA had developed these procedures to overcome the tremendous complexity of manned space flight in general, and the space shuttle and its many experimental technologies in particular. The significance of the *Challenger* case stems from the occurrence of catastrophic failure despite such a demonstrably deep historical concern for safety. How did the problems that led up to the *Challenger* disaster slip through so many seemingly robust safety nets?

THE DILEMMA OF "WEAK SIGNALS"

Contrary to the belief of many nontechnical people, most technology is "unruly." That is, it is not always well behaved. Often, technological innovators do not fully understand the behavior of the systems they are creating. In particular, they may not understand the conditions that cause radical changes in performance, nor do they fully appreciate the results of interactions among components they have not had an opportunity to observe. This unfamiliarity is especially prevalent with emerging technology that has not had time to accumulate a substantial body of experience through use under varied conditions, and in large-scale projects, such as the space shuttle, that possess many potential interactions that cannot be exhaustively tested.

Consequently, as sociologist Diane Vaughan explains in *The Challenger Launch Decision*, an engineering truism has it that "change is bad." That rule of thumb stands in sharp contrast to the public image of design engineers as innovators, but it reflects the sober recognition that alterations to design, materials, fabrication, and testing introduce changes in performance that are often impossible to predict. In fact, the design of the joints used to connect the separate sections of the shuttle's tall solid rocket boosters were a modest modification of the one used in the reliable Titan III rocket.

Based on the design of the Titan II ICBM, the Titan III had, from the mid-1960s onward, become the workhorse of reusable launch vehicles. In different configurations, Titan rockets had launched 360 times and were considered "very reliable," with an average of one failure every ninety launches. True to the engineering maxim that "change is bad," however, the relatively minor modifications introduced by Utah-based contracting company Morton Thiokol to the United Technologies Titan solid rocket booster design changed its behavior in unexpected ways.

In spite of its fatal flaw, the solid rocket boosters were only one of many developmental technologies incorporated into the massive, bewilderingly complex machine known as the space shuttle. Out of necessity, NASA and its contractors approached risk management systematically by using scientific, data-based methods to identify problems and develop solutions. While intuition plays an important role in technical work, it served here mainly as a guide to diagnosing problems and developing solutions. Throughout NASA, the necessity of "hard facts" based on the quantitative analysis of actual flights and rigorous testing was deeply entrenched in its culture, and it was a sine qua non to establish proof of the existence of a problem, isolate its causes, and provide evidence of the efficacy of proposed solutions.

This ingrained approach has one obvious shortcoming. Engineering personnel might have a hunch about a particular risk but lack culturally acceptable proof that the risk is real. In such a situation, the organization can behave as if conditions are safe until the hunch can be verified as a real risk through further testing or a real-life accident. Conversely, the organization can assume that flights are at risk until it can be proved that it is safe to fly. The ambiguity about how to interpret signs of potential but unconfirmed danger—proving a negative, as it were—constitute the *weak signals dilemma*. This issue is intimately related to similar risk issues seen in earlier chapters.

Historically, NASA had always been conservative, requiring proof that it was safe to fly. They presumed that an unproven case was an unsafe one. However, on the evening before *Challenger*'s launch, NASA took what appeared to be the opposite view: In the absence of confirming hard facts, NASA ignored the most knowledgeable Thiokol engineers' fears about the potential adverse effects of cold temperatures on the rubber O-rings that sealed the joints between sections of the giant solid rocket boosters. These boosters were known variously within NASA as SRBs, SRMs (for solid rocket motors), boosters, or simply "the solids"—they lifted the shuttle off its launchpad with nearly five times the thrust of the shuttle's main engines.

NASA also ignored the advice of another contractor, Rockwell, whose engineers were worried that the ice that had formed overnight and now covered the launch gantry might be shaken loose by launch vibrations and damage the shuttle's fragile heat-absorbing tiles, creating a risk of burn-through during reentry. (Ice had formed as a result of an ill-fated decision to let water lines drip instead of draining and refilling them, a more time-consuming process.)

Rocco Petrone, president of Rockwell's Space Transportation Division, was called from the Kennedy Space Center at 7:00 A.M. EST by Robert Glaysher, his company's representative at the launch site. "Make sure NASA understands that Rockwell feels it is not safe to launch," Petrone instructed Glaysher. When Glaysher relayed the concern, NASA chose not to heed Rockwell's alarm.

THE SHOW MUST GO ON

The night of January 27, 1986, was not the time NASA managers wanted to hear about the insufficiently understood yet possibly dangerous effects of cold temperature on O-rings. The Teacher In Space Program, in which McAuliffe was to be the first civilian member of a space shuttle crew, had generated a great deal of favorable publicity. Through constant press and TV coverage, the world was watching NASA's every move. But difficulties during the leadup to the launch had already taken much of the bloom off the rose by the night of January 27. The launch was, in fact, originally scheduled for the day before, Sunday, January 26, but had to be delayed after a forecast of bad weather.

That delay turned into an embarrassment when the weather on the morning of the January 26 proved perfect for a launch. By then, however, the launch had been scrubbed. Likewise, on January 27, a stuck hatch bolt locked the astronauts out of their capsule, a problem exacerbated by a series of faulty batteries used to power the portable drills needed to extract it. By the evening of the 27th, as the next day's weather forecast called for unusually cold overnight weather, "It's too cold to launch" was not a message anyone wanted to deliver to NASA or to the army of expectant reporters and crowds of family, dignitaries, and well-wishers who had jammed the visitors' grandstand for each prior launch attempt.

Challenger's launch scheduling had already created a number of peculiarities, particularly the skipping of January 26 in favor of the 27th, a decision made personally by NASA's acting administrator, William Graham. But the big unanswered question—one that has puzzled people for two decades—was why, after the delay on January 27, was *Challenger* launched amid icy conditions on January 28, and over so many objections?

One compelling answer to that question is that when objections were raised, NASA managers were not receptive to hearing them. During an unusual teleconference on the evening before the launch, Lawrence Mulloy, the Solid Rocket Booster Project manager at NASA's Marshall Space Flight Center in Huntsville, Alabama, infamously asked the concerned engineers, "My God, when do you want me to launch, Thiokol, next April?" Both Morton Thiokol, the rocket booster contractor based in Brigham, Utah, and NASA's own engineers had been worried about the effects of cold weather on the SRB's O-rings since the beginnings of the space shuttle program. While they didn't have indisputable evidence of a clear and present danger, they did have reasons for concern. The mystery is why those misgivings were overlooked.

EARLY WARNINGS

The Kennedy Space Center (KSC) is located in Cape Canaveral, Florida, on the Atlantic Ocean at approximately the same latitude as Orlando. The winter weather at the KSC is generally mild with average January high temperatures in the low seventies F and lows in the fifties.

Extreme cold weather was not on the radar screen for the engineering teams working on the O-ring sealing problems of the solid rocket booster joint. In fact, prior to *Challenger*, only one incident of severe cold weather had threatened a launch. In late January 1985, a year before *Challenger*, the flight designated STS-51C raised low temperatures as a distinct risk factor when a hundred-year-record cold snap plunged overnight temperatures to 18 to 22 F for several days prior to the January 24 launch. When the boosters were recovered from the ocean and examined after the launch, significant amounts of erosion and a type of joint hot gas leakage known as blowby were observed on two field joints. (A so-called field joint is one assembled in the "field," that is, at Kennedy Space Center in Florida, rather than at Morton Thiokol's factory in Utah. This was done because the 150-foot-long, 12-foot-diameter solid rocket boosters containing one million pounds of solid propellant are too large to be shipped cross-country already assembled.)

That was not the first time O-rings and temperature had been correlated. The first official mention of the connection appeared a full six years prior to the *Challenger* disaster, in a 1980 NASA report that requested "additional verification at temperature extremes."

After the temperature issue was raised by shuttle flight 51C, NASA requested a detailed briefing on O-ring erosion, which was held on February 8, 1985. Thiokol's presentation primarily dealt with the existing set of facts and only superficially with temperature, since there was little in the way of hard evidence to support the assertion that low temperatures contributed materially to risk. At that time, Mulloy dismissed even the limited mention of temperature in the report, employing the mantra "prove it to me with facts" by arguing that there were many possible causes other than temperature that could explain an increase in erosion.

Those who don't work as engineers may not appreciate that the introduction of temperature added significant complexity to a problem that was already technically very complicated. Formulating a more complete conceptual model of O-ring behavior meant that additional study was necessary before flights could continue. Acknowledging the role of temperature left Marshall managers between a rock and a hard place with a joint whose behavior they could no longer claim to understand.

Why were they so concerned?

First, the space shuttle had been declared an operational rather than a developmental program. At that point, surprises that grounded the fleet over safety concerns were not supposed to happen. Deep embarrassment was certain, and nobody wanted to be the one to provoke humiliation. An aversion to being shamed is a powerful motivator.

Second, beginning with its planning phases in the early 1970s, the space shuttle had increasingly become militarized. The initial changes were technical, including an enlargement of the payload bay to hold larger military satellites and a change in the wing design from straight wing to delta wing to permit the use of Vandenberg Air Force Base in California, a location essential to the launching of military payloads into polar orbit. A West Coast capability was also essential to launch satellites that could spy on the Soviet Union. Thus, by the mid-1980s, NASA was dependent upon the air force for funding as well as for garnering political support from Congress.

Vandenberg—located on California's central coast sixty miles north of Santa Barbara—is considerably colder than the Atlantic coast of

Florida. On many early mornings, temperatures fell below the lowest possible temperature within NASA's launch experience. Temperature-related "launch commit criteria"—the space agency's parlance for rules that would have precluded cold-weather launches—might have endangered NASA's critical Defense Department funding because in that case the air force could not totally rely on the shuttle to launch satellites and space-based weapons like the missile defense initiative popularly known as "Star Wars."

Third, from the space shuttle's first launch, it had become a Reagan administration public relations vehicle. President Reagan visited mission control in Houston, personally attended the landing of *Columbia* on the Fourth of July in 1982, and Vice President Bush made various NASA visits (including one planned for the *Challenger* launch). President Reagan and German Chancellor Helmut Kohl had even established a live TV link with *Columbia* astronauts on November 28, 1983, as they were on their way to Spacelab, a space laboratory built by the European Space Agency.

During a test of the TV hookup, astronauts Owen K. Garriott, Robert A. Parker, and Brewster H. Shaw lined up in a "see, hear, and speak no evil" pantomime to protest the White House's tight scripting of the event. That was a rare sort of civil disobedience in space. Clearly, President Reagan and his handlers took public relations and the space shuttle *very* seriously.

As winter ended in Florida in early 1985, the immediate worries about cold-weather launches faded. Nevertheless, problems with the joints continued, although all were nationalized within the existing understanding of the SRB O-rings, which included a number of assembly and testing variables representing all known risks that affected their reliability.

At the same time, the investigation into temperature effects continued, albeit at a low level. Nevertheless, tests performed in March 1985 showed that "the seals would lift off their sealing surfaces for several [2.4] seconds at 75 degrees Fahrenheit and in excess of 10 minutes at 50 degrees Fahrenheit." Those results showed that temperature could have an exponential impact on O-ring behavior, the very same point recognized five years earlier by NASA researchers.

Flight STS-51, a mission on which Senator Jake Garn was a passenger, was launched on April 12, 1985. After the SRBs were recovered, they showed the largest amount of erosion of any flight to date. Although the erosion was severe, a preflight increase in the leak test pressure for that particular joint (it was a nozzle joint, not a field joint, and thus was differently designed and assembled at the Morton Thiokol factory) provided a satisfactory explanation. Erosion was deemed within "acceptable safety margins," and thus no further action was considered necessary according to NASA's strict protocols for problem identification, which did not reintroduce "known problems" once they had been thoroughly reviewed.

O-ring erosion on flight 51-B, which launched on April 29, 1985, created even greater concern, although it, too, was ultimately explained within the existing paradigm. The primary O-ring of the left nozzle joint of 51-B had burned all the way through, and blowby effects had reached the joint's second O-ring, the so-called secondary seal, suggesting the possible loss of the joint's backup O-ring protection, and catastrophic failure if this second O-ring were to burn through, thus allowing the escape of high-temperature propellant gases.

After further study, NASA gave verbal approval in July to incorporate a "capture feature" into the SRB design that would improve secondary O-ring performance by limiting "joint rotation," a phenomenon whereby the high-pressure gases created by the burning rocket fuel slightly ballooned the booster casing and widened the gap filled by the O-rings. The new safety feature had been undergoing tests since October 1984 and was considered worthwhile by NASA Marshall.

Incorporating capture was a long-term solution, however, and would take twenty-seven months to implement, since it involved changes to the SRB's metal castings. (The capture feature was one of the changes made after the *Challenger* explosion.)

Dissatisfied with what he perceived to be a lack of urgency dealing with this problem, Thiokol O-ring expert Roger Boisjoly wrote a strongly worded memo to pressure Thiokol management into creating a dedicated team to study the seal failures. The team had its first meeting on August 15, 1985, at which it proposed twenty alternative designs for the nozzle joints and forty-three designs for the field joints. Perhaps because these were such ambitious proposals, the shuttle would fly "as is" until NASA could decide upon and then incorporate needed changes. Clearly, that premature go-ahead was a fatal mistake.

In the meantime, flight 51F had flown successfully on July 29, 1985, with no erosion, although a gas path was found cutting through the special high-temperature putty that was used inside the boosters to help seal the joints. The conclusion drawn was that the various technical and procedural changes were working. While NASA and Thiokol had been tinkering with the details of the joints in order to improve their performance, 51F's lack of erosion should hardly have been considered conclusive. Nevertheless, there was a willingness to accept one instance as proof that problems had been solved. Here was an obvious contradiction to the data-based rational methods so strongly espoused by NASA in the past. Wishful thinking was clearly at work.

In early October 1985, Thiokol's Boisjoly again expressed urgent concerns in his weekly activity report describing the difficulties the O-ring task force was having getting things done. While most of Boisjoly's complaints were directed at familiar red tape problems facing any large bureaucratic organization, those problems nevertheless slowed the progress of the task force. Increased senior management support would likely have cut through the red tape, but it was not forthcoming.

On October 30, 1985, flight 61-A was launched in warm-weather conditions with a calculated O-ring temperature of 75 F. This flight had significant leakage in one of its field joints. While the results of 61-A were similar to past problems, the observed leakage on a field joint in warm weather would confuse the relationship between temperature and O-ring leakage during the all-important evening conference call three months later just before *Challenger* flew. Ironically, even though there was considerable damage, 61-A was hailed as support for the relative safety of "acceptable risks."

By January 1986, then, concerns about the joints were at an all-time high. At the same time, as a practical matter it was believed that as long as strict attention was paid to assembly and preflight testing, both field and nozzle joints would perform within acceptable risk parameters. Experience suggested that there was likely to be some blowby and erosion, although the presence of these effects in random putty irregularities made specifics impossible to predict. While temperature had been established as a complicating factor, albeit one whose impact was not fully understood, it was not considered a serious concern because the record "hundred-year" cold of the previous January was not considered likely to recur. Unfortunately, Mother Nature threw NASA a deadly curve.

THE CONFERENCE CALLS

On the evening of January 27, weather forecasts indicated likely temperatures would be in the low twenties prior to launch the next morning. Thiokol vice presidents Robert Lund and Joseph Kilminster agreed that NASA should be contacted. Alan McDonald, Thiokol director of the Solid Rocket Motor Project, informed Cecil Houston, Marshall's resident manager at Kennedy Space Center, that Thiokol's engineers did not know whether the launch should go ahead. An impromptu three-city telephone conference between officials at Thiokol in Utah, Marshall in

Huntsville, and Kennedy Space Center in Cape Canaveral, Florida, was arranged for 5:45 P.M. EST to discuss the issue.

The teleconference lasted about forty-five minutes. Thiokol took no official position, although its representatives stated that the launch should be delayed until noon or afterwards so the weather could warm up. Unfortunately, the telephone connection was bad, especially for people reached at home or at their hotels.

Over the years, organizations have come to rely on audio and video teleconference facilities to guide important decisions as well as to conduct more routine meetings. Such conferences were and often still are plagued with problems. People in leadership roles are permitted the floor most of the time while people lower in the hierarchy often don't get the opportunity to speak, or they avoid airing complaints or bad news they are aware of. Participants regularly complain about the difficulty of hearing and being heard by others, and the lack of last-minute printed materials is often a problem for the participants who are on the road. Nevertheless, despite the many difficulties, important decisions are often made while this balky medium is in use. *Challenger*'s fate hung in the balance of such a call.

Logistics also complicated the first teleconference that evening. Lawrence Mulloy, NASA's SRB project manager and an essential decision-maker, could not be reached. A second conference call was therefore scheduled for 8:45 P.M. EST so that more personnel could be involved, with engineering data sent in advance.

After the first conference call ended, Stan Reinartz, Marshall shuttle projects manager, ran into Mulloy having dinner at the hotel near the Kennedy Space Center in which all the Marshall personnel were staying. However, Reinartz did not inform Mulloy or other NASA upper-level management that based upon Thiokol's unofficial recommendation there might be a launch delay, later testifying that "We did not have a full understanding of the situation. . . ."

At Marshall, people with the relevant skills were told about the later conference call. However, some personnel could not be located. In particular, Leon Ray, the person at Marshall most knowledgeable about the joints, was not contacted because he was assumed to be on his way to Florida to watch the launch. He was actually at home in Huntsville, but no one had bothered to call him.

At Thiokol, the relevant people with technical expertise were available because they had been contacted earlier in the day. After the first conference call, the engineering staff worked to prepare presentation materials to make its case that *Challenger* should not be launched.

At 8:45 P.M., the second call began. At Morton Thiokol in Utah, the attendees were Jerald Mason, senior vice president, Wasatch Operations; Calvin Wiggins, vice president and general manager, Space Division, Wasatch; Joe Kilminster, vice president, Space Booster Programs, Wasatch; Bob Lund, vice president, Engineering; Roger Boisjoly, Thiokol's most experienced SRB engineer and its local seal expert; and Arnie Thompson, supervisor, Rocket Motor Cases. At Kennedy were Stanley Reinartz, manager of the Shuttle Projects Office at Marshall; Lawrence Mulloy, manager, SRB Project at Marshall; and Alan McDonald, director of the Solid Rocket Motor Project for Morton Thiokol. At Marshall in Huntsville were George Hardy, deputy director, Science and Engineering, and Judson Lovingood, Reinartz's deputy, completed the group.

Buried among the Thikol engineers' presentation materials were some potentially launch-stopping data. The predicted O-ring temperature, based on a Thiokol analysis of the effect of overnight cold and other factors, was 29 degrees F, 24 degrees below the lowest temperature of an actual launch to date. (It would later turn out that the actual temperature was even lower than that because of the cooling effect of the shuttle's external liquid fuel tank.)

The Thiokol engineers felt that this projection suggested risks for several reasons. First, the cold O-rings would be less flexible and less able to fill the gap between the sections of the SRB casing; second, the grease used to lubricate the O-rings would be less viscous, slowing their movement into sealing position; and third, the pre-ignition compression on the O-rings would be lessened due to shrinkage—in other words, the O-rings might be starting out too small to seal effectively. The combined effect, reasoned the engineers, would be to increase the time needed for the primary O-ring to establish its seal. That lag might possibly exceed the time available to complete the sealing process due to the joint expansion that occurred during the fraction of a second of the SRB's ignition pressurization.

Of course, the argument was hypothetical, since the actual behavior of the joints as a function of temperature was still unknown. In fact, test firing of the SRBs was performed only with the boosters in a horizontal position. Only extensive tests and analysis work on low-temperature seal dynamics could answer the question of how the various joint designs would actually behave under the forecast low-temperature conditions. The data in hand were incomplete since there had been only one launch at low temperatures and no real-life low-temperature testing. Clouding the picture still further was the fact that in the two instances of field joint blowby that had been observed, only one had taken place under relatively cold O-ring conditions, while the other had occurred under warmer conditions in October 1985. In the absence of strong technical arguments backed by solid facts, the Thiokol group formulated a compromise recommendation. It proposed that 53 degrees Fahrenheit—the conditions of the troubled launch of flight 51C in January 1985—be the minimum temperature for *Challenger*'s flight, since it represented the coldest temperature of any previous launch.

Despite the strength of some of the engineers' convictions, there is no doubt that the evidence about the role of temperature was incomplete.

During the second conference call, NASA's Mulloy focused on the dearth of proof, strongly invoking the principle central to NASA culture that facts, not suppositions, mattered most. Mulloy dismissed the Thiokol engineers' temperature concerns as "incomplete." George Hardy, Marshall deputy director of Science and Engineering, drove the nail in farther by stating that he was "appalled" by Thiokol's recommendation.

According to later interviews and testimony before the Rogers Commission—the group led by former secretary of state William Rogers, which Reagan had created to investigate the accident—many at Thiokol perceived those statements to be "turning the tables." That is, they felt pressured to prove that it was *unsafe* to fly. Of those experiencing such pressure, none may have felt it more strongly than Roger Boisjoly, perhaps the most strenuous no-launch advocate as well as one of the people most knowledgeable about the behavior of the joints. After the accident, Mulloy and Hardy testified that it had not been their intention to put pressure on anyone, a sentiment reinforced by others at NASA who attended the teleconference. NASA's position was that they were simply seeking a fact-based engineering rationale for Thiokol's position, just as they had always done.

Since that was the first time Thiokol had made a no-launch recommendation, it may have felt to them that they were being challenged in a different way. Unlike a classical debate, in which each side has to prove its case, many at Thiokol assumed that launch safety possessed an asymmetrical proof structure similar to the "presumption of innocence" foundation of the U.S. and many other criminal justice systems. In that light, if the launch was considered unsafe until proved otherwise, even a weak argument should have prevailed. However, over time and through the accumulation of experience, engineering evidence, and many management reviews, NASA's view was that the SRB O-ring seals represented an acceptable risk. But there was more at work here than reason.

During a critical half-hour caucus among Thiokol personnel while the conference phones were muted, speculation at the two NASA sites was that Thiokol would come back with a modified version of its no-launch recommendation, perhaps one with a lower temperature threshold. Most people expected a 40-degree minimum because that temperature was the lower end of the range for which the solid rocket motors were "qualified," NASA's term for safety and technical approval. Such a recommendation would have been difficult to dispute, as it would be "within the rules," require no additional evidence, and thus be politically bulletproof. Of course, NASA might have requested and obtained a "waiver" for that condition. For the *Challenger* launch, other waivers pertaining to the external fuel tank and the entire shuttle system had already been obtained. For reasons still unexplained, pushing the limits in spite of the risks appeared to be okay for that particular launch.

Ultimately, therefore, and despite strong protests from its engineers, Thiokol's management reversed its previous no-launch position, adopting Mulloy's counterarguments. In particular, it placed great stock in the redundancy provided by the secondary seal even though that seal might also be compromised by the effects of the freezing-cold temperatures.

THE LAUNCH

The next morning, the launch went ahead as scheduled, despite additional opposition by Rockwell, a second contractor, and to the surprise of the astronauts, who never expected to fly that day because of the weather. Just after liftoff, 0.68 second into the flight, a strong puff of dark smoke spurted from that part of the aft area of the right solid rocket booster that faces the external fuel tank. As the spacecraft ascended, eight additional puffs of smoke occurred at the rate of four per second, approximately the frequency of the structural load dynamics and joint flexing of the accelerating shuttle. At that point, the black color of the smoke suggested that grease, joint insulation putty, and rubber O-rings were being burned by escaping hot high-pressure propellant gases.

Approximately thirty-seven seconds into the flight, *Challenger* encountered severe high-altitude wind shears that lasted twenty-seven seconds. The shuttle's guidance and control system sensed and corrected for the effect, but the SRB's steering system had to be more active than in previous flights, increasing the stress on the spacecraft and aggravating the joint failure.

At 58.8 seconds, as the shuttle increased its thrust, a small flame appeared near the aft field joint in the same region as the source of the original smoke. The flame grew rapidly and became well defined within a second. Independent telemetry revealed that the right solid rocket booster was operating at lower pressure, confirming a propellant gas leak. At that point, if not before, the O-rings had clearly failed.

The flame continued to grow, and aerodynamics and the spacecraft's physical structure directed it toward the external fuel tank and the attachment strut between the SRB and the external tank. At 64.7 seconds, the flame breached the shuttle's large external hydrogen tank, causing the highly combustible fuel to leak, mix with surrounding air, and burn.

At 72.2 seconds, when *Challenger* was at Mach 1.9 and forty-six thousand feet, a rapid chain of events unfolded, resulting in the destruction of the spacecraft. First, the right booster became detached from the external fuel tank assembly when its attaching strut lost structural integrity. That caused the booster to begin to rotate around its remaining upper connecting strut. Less than a second later, the entire external hydrogen tank rapidly lost its structural integrity, resulting in the release of massive amounts of liquid hydrogen, which immediately ignited as it mixed with the surrounding air.

The expansion of the burning hydrogen propelled the hydrogen tank rapidly upward at approximately the same time as the rotating right SRB impacted the intertank structure and its adjacent external oxygen tank. Within milliseconds, there was a massive, explosive burning of the hydrogen and oxygen released from their respective ruptured tanks. The spacecraft was totally enveloped in the explosive burn, and its reaction control system ruptured shortly thereafter, causing its propellants to burn as well.

Under those massive aerodynamic loads, the spacecraft broke into a number of large sections as it emerged from the fireball. The crew module separated intact from the explosion and began its fatal free fall toward the ocean nine miles below.

When the SRBs were recovered, the right one displayed a hole big enough for a man to crawl through.

WHAT CAUSED THE ACCIDENT?

In the case of *Challenger*, three types of causes interacted to produce tragic results. The first type consisted of inherent design weaknesses in the shuttle. We might call them "cold" causes because they are unintentional mistakes, although not unimportant ones. While cold causes may be critical accident contributors, they do not evoke a high degree of emotion, at least not compared with what we might call "warm" and "hot" causes.

Warm causes include ignoring weak signals of danger and other bureaucratic inefficiencies in response to indications of risk. These choices appear less innocent than many design errors because they involve decision-makers' priorities and judgment in the face of explicit, identified risks.

Finally, we move on to hot causes: deliberately subordinating safety to financial and political pressure. With hindsight, such decisions often appear unethical or even immoral. As was the case in *Challenger* and the Vioxx case in chapter 6, hot causes often consist of conscious decisions that may well expose people to harm without their knowledge, and certainly without their consent.

Cold Causes

Challenger possessed inherent weaknesses in its technical design. The alterations by Morton Thiokol to the original United Technologies Titan III solid rocket motor design were made for logical reasons—increased power and improved safety—but they introduced unanticipated performance changes, as alterations often do. It took considerable time for NASA's contractor engineering community to figure out what was happening with the joints, and to develop an assembly and testing protocol that was reasonably reliable. Nevertheless, even at their best, the SRBs did not perform the way they were supposed to. The technical origin of the accident must start with that.

As we will explore in greater depth in the next chapter, design errors are central to many accidents. Design mistakes, per se, usually do not cause accidents unless they are completely invisible until tragedy strikes. As *Challenger* shows, however, there are usually signs that things are amiss, but the key factor is what people do when those signs are revealed.

Warm Causes

In contrast with tragic yet unintended design flaws, NASA's and Thiokol's response to danger signals does not appear to have been innocent.

Instead of redesigning the joints or, at a minimum, thoroughly understanding the joints' behavior and the conditions under which they might fail, over time Thiokol and NASA came to accept their behavior.

I am using the word *accept* in the sense of "become acclimatized to" rather than "approve of." Sociologist Diane Vaughan, in her meticulous study of the *Challenger* case, refers to this process as "the normalization of deviance." Vaughan shows how both Thiokol and NASA personnel gradually developed comfort with the anomalous behavior of the joints, including their nonstandard extrusion sealing method, the presence of random blowby incidents, and a tolerance of erosion. With each successful flight, acceptance of blowby and erosion grew, even though those symptoms were clear signs that the joints were not sealing as they were designed to do. However, no matter how many rounds of Russian roulette one might successfully survive, the game is never "safe." Unfortunately, NASA had forgotten how to be afraid.

A different approach would have been to treat each new incident of blowby and erosion as a near miss that demanded energetic investigation, a vigorous unearthing of the root causes of the problem, and a definitive remedy. Rather than increasing comfort by focusing on past successes, which had occurred despite evidence of sealing problems, NASA could have escalated concern based on the persistence of signals of "potential failures" despite its best efforts to eliminate them. That would have been a radically different mind-set and, while it would have doubtless led to delays and greater cost, such a course of action would have ensured much higher reliability.

During the evening teleconferences, Thiokol's Boisjoly and a few others were trying to impose some reflective thinking on a problem that for many months had been subject to relative indifference. What happened, of course, was that time pressure created the opposite effect: a crisis mode, not a thoughtful review. It probably goes without saying that eleventh-hour meetings are generally ineffective environments in which to consider unpopular theories supported by scanty evidence. With tragic irony, seal task force investigations had progressed with bureaucratic slowness, so there was no additional evidence to bring to this crisis meeting, although there has been considerable criticism in the years since the accident that more evidence could have been mustered than was made available.

For its part, Thiokol management was feeling production pressure, and its perceptions were probably exaggerated by the last-minute nature of the meeting and the apparent displeasure of NASA personnel. In such a frame of mind, it is difficult to take a step back, especially to admit that one's overall understanding of the problem is much less thorough than needed, and that having placed greater priority on the seal task force would have been a good idea. In the end, Thiokol management did not know—and could not have known—how the joints would behave under low-temperature conditions. Despite their lack of understanding, individuals made a decision "with their management hats on," but in truth it was little more than wishful thinking. Actually, they were doing what they were told.

As for NASA, to truly understand the organization's approach to risk and the decisions that flowed from managers' beliefs, we must understand its organizational culture, particularly the assumptions that operated at a deep level to guide not only how people acted, but also how they thought. Like all organizational cultures, NASA's evolved from its mastery of the challenges it had faced—its successes, in other words. In developing this mastery, NASA promoted its methods and espoused its values beyond mere institutionalization to become simply "the way we do things." While these largely transparent assumptions sometimes became visible (as they did during the evening teleconference), most of the time they remain quietly beyond questioning—and accepted by virtually all involved. It was simply unthinkable that NASA's ways of doing things were themselves sources of risk rather than reducers of risk.

The dominant NASA worldview was that its fact-based methods would "capture the problem," even in the absence of a comprehensive model of joint behavior or a comprehensive redesign that would cause the joints to seal properly. In other words, even though they lacked an integrated picture of how the joints behaved, NASA and Thiokol management believed they understood the risks well enough to fashion a day-to-day working solution within acceptable risk.

Yet, as has been described, there were signs that things were wrong. Blowby and erosion meant that the joints didn't seal, and deeply knowledgeable people were worried about the effects of temperature. They had some facts, although far from conclusive ones.

Unfortunately, as *Challenger* illustrates, ignoring weak signals is the norm in many organizations; it occurs in business and public policy, as well as in science. A small number of high-hazard organizations in the military (aircraft carrier flight operations) and in civilian life (nuclear power plants) avoid that pitfall, but they are extremely rare. In fact, the extensive methods such organizations employ to ensure that weak signals are amplified rather than suppressed illustrate how fragile such information is in ordinary settings.

Complicating the problem, NASA was subjected to other pressures beyond the failings of bureaucracy and normal psychological denial. The *Challenger* launch harbored a number of guilty secrets.

Hot Causes

Lawrence Mulloy was an effective NASA pitchman and an energetic advocate for the priorities of the solid rocket program. One such priority was the so-called filament wound case (FWC), an alternative to the steel casings that made up the sections of the existing SRBs. The FWC was manufactured by spinning cocoonlike casings out of graphite-epoxy fiber using giant spinning machines. Though these casings were extremely strong yet much lighter than steel, graphite-epoxy was prone to crack under pressure. A 1985 high-pressure water test of a full-size FWC cracked the case below the high pressures needed for a safe launch. If a case cracked on the launchpad, it would probably destroy the launch complex as well as the shuttle.

Despite those risks, Richard Cook reports in Challenger *Revealed: An Insider's Account of How the Reagan Administration Caused the Greatest Tragedy of the Space Age* that "Mulloy repeatedly asserted, without offering data, that despite the [filament wound case] failure, the case was safe and would be proven so when retested."

Mulloy's enthusiasm for the FWC—as well as his lobbying in 1985 that SRB joint temperature not become a criterion that had to be met before launching—were both linked to the importance within NASA of military payloads. A temperature-based precedent set by the *Challenger* launch would have been potentially devastating. Morton Thiokol, the SRB contractor that produced the solid rocket motors, also had an obvious stake in ensuring the success of the Vandenberg launches and the expansion of the Space Shuttle Program they represented.

Despite the militarization, there is still no answer to the question of why *Challenger* had to launch the morning of January 28 rather than a few days later. Shuttle delays were common, even those that had scrambled the launch schedule. For that answer, we need to return to the politics of the space shuttle, and to the president of the United States and the American heroes who had become a hallmark of his State of the Union addresses.

Ronald Reagan's heroes were individuals who exhibited bravery, self-sacrifice, and indomitable spirit. They were battlefield heroes, breakthrough entrepreneurs of humble origins, inspirational clergy, and immigrants with bright futures despite their hard-luck pasts. They were, in short, quintessential American success stories.

Reagan's 1986 State of the Union was scheduled for Tuesday, January 28, 1986, two days after *Challenger*'s scheduled launch on January 26—the launch that NASA administrator William Graham inexplicably canceled the night before due to forecast bad weather. At

Graham's direction, NASA had prepared a draft for the White House for Reagan to insert into his speech. Naturally, the main feature of NASA's draft was Christa McAuliffe, the Teacher in Space, who was to be cited in the speech as one of Reagan's quintessential heroes.

After the accident, however, the White House denied that McAuliffe was to have been mentioned in the televised speech. Questioned directly on the application of pressure by the White House, the president denied any role in NASA's launch decision, disclaiming any suggestion that "somehow they [NASA] were pressured to go off beginning with myself, no such thing has ever taken place. We don't know enough about that kind of thing to know whether we should advise them to take off or not."

In light of the powerful role model that McAuliffe represented, Reagan's fondness of the space shuttle as a public relations platform, and the relative ease and reliability of telephone hookups to the shuttle, a live telephone call during the speech seemed an irresistible public relations coup. For that to work, however, the shuttle had to be settled into orbit, as it should have been. But after the unexpected and embarrassing failed launch on the 27th due to the stuck hatch bolt, the shuttle had to launch on the 28th, and no later.

Despite all the official denials of pressure from the White House to launch in time for Reagan's speech, there was a significant amount of telephone conversation between NASA, including the Kennedy Space Center, and the White House during the days leading up to launch time. Although there are many possible reasons for those conversations other than the application of political pressure, White House callers included NASA General Manager Philip Culbertson; Associate Administrator for Space Flight Jesse Moore and his deputy, Michael Weeks; Director of NASA's Marshall Space Flight Center William Lucas; and NASA Public Affairs Director Shirley Green, a political appointee with White House connections.

One unexplained call originated from the office of Richard Smith, Kennedy Space Center director, to Acting NASA Administrator William Graham. According to Rogers Commission documents, participants might have included Philip Culbertson, Jesse Moore, and Richard Smith. When interviewed, none of the participants recalled anything distinctive about the conversation beyond a routine discussion of the launch, although the call appears to have taken place after the warnings about weather and freezing conditions would have gone out.

Other phone calls between NASA and the White House were also logged, including one that establishes a link between Kennedy and President Reagan's scheduling office, a relationship the White House stated did not exist.

The final piece of the *Challenger* launch puzzle fell into place from an unlikely, and some might think dubious, source. Ed Helin, one of Ronald and Nancy Reagan's astrologers who had been providing advice to them since 1949 and who was paid by the Republican National Committee, repeated in a number of interviews that he advised the president about the launch of *Challenger*. Richard Cook's reportage goes as follows:

> *"Did you talk to the president before the* Challenger *launch?" I [Cook] asked.*
>
> *"Yes," Helin said.*
>
> *"Did you talk to him or his aides?"*
>
> *"Oh, I talked directly to the president," he said. "He had called me."*
>
> *Helin now explained that he had advised President Reagan that, astrologically speaking, January 28 was not a good day to launch* Challenger. *He said that the horoscope viewed the weather as a problem.*

I was stunned to hear this. Not only were the experts at NASA and its contractors saying not to launch because of the weather, but so was the president's astrologer. Helin now digressed to talk about how he told the president that he saw incompatibilities in horoscopes between him and Chief of Staff Donald Regan. This was interesting, but I wanted to return to Challenger. *I asked, "Did the president know that NASA had cold weather concerns?"*

"Yes, he did."

"Well, then, who decided to launch?"

"The president."

I wanted to be sure I heard him correctly. "Sir," I said slowly. "You are telling me that the president personally made the decision to launch Challenger *in spite of what he knew were NASA's concerns with cold weather. Is that right?"*

"Yes," Helin said. "That's correct."

Cook continues that Helin speculated that President Reagan was getting pressure from the television networks to launch because of the money they were spending. While perhaps true, Reagan might not have confided to Helin his plans to call the Teacher in Space during his speech. Whatever Reagan's reasons, the evidence provided by Helin's story opens one more possible explanation for NASA's otherwise inexplicable rush to launch *Challenger* that frigid morning in the face of so many risks.

While the normalization of deviance, pushy middle managers, strong financial incentives, and an impatient media would have encouraged launching *Challenger* sooner rather than later, it is possible that the express wishes of the president of the United States provided the final explanation. The *Challenger* may have exploded because of a publicity stunt.

CHAPTER 5

CHERNOBYL, FAULTY DESIGN, AND THE INTERPLAY OF HUMANS AND TECHNOLOGY

One of the questions that has plagued humankind since August 1945 is this: Can we prevent the events that took place at Hiroshima and Nagasaki from ever recurring? The answer is no. No, because they already have recurred. Indeed, far worse—in terms of atomic fallout and long-term harm to human populations—took place on April 26, 1986, in northern Ukraine. At 1:23 A.M. on that date, Reactor 4 of the Chernobyl Nuclear Power Plant exploded, sending radioactivity ninety times greater than the Hiroshima and Nagasaki bombs into the surrounding countryside. This toxic and carcinogenic plume contained large quantities of radioactive uranium, graphite, iodine, and cesium.

Exacerbating the nuclear disaster, the plant was located in the middle of a densely populated area, 12 miles north of the town of Chernobyl (pop. 12,500), 2 miles from the town of Pripyat (pop. 45,000), and 122 miles north of Kiev (pop. 2.5 million), the modern capital of the region, then still a part of the Soviet Union.

Many of the victims of the disaster were children, largely because high concentrations of radioactive iodines continued to spew into the atmosphere for days after the explosion, doing untold damage to the growing thyroid glands of the youngest and most vulnerable victims.

Though stable iodine tablets can reduce the risk of long-term cancers, they need to be taken before such disasters strike. For a variety of reasons (including the Soviet Union's planned May Day celebrations), stable iodine tablets were not distributed until four days after the accident, by which time the most dangerous iodines were already absorbed by local populations from the air, drinking water, and milk from cows on farms in the region.

Beyond the immediate explosion, contamination of the site, and the deaths of a number of Chernobyl plant, firefighting, and emergency personnel, the behavior of governmental authorities compounded the damage done by the accident. Large amounts of contaminated meat and milk were sold before the government admitted the danger to the public. Evacuation delays also caused the population to breathe contaminated air and consume tainted food for eight days. Furthermore, as the radioactive cloud drifted north into northern Ukraine and southern Belarus, the radioactive iodines and cesiums were absorbed by populations there, through rainwater and, later, from crops grown in contaminated topsoil. According to the World Health Organization (WHO), four thousand people are eventually expected to die from radiation exposure resulting from the Chernobyl accident.

In the more than two decades since the Chernobyl disaster, follow-up studies have indicated a systematic increase in thyroid cancer among children in the affected region as well as stomach problems associated with the cumulative effects of consuming locally grown produce contaminated by the radiation. In particular, nearly five thousand cases of thyroid cancer in children have been reported, according to WHO. Fortunately, despite the long-term nature of their disease, the children are experiencing high survival rates: There have been only nine deaths as of 2005. On the other hand, because of the Chernobyl disaster, large parts of the entire region have been rendered a "dead zone," uninhabitable for the next six hundred years.

Nevertheless, according to WHO and Soviet authorities, 270,000 people continue to live in "strictly controlled zones," exposed to unsafe levels of radioactivity.

AGENCY VERSUS STRUCTURE

When looking to explain how disasters occur, humans usually want to find who was "at fault," some agent who acted inappropriately and whom can be blamed. Chernobyl, like most disasters, provided plenty of people to play that role. Yet the disaster also gives a framework for examining the way in which organizational and mechanical design—the preexisting "structure"—interacts with real-time decision-making to create disasters. In this section, we will separate the two, then bring them back together to see how they interact.

Operator Mistakes

The Chernobyl disaster occurred, ironically, during a test of its backup power-generating safety system. Several years before the accident, Chernobyl's plant engineers had recognized that the reactor's backup diesel generators required a dangerously long thirty-second delay before supplying power to the reactor's main pumps in the event that external power was lost. They had proposed a new safety system that would tap the residual momentum from the plant's generator turbines to bridge this delay in starting up the backup generators. At the time of the accident in April 1986, engineers were testing their ideas for the second time. (See figure 5.1 for an overview of the system.)

The previous test had been performed on Reactor Unit 3 with no ill effects. However, in this first test, the power rates dropped too quickly to power the reactor's main pumps during the bridge period. Consequently, engineers were testing redesigned electrical components in a modified system during the evening and early morning of April 25–26, 1986, when the disastrous explosion in Reactor Unit 4 occurred.

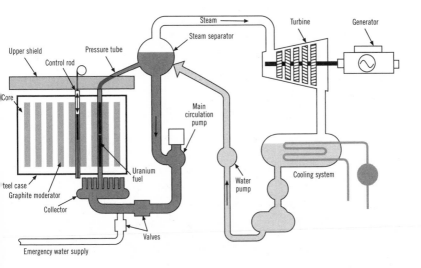

Figure 5.1 *Schematic diagram of the Chernobyl RBMK-1000 nuclear reactor.*
Credit: Courtesy Atomic Energy of Canada Limited (AECL). Adapted from original.

Their test required the reactor to operate at less than half power (the test was planned for 25 percent power) to allow all its steam to be diverted to a single turbine. This turbine would then be disconnected, allowed to spin down, and the electricity generated by the slowing turbine would be used to power four of the reactor's eight main pumps.

Since the reactor had to be run at reduced power, the Chernobyl plant's ordinary production requirements relegated testing to the period just before the annual shutdown for routine maintenance. If the test could not be completed during that time, the plant's production demands required the engineers to wait another year before a test could be attempted. The test on April 25–26 was, therefore, important.

To conduct the test, a series of careful steps were required to power down the reactor. These steps began at 1:00 A.M. on April 25, the day before the accident. Twelve hours later, at 1:00 P.M., the reactor was reduced to 50 percent power, and its steam output switched to a single turbine. The power-down process was then interrupted by an unexpected increase in demand for electricity. To meet the demand, plant managers kept the reactor at 50 percent power for nine hours.

At 11:10 P.M., permission was finally granted to recommence the power reduction. Unfortunately, the unit operator made a mistake with a control, and the reactor fell to about 1 percent power—far too low for the test and well outside normal operating limits.

From such a low level of power, plant operators faced two hurdles in getting the reactor back up and running for the test. First, the rapid decline in power had released a significant amount of xenon gas as a natural by-product of the reaction. Xenon absorbs neutrons, and its presence not only impeded the power-up, but it also threatened to shut down the reactor completely, a phenomenon known as "xenon poisoning."

The second hurdle was that, due to unusually low power levels, the water in the reactor had fallen below the boiling point. In its liquid (rather than steam) state, the water was a better neutron absorber and, thus, a reaction-dampener. To compensate for these two brakes on the reaction, the unit operator pulled out almost all the reactor's 211 control rods. That unusual step succeeded in raising the reactor to 7 percent power, but at the cost of a clear violation of safety procedures, since this type of reactor was never supposed to be run with as few as six or eight control rods. With most of its control rods removed, the reactor's emergency shutdown procedure would be slowed should that step be needed.

Operating at low power with its core filled with water, Chernobyl's Reactor Unit 4 was now unstable, since small variations in flow and temperature dramatically affected power levels as a result of the reactor's "positive void effect," a self-reinforcing phenomenon explained in greater detail below. Furthermore, with little steam being produced, the reactor's automated pumping system was having difficulty controlling the turbine's return water flow. (This water comes from steam that is cooled subsequent to powering the turbine.) The operator tried manually stabilizing the water flow, to no avail. Since the reactor was at risk of being shut down by its low-water-level safety system, the operator disconnected this system to avoid a shutdown that would abort the important turbine spin-down test.

After half an hour of adjustments, the operators decided that the reactor was stable enough to begin the turbine test. However, one further problem needed to be solved. Several turbine tests might be required, and the reactor was configured to shut down if its remaining turbine was disconnected from its steam output. Consequently, that safety system was also disabled. At this point, only abnormal power levels would trigger an automated shutdown.

When the test began, electric power from the disconnected and slowing turbine successfully continued to power four of the eight main reactor pumps. However, in the reactor's highly sensitive low-power state, the gradual reduction of pumping strength as the turbine spun down produced a modest but rapidly increasing level of reactor activity after twenty seconds. In response to the reactor's rapid rise in power (or perhaps in reaction to an automated lowering of the control rods by the single remaining safety system), the operator pressed the shutdown button that would drive the control rods down and stop the reaction completely. That action might have worked had the lowering of the control rods been done with a normal number of control rods already partially inserted into the seven-meter-high (twenty-three-foot) cylindrical graphite core.

Unfortunately, an unexpected aspect of the control rods' design caused them to have an effect opposite from the one desired. (See figure 5.2.) Specifically, each rod consisted of two sections, an upper part of neutron-absorbing material and a lower part made of graphite that is transparent to neutrons. The purpose of the graphite is to take up space in the control rod tubes that would otherwise be filled with

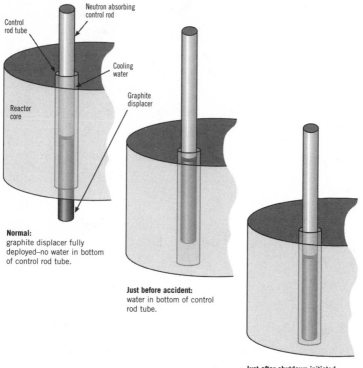

Figure 5.2 *Effect of Chernobyl's shutdown rods at the time of the accident.*
Credit: Courtesy Atomic Energy of Canada Limited (AECL). Adapted from original.

liquid cooling water, itself an effective neutron absorber. This two-part design increased the effectiveness of the control rods by eliminating the water in the lower section of the control tubes that would otherwise be absorbing neutrons.

With the control rods fully withdrawn to try to restore power to the xenon-filled reactor, the bottom of each control rod tube was, in fact, filled with water, not occupied by graphite. Therefore, as the control rods were lowered, the first effect was to push out the remaining water, replacing it with the graphite that constituted the lower section of the rods. That meant the control process was effectively operating in reverse. This effect would last until the total neutron absorbency of the upper part of the rods that were being lowered exceeded that of the water forced out by the lowering control rods. As it would turn out, there would never be enough time for that to happen.

There was an additional complication. In general, the lower part of the reactor was the least active. However, under low power, it was the most active area of the reactor. In fact, the bottom part of the reactor was behaving as if it were a separate mini-reactor, largely independent of what was going on elsewhere in the core. It is believed that the effect of graphite and water replacement was most severe in this localized area, and that this was the actual source of the explosion.

Within four seconds of the rods' initial descent, the reactor's power level spiked to one hundred times full power, creating a massive heat surge. The heat surge caused the uranium fuel to fracture into small pieces, immediately transferring heat to the surrounding water and causing it to explosively vaporize. The resultant steam explosion burst some of the reactor's 1,661 pressure tubes that contained the fuel, ruptured the steel container around the high-temperature graphite, and lifted the shield on top of the reactor core, an action that broke the remaining pressure tubes, all of which were attached to this shield, a steel-and-concrete structure that sat just below the reinforced floor of the ordinary industrial building that sat atop the reactor proper.

In addition to the steam explosion, it's possible that the energy transfer was so intense that the water partly decomposed into hydrogen and oxygen. Thus, there may also have been a hydrogen explosion.

Whatever its cause, the explosion engulfed the reactor building itself and started graphite and conventional fires as high-temperature radioactive debris was thrown from the core. Some of the fires burned for the next ten days, and the combination of the explosion, fires, and heat from the reactor continued to push contaminants into the environment during that time.

Faulty Design

It would be easy to blame everything on the unit operator for his error in bringing the power down to 1 percent. And, of course, he does deserve blame. Yet, it is fair to ask why the building was so ill equipped to handle an explosion. And why were there no backup measures within the design of the building in case of fire?

According to John Carroll, professor of behavioral and policy sciences at MIT's Sloan School of Management, people tend to "reason back from the sharp edge." This is a form of *hindsight bias*. When we analyze an accident, it seems logical to trace events in reverse order until we locate the cause. Furthermore, it appears to us that events closest to the accident are more likely to be causes than those more distant. This attitude is especially strong when human mistakes appear to be the cause. Pilot error is clear, simple, and final. We can move on with the satisfaction that we have located what went wrong.

But even ordinary accidents may be more complex than they seem on the surface. For example, we're all familiar with intersections or dangerous corners that have a higher accident rate than is reasonable for their traffic flow. Limited visibility, distractions, confusing traffic signals, and slippery road surfaces may all contribute to these higher-than-normal accident rates. Since none of these contributory factors was happenstance—they were design decisions made by someone, although not necessarily deliberately—such factors can be claimed as contributors to every accident that occurs at that intersection or corner.

Of course, we prefer to blame people, not situations. "She was driving too fast" is a more satisfying explanation than "the road designer should have known better." Yet, both contributors are important; in fact, both are necessary for the accident to have occurred.

However, in more complex systems—such as those within which many of the disasters in this book occurred—the web of cause and effect is more complicated and stretches back in time and space from the final accident.

In the case of Chernobyl, the web stretches back decades.

The Chernobyl reactor was a Soviet-specific design originally commissioned in the 1970s as part of the USSR's nuclear weapons program. It was designed to produce plutonium as well as to generate electric power. In its role as a weapons facility, the Chernobyl reactor required frequent removal of its fuel rods via a crane at the top of the structure (the building was seventy-one meters, or 233 feet, tall), and this design was viewed as precluding a conventional containment structure employed in Western and other Soviet power-generating facilities. Consequently, when the reactor was subsequently converted to civilian use, it lacked an important safety feature. At the time of the accident, no regulations prevented the use of this unprotected design.

In addition, the reactor's basic technical design (designated by the Russian acronym RBMK) contained four intrinsic risks, not all of which were fully understood by operating personnel.

1. *Functionally, nuclear reactors in power plants do little more than convert water to steam that is then used to turn a generator via a turbine. Whenever a RBMK reactor's water boiled more actively, such as during a power surge, the pace of the reactor increased as neutron-absorbing liquid water was replaced by steam. This change led to higher reaction rates (via lower neutron absorbency) and greater steam production (because of higher heat output). That positive feedback loop is called a positive void effect and it contributed to instability, especially at low power levels when there is proportionally more water in the reactor's core.*

2. *The reactor's "moderator" (the material used to reduce the speed of the reactor's neutrons to increase efficiency) was combustible*

graphite operating at high temperatures (700 degrees C) rather than plain water or heavy water. Because graphite can burn, it was sealed inside the steel reactor vessel to avoid exposure to air, which could cause combustion.

3. *The reactor was at its most unstable while operating at low power levels. Due to the operator error, it was unintentionally placed in that state immediately prior to the accident.*

4. *The reactor's control rod design could, under unusual and unauthorized operating circumstances, act to initially increase the reaction rate rather than reduce it when the rods were activated to shut down the reactor. The Chernobyl disaster on April 26, 1986, took place under such adverse conditions.*

Design weaknesses often fall into two categories: the obvious and the subtle. If a building is designed without adequate safety provisions, it will come as no surprise when it fails if subjected to certain kinds of stress. That was the case in the Chernobyl reactor building, which was not designed to contain a reactor explosion.

Less obvious, however, is that virtually all design problems arise from a design decision at an earlier point in time. Such decisions may be the consequence of deliberate compromises arising from any number of pressures, an incomplete understanding of the technology in use (such as *Challenger*'s O-rings), or negligence. Faulty design creates latent unsafe conditions that can result in an accident under particular circumstances.

While the most common explanation for an accident is operator error, a more frequent cause is faulty design of the *sociotechnical system* (that is, people and technology in combination) in which the operator is embedded. All the accidents examined in this book demonstrate such weaknesses, although the sources of the design flaws vary, as does the ease with which they could have been uncovered in advance.

Beyond these basic issues of technical design and operations, the belief that pervaded all Soviet nuclear energy facilities was that they were so safe that accidents couldn't happen. Underscoring this belief, the plant lacked protective clothing, radiation monitors, and other safety equipment that are routine precautions in Western facilities. Furthermore, Soviet operators were not trained in safety procedures, nor were they educated in the fundamental risks inherent in the technology they were operating.

While it is not my purpose to delve deeply into the origins of these oversights, they stem from the policy level of the Ministry of Medium Machine Building, a government agency in charge of facilities associated with the Soviet nuclear weapons program. Without an institutional recognition of risk, an emphasis on safety is unlikely, and in the absence of a focus on safety, it is impossible to achieve it. We will see a number of examples of insufficient concern for safety in this chapter.

Regardless of the underlying systemic flaws of the Soviet nuclear program, the value of Chernobyl as a case study is lost if we simply label the Soviet government irresponsible and arrogant or decry the incompetence of local plant management, tempting though that may be. Rather, it is likely that the responsible decision-makers had other priorities and limited funds, that their behavior existed in a bureaucratic framework and political culture that promoted and reinforced it.

Policy-level management may not have fully appreciated the risks of the RBMK reactor design, especially in combination with an inexperienced and inadequately trained workforce. That is not an excuse, merely an observation on the facts of life within large, centralized bureaucracies. While fully appreciating the risks before an accident takes place is more complex than it appears in the wake of an accident, it is an essential step in preventing future disasters.

THE HUMAN–TECHNOLOGY INTERACTION; OR, IT IS NOT ALWAYS "PILOT ERROR"

For generations, technology has been considered a solution to the unreliability and expense of using human beings. Machines allow capital to substitute for labor. Machine efficiency and reliability have dramatically increased production, powering the world economy for more than a century. Despite obvious gains, these benefits have not come without unexpected costs, since progress inevitably engenders risks.

Maritime radars, for example, have considerably expanded the conditions under which ships can go to sea. At the same time, their proliferation has also increased risk-taking under fog and storm conditions previously considered too dangerous to leave port. Similarly, in our everyday lives we find that the proliferation of four-wheel-drive vehicles allows us to drive under adverse conditions and travel to places inaccessible to the ordinary family car. As a result, we still get stuck in the mud and have accidents on icy roads. Improving safety also encourages risk-taking.

Within the commercial airline industry, especially in the computer-display-based "glass cockpit" that has been the focus of considerable engineering attention, the interplay between humans and machines is especially complicated. There is no doubt that automated flight management systems (FMSs) have made it much easier to fly modern aircraft. In fact, it is unclear whether these aircraft can be safely flown without these systems, especially with the two-person crews that are now standard. At the same time, the systems themselves have been implicated in a number of accidents.

While the official root causes of commercial airline accidents have remained steady over a forty-year period—70 percent are attributed to pilot error—more recent pilot errors tend to be associated with the operations of automated flight management systems, especially with their vertical navigation/speed control functions during takeoffs and landings.

The "1996 FAA Report on the Interfaces Between Flight Crews and Modern Flight Deck Systems" highlighted the causes and consequences of pilot confusion about the behavior of these systems. The essence of the problem is the conflict between pilots' understanding of the automated system's "intentions" and the actual behavior of these systems.

That type of confusion is easy to illustrate. Each of us has encountered a door or cabinet that seems to say "pull" when, in fact, it needs to be pushed. Studies show that people develop expectations of how objects are supposed to behave. Difficulties arise when they don't behave as expected, particularly when people are under stress. If the door that opens the wrong way happens to be a fire exit, the cost of confusion can be lethal. Flight management system interfaces and operations are analogous, but considerably more complex.

Flight management systems facilitate the operation of the aircraft. In some cases, they actually take full control. Thus, rather than directly flying the plane themselves, the flight crew often programs and directs the computers that do the actual flying. In that respect, modern commercial aircraft are much like the space shuttle, most of whose operations are far too complex for manual control, even in an emergency.

In essence, pilots share physical control of the aircraft with the flight management system. What this really means, of course, is that they are sharing control with the designers of the hardware and software that operate these systems. That is not just a semantic distinction between objects and the people who create them. Indeed, if something goes wrong, a new group of actors must be brought into the diagnosis, pushing the causal chain back in time to the development and testing of the hardware, software, and data.

To avoid testing everything from scratch with each new enhancement, most flight management systems are created in increments. Consequently, many systems do not have top-down design coherence. That means FMS operations are not always obvious to the pilots who use them. In particular, those systems operate in a variety of modes that determine the types of inputs they will accept, the aircraft controls they operate, and the objectives they will try to achieve (for instance, maintaining a specific compass heading or descending to a particular altitude).

Modes can be interrelated. Some modes are accessible only from other modes (you have to set a compass heading before you can maintain it), while others are entered automatically according to parameters set into the system. In particular, certain in-flight situations are presumed by FMS designers to be inherently dangerous, and thus engage automatic corrective actions not under pilot control. Under certain circumstances, pilots have been known to fight with the flight management system, unable to disengage it or quickly figure out how to get it to do what they want. If you've ever gotten stuck while programming your VCR or mobile phone, you have a taste for that experience. Now imagine that you're a pilot in a jam with little time to solve the problem and the lives of 250 people at stake as you perform.

Fortunately, the vast majority of flights operate within normal parameters. Nevertheless, during the steep learning curve associated with a new generation of aircraft, the number of incidents and accidents is considerably higher; many never make the news because they don't result in crashes, but they are accidents nonetheless. And some, of course, end in tragedy. That was the case during the first few years after the Airbus (A319/320/321) was introduced. In 1994, China Airlines Flight 140 from Taiwan to Nagoya, Japan, crashed during its landing approach when the flight crew became confused by the flight management system.

The accident was precipitated by the inadvertent activation of the "go-around" button—a safety feature—by the flight engineer as the aircraft approached the runway for landing. The button was badly located near other controls and was prone to being pressed during routine actions, and that inadvertent pressure engaged automated systems programmed by Airbus engineers to make the aircraft climb rapidly.

Fully disengaging the system required several steps, not all of which were known to the flight engineer or pilot. Equally important, the steps required were similar to those on the Boeing 747, the aircraft on which both pilots had spent a great deal of time, but different enough to still cause confusion. Consequently, the crew applied a remedial half measure that left the aircraft in an unsafe out-of-trim condition in which the aerodynamic forces on the aircraft were out of balance and incompatible with landing. Unaware of the danger posed by the still-operating flight control system—it did not warn the crew that it was still engaged—the plane stalled on its approach and crashed into the runway, killing 260 people.

Similar incidents had occurred before with the Airbus, though without fatalities. Unfortunately, Airbus management did not consider the incidents critical enough to demand immediate attention by customer airlines. Had the problems been dealt with differently at the administrative level, the crash of Flight 140 might have been averted. Since informing carriers of dangerous incidents is a routine defensive measure, this is a clear example of a gap in the safety system, one that can also be linked to Airbus's natural desire to protect the reputation of the company's new airplane.

Glass Cockpit on Terra Firma

Lest we think that screen-based glass cockpits and automated control systems (including their associated problems) apply only to high-tech settings, many other circumstances fit this profile, more often than we might think. The 1987 U.S. stock market crash, known as Black Monday, which resulted in the largest single-day down market in history, was caused by the widespread use of computer-automated trading systems and portfolio insurance mechanisms whose interdependent behavior during a frenzied period of selling was not understood until it contributed to the collapsing market that day.

While automated trading systems and portfolio insurance did not directly cause the market crash, they made the situation far worse. The market had been off for several days before the crash. The economic conditions were not sanguine. As heavy selling began, the market's primary computer systems could not keep up with the pace of automated trading systems pumping out more sell orders while the market plunged.

As published prices lagged behind orders, the price of exchange-listed stock options (financial instruments that provide the rights to buy or sell stock at a previously agreed price) diverged from the price of the underlying securities on which they were based. That made the overall market conditions more uncertain, and interfered with the portfolio insurance mechanisms using options as part of their protection scheme. Without accurate prices, traders' calculations of how much insurance they needed to buy were incorrect. When the dust settled, many who thought they had been protected lost fortunes.

The financial sector has long been at the forefront of change. Finance is largely—almost completely—information-based, and thus it was one of the first businesses to use computers, to globalize, to invent "synthetic" products, and to create fresh fortunes in new ways. Not surprisingly then, finance has also given rise to new ways to fail catastrophically for investors, companies, banks, markets, and even countries (as we will see in chapter 10). As more and more operations and logistics systems evolve and create higher levels of automation, it's likely that more subtle but also more potentially devastating disasters will emerge. As the rest of the business world catches up to finance—and it is moving in that direction quickly—we should expect these new types of hazards to spread.

"NORMAL ACCIDENTS"

In 1984, Charles Perrow, a Yale professor of sociology, added an important idea to our understanding of the ways in which the design of systems interacts with human decision-makers to create accidents. Perrow's idea was summed up by the phrase *normal accidents*. His notion is that systems that are characterized by both high interdependence and "tight coupling" (a propensity to exhibit an uncontrollable domino effect that will be explained in more detail below) are the most vulnerable to accidents. In a statistical sense, accidents are unavoidable when these conditions are present.

An interdependent system can best be illustrated with an example as common as the weather outdoors. That is, if a major snowstorm arrives at midday, not only are planes grounded and roads clogged, but hotels are jammed as trapped travelers scramble for places to stay, their former rooms now occupied by people who arrived during the morning. The storm also means that people's affairs are interrupted, meetings must be rescheduled, and social engagements canceled.

For some people, the consequences may be more severe. Ambulances may have difficulty getting people in need to the hospital, and health workers may have difficulty getting to work. This affects patient care and potentially forces the cancellation of time-critical operations or other important medical procedures.

Tight coupling, Perrow's second criterion for accident-prone systems, characterizes situations in which hazardous activity escalates faster than people's ability to keep up with it. A system is, in other words, "overtaken by events," or OBE.

OBE is a function of relative time, not absolute time. For example, the pace of government policy-making on important problems like climate change, genetic engineering, and public education might be decades-long. However, success or failure depends on whether appropriate actions can be fashioned before the situation turns into a crisis.

If responses take decades but hazards take far longer to develop, all is well. If the relationship is reversed—as was the case with New Orleans's flood-protection strategy prior to Hurricane Katrina—then things may end in disaster.

Sometimes, a crisis situation unfolds in minutes. As we will see in the Black Hawk shoot-down in chapter 7—the most serious friendly fire accident in the modern U.S. military—the time between first radar contact and the destruction of the army helicopters by friendly F-15s was just eight minutes, and included multiple radio interactions and two visual identification passes by the fighters.

Perrow's interdependence and coupling are also interrelated. Both make the system more difficult to understand, complicating diagnosis and the development of solutions when something goes wrong. In many organizations, decisions have to be approved by higher-ups, a process that inevitably slows things down. In complex, tightly coupled, and high-risk systems, the situation is likely to spin out of control unless the diagnosis, solution approval, and execution process fits the speed of events, whether the objective pace is fast or slow.

An important class of normal accidents involves critical infrastructure. In the cases examined so far, the damage was described in terms of "first-order" impacts—the people and circumstances directly affected. Other scenarios are more troubling. After the 9/11 World Trade Center attacks, there were serious concerns about whether the U.S. stock markets could reopen, a potential catastrophe for the U.S. and global economies. In addition to the New York Stock Exchange, which was located near ground zero, many Wall Street firms were crippled by the communications disruptions caused by the collapse, since the World Trade Center sat atop one of the most important concentrations of telecommunications equipment in the world. Without the reestablishment of vital systems, there would be no trading.

Fortunately, following the near miss of the 1993 World Trade Center bombing that did relatively modest damage, changes were made to speed the restoration of telecommunications and computer systems after a disaster. However, many area financial firms still had to solve high- and low-tech problems of their own—such as getting their employees to locations from which they could work. For security and cost reasons, backup sites are often remote from home offices, complicating employee access immediately after the attack. It was nip and tuck whether all the firms could be ready on time.

Thank Heavens, Another Disaster Averted

A similar case of infrastructure disruption occurred when the PanAmSat Galaxy IV communications satellite rotated out of its orbit on May 19, 1998. That unforeseen event disrupted 90 percent of the digital pagers in the United States, as well as cable and broadcast transmissions, credit card approvals, and ATM transactions. The failure affected the lives and work of fifty million people. If there had been a serious public emergency while the satellite was offline, doctors and other caregivers would have been more difficult to reach and thus less able to get to where they were needed. Fortunately, such a scenario did not unfold.

Paging service providers as well as PanAmSat (at the time, majority-owned by Hughes Electronics, the maker of the satellite) had allowed pager services to become concentrated on a single device. Furthermore, since no communications satellite had ever failed, the vast majority of customers did not have backup facilities, and many lacked contingency plans. In retrospect, the assumption of perfect reliability combined with no redundancy and no just-in-case strategy seems irresponsible and naive, but it is consistent with the way many people manage low-probability risks, as described in chapter 2.

As it would turn out, the design of the Galaxy IV was flawed—along with thirty-five other similar satellites, including one owned by

SatMex, which failed in a similar way over Mexico two years later—causing a short circuit in the control computer that pointed the satellite's antennas toward Earth. Unknown to the operators, the satellite's backup computer had also failed a year earlier due to an electrical problem. The failure of both the primary control computer and its backup effectively cut the satellite's life in half.

Though there were no backup plans for the now defunct Galaxy IV, there was some good luck because of spare capacity on other satellites—including a Galaxy IIIR nearby in space. Thus, paging providers and other customers could manually redirect their antennas to point to the alternative satellite. But with some antennas on mountaintops and many tens of thousands requiring manual realignment, the complete redeployment of services took nearly a week despite thousands of technicians dispatched to the field.

CHALLENGES AT THE "CRITICAL POINT"

As we have seen, the challenge of eliminating accidents is formidable, and perhaps impossible. Even safety precautions like maritime radars and state-of-the-art automation systems have nonobvious complications. Where does it all end?

The Danish theoretical physicist Per Bak and his colleagues at the Brookhaven National Laboratory in Upton, New York, made an important contribution to our understanding of complex systems and the accidents to which they are prone. True complexity—typified by ecologies, economies, and large organizations—arises over an extended period through the complex interplay of driving and restraining forces.

A common pile of sand is deceptively simple, but it provides an accurate illustration.

Unlike tiny, polished glass beads, grains of sand are irregular, and thus lock into one another, resisting movement in unpredictable ways.

If one gradually adds sand to a tabletop sand pile, for example, the sand will initially stay where it falls. When the height of the pile reaches a "critical point," however, adding more sand does not always have the same effect. Sometimes the new sand simply trickles down locally, other times it sets off modest avalanches in both near and far locations, and occasionally small amounts of new sand may precipitate a catastrophic avalanche that affects the pile as a whole, an unpredictable consequence far out of proportion to the triggering event.

Bak's key insight is that systems characterized by interconnectedness and constant driving forces—like the tectonic pressures at the earth's crust—naturally evolve toward such critical points. Once there, "good" avalanches—such as technological breakthroughs—and "bad" ones—such as earthquakes and tsunamis, the Great Depression, or the fourteenth century's black death, which killed half the population of Europe—occur according to predictable probabilities called *power laws*.

Power laws describe the well-known inverse relationship between the intensity and frequency of earthquakes. They also describe the distribution of city size and company sales figures, the degree of improvement in technology breakthroughs, and many other phenomena. While violent earthquakes occur predictably less often than small tremors, the timing, intensity, and location of the next major event cannot be forecast. The same is true for predicting the next Microsoft or Google, medical breakthrough, or athletic superstar. A common characteristic of all these phenomena is that if you wait long enough—sometimes millennia, sometimes one day—an even bigger event will come along. This rule also applies to disasters.

Fortunately, the preponderance of natural and man-made critical systems does not mean that many of the accidents to which these systems are prone can't be prevented, although the challenges become greater as complexity rises. Systems at the critical point often display subtle, sometimes baffling behavior, since the size and location of consequences may be only distantly related to their causes.

Nevertheless, redundancy is often the key to risk protection. However, there are some particular challenges that plague highly complex systems.

By both design and happenstance, many contemporary systems involve a bewildering blend of people, technology, and idiosyncratic circumstances. In well-defended systems, failures often arise from an interaction of elements. Therefore, increasing the reliability of individual parts will not necessarily remedy the vulnerability of the whole.

Specific history matters. Not only can rare combinations conspire to create an accident, the specific sequence of events can put the overall system into a particular state in which accidents are more likely to occur. The inadvertent press of the go-around button in China Airlines Flight 140 activated a particular mode in the aircraft's flight management system requiring a specific set of steps to be disengaged. If not for that mode, standard procedures would have averted the accident.

Redundant systems—and the monitoring, maintenance, and automated controls that often go with them—can significantly increase overall system complexity as well as introduce new failure scenarios. In some cases, the redundancy and defense-related systems are more complex—and thus more error-prone—than the systems they are designed to protect.

As described in chapter 4, the effectiveness of the backup O-ring in the *Challenger* spacecraft's solid rocket booster could not be tested and could only seal if the primary O-ring failed during the first part of the brief ignition cycle. Like the primary O-ring, its effectiveness also depended on something as simple as the weather—that is, the air temperature. Ironically, it failed when it was most needed.

So-called social redundancy, in which people are trained to back up one another, is prone to its own unique complexities. Authority relationships (which may be based on position, status, perceived knowledge, or other factors) tend to distort the vigilance on which social redundancy relies. Otherwise desirable factors like trust, loyalty, and prestige can easily backfire, neutralizing the effectiveness of a double check. In a number of airliner crashes, for instance, lower-status ground staff did not challenge the actions of higher-status flight crews. That phenomenon was clearly evident in the Mission Management Team meeting during the *Columbia* space shuttle accident described in chapter 1, and it is common in all hierarchical organizations. It was critical between the F-15 pilots and the AWACS crew during the friendly fire shoot-down of the Black Hawk helicopters to be described in chapter 7.

Many accidents can be traced to various faults with monitoring and control systems. The 1979 nuclear power plant meltdown at Three Mile Island in central Pennsylvania was caused by a combination of faulty monitoring and control system design, operator information overload, and inadequate staff training. In particular, operators could not directly monitor the status of key safety aspects of the plant, such as coolant levels in the reactor and the open or closed position of vital valves. Similar monitoring and control failures were directly involved in the chain of events leading to BP's Texas City refinery calamity of 2005. As a result, operators never realized that they were dangerously overfilling equipment. Finally, monitoring problems were also central to the *Columbia* space shuttle accident, since certain key launch monitoring cameras were not working to observe the impact of the foam, NASA refused to take advantage of Defense Department long-range photographic resources, there were no sensors to measure certain critical parameters within the interior of the wing, and the astronauts lacked any way of remotely examining the shuttle for damage.

The shift to software-intensive systems has made man-machine partnerships far more complex than we fully understand. Highly reliable technology makes people less vigilant, since human beings are not effective monitors of situations that rarely fail. Ironically, employing more comprehensive and reliable systems only exacerbates the problem. Although such systems are more reliable, they are more boring to monitor as well as more difficult to diagnose. While more effective software design, increased personnel training, and improved diagnostic systems would improve the situation, those steps are at least as demanding—and expensive to implement—as the problems that prompted the increase in automation in the first place.

Ultimately, those complexities mean that, at the critical point, improvements to any interdependent and well-defended system are made only in increments. There may be many small steps forward, but only rarely do breakthroughs occur. Regular setbacks, and a small number of large-scale accidents, are also inevitable.

Nevertheless, we must relentlessly press on, taking every advantage to rationally reduce risk despite the difficulty, the short-term cost, and the politics. Complex, critical systems are, by definition, driven by man and by nature. They do, however, eventually yield to our efforts to tame them, but not easily or automatically, and never without the occasional nasty surprise.

THE HYATT TEA DANCE DISASTER: FAULTY DESIGN, PURE AND SIMPLE

So far, the examples we have examined in this chapter have illustrated the effects of faulty designs combined with human error at the time of a disaster. Now we will examine one disaster that—in contrast—resulted from faulty design alone. For a change, no one at the time of the disaster could be blamed. It was just a bad design for a hotel, and by all rights should have been caught by the engineers while the design was still on paper, or at least during fabrication or construction.

The disaster itself occurred on the evening of Friday, July 17, 1981. At the time, the newly built Kansas City Hyatt Regency was hosting a dance contest in its lobby. A big band performed Duke Ellington's "Satin Doll" while glasses clinked and people chatted excitedly. With two thousand people looking on, contestants competed on a dance floor inside the main hall of the Missouri showpiece owned by billionaire Donald Hall, heir to the Hallmark Cards empire. Far above the contest, on the three skywalks inside the Regency's atrium, many more spectators kept time to the music, or tried to dance as best they could on the narrow concrete-and-steel walkways.

At 7:05 P.M., a loud crack, likened by many witnesses to a rifle shot, stopped all the dancers in their tracks. Within moments, the fourth-floor skywalk—the uppermost of two interconnected walkways—collapsed, falling onto the skywalk immediately beneath it, causing both to fall to the ground floor, crushing people below and hurling others from the walkways to the lobby floor. When the dust settled, 114 people were dead and more than two hundred injured in the worst hotel structural failure in U.S. history.

Unlike other structural collapses caused by shoddy construction or unanticipated loads from snow, rain, or wind, the Hyatt Regency disaster was exclusively a case of poor structural design.

What Caused the Hyatt Disaster?

Ever since architect John Portman created the spectacular Regency Atlanta in 1967, Hyatt had used his sweeping interior space as the signature of its hotel chain. Thus, in all subsequent designs, Hyatt architects and engineers emulated Portman's sense of interior drama. To create that effect in Kansas City, the new Hyatt featured aerial walkways that traversed the atrium high above the lobby. (See figure 5.3.)

In addition, a grand freestanding staircase majestically graced the atrium, rising seemingly without support from the second to the third

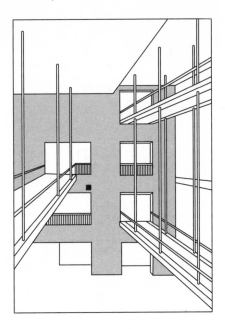

Figure 5.3 *Kansas City Hyatt Regency atrium looking south.*
Credit: Original drawing by Kevin Woest. Adapted with permission.

floor, while the proposed and aptly named skywalks echoed the sense of floating on air by using a series of light-colored steel rods to hang the walkways from the atrium roof against the glass exterior wall behind them.

In the structural engineers' original design, two sets of three long vertical rods carried the bulk of the weight of the interconnected fourth-floor and second-floor skywalks. Each of the sixty-five-thousand-pound concrete-and-steel walkways was structured as a horizontal ladder on which the side rails were hefty I-beams and the rungs were box beams formed by welding two steel channels to each other toe-to-toe. The skywalks were fixed at one end, welded to a steel plate attached to one wall. At the other end, they were held in place by a roller joint, which was designed to provide for thermal expansion. Crossing the center of the atrium, the third-floor skywalk was similarly designed, but had only one level. With all that steel, welding, and roof support, the skywalks were thought to be secure. But how would one know for sure? Making that determination was the job of the structural engineer, Jack D. Gillum and Associates.

As the project progressed, Havens Steel, the steel fabricator responsible for the hanging assembly, proposed a design change. The company's rationale: It wanted to simplify the production process and minimize the risk of damage during construction. Havens proposed shifting from a single-rod hanging system to a two-rod design to avoid cutting threads in the lower half of each rod's length to attach the nuts and washers that held up the walkways.

At first glance, that seemed like a straightforward change. However, a postdisaster analysis of the forces on the upper walkway's connections showed that the stress on the lower nut, washer, and box beam was doubled by this change because the joint now had to carry the weight of the walkway below as well as its own. (See figure 5.4.) In addition, even without that change, the positioning of the supporting nut and washer over the box beam welds was a gross error, since it was the

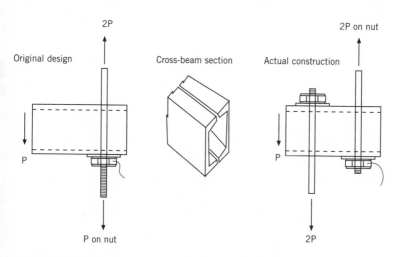

Figure 5.4 *Kansas City Hyatt Regency skywalk hanger assembly design.*
Source: Wikipedia Commons.

weakest part of this structural element. Unfortunately, the implications of both those design decisions went unrecognized by the structural engineers, although court documents show their formal approval stamp on the fabricator's revisions to Gillum's original design.

Beyond that, the analysis showed the design of the connection between the hanging rods and the box beams was preliminary, not final, and was not designated by the engineers as a "special connection" and thereby deserving of additional scrutiny by the fabricator. Instead, Havens designed them "by the book," using the American Institute of Steel Construction (AISC) guidelines and standards for the design of steel-to-steel connections. Since it is the structural engineers' responsibility to ensure the proper design of load-bearing connections, in an administrative hearing, the Missouri Board of Architects, Professional Engineers, and Land Surveyors found the engineers employed by Jack D. Gillum and Associates who had signed off on the final drawings liable of gross negligence, misconduct, and unprofessional conduct in the practice of engineering. While the engineers lost their licenses to practice in Missouri and Texas, they still practice in other states and were not held to be criminally negligent.

The accident might not have occurred, even with the fabricator's change in design, had the structural system been originally designed within Kansas City's building codes. As it was, it lacked a sufficient safety factor and could barely support the weight of the walkways, since Gillum's original design contained only 60 percent of the city's building code requirements. Although the walkways might have survived the Tea Dance intact if built exactly as the engineers specified, it is impossible to say how long they would have held up.

Design is creative problem-solving and central to all productive systems. Thus, design issues are always important to the understanding of any accident. Designers work with a wide range of materials to create a specific result, often seeking to discover the best balance among conflicting objectives. While scientists investigate existing forms and seek to develop general laws, designers endeavor to formulate novel solutions by focusing on specific cases.

In advance—and often even when completed—it is impossible to prove that a given design is optimum, or even if it fully meets its articulated design objectives. One of the ironies of design—experienced by all designers at one time or another—is that a project can fulfill all its stated objectives yet fail to please its clients. For this and other reasons, design problems are often characterized as "wicked," lacking both definitive formulation or solution.

In the case of the Hyatt walkways, design issues were fatally wicked. We can see that the architects and structural engineers sought drama in their creation while being constrained by both safety and cost. Drama encouraged innovation and a rejection of conservative structural options (such as pillars), while cost constraints limited testing, independent engineering reviews, and other activities that might have prevented the accident. Unfortunately, the most significant trade-offs made by the designers in Kansas City were invisible to the naked eye. The Hyatt skywalk system lacked redundancy, the ability to survive when one or more of its structural elements fail. Redundancy is essential to safety, and its absence or failure is central to virtually all accidents. Redundancy, alas, is always a matter of design.

The case of the Hyatt Tea Dance disaster emphasizes the critical role that design plays in every accident. The walkway system's avant-garde appearance belied its basic engineering weaknesses—mistakes that could have been remedied by a few simple changes and by adding redundancy. Many of the disasters in this book also reflect engineering mistakes, while others exemplify errors in rules, procedures, and management practices. In every case, the question arises: How did these mistakes slip through the protections that should have caught them?

HAZARDS, HOLES, AND THE DESIGN OF DEFENSES

As the Chernobyl plant disaster, the Galaxy IV failure, and the Hyatt walkway collapse all illustrate, designers must consider the dynamics of failure as well as those of meeting a contract deadline. These precautions are especially pertinent to complex systems that involve the interaction of people and technology. Today that means virtually all productive systems have a reasonable potential for risk.

British psychologist and safety expert James Reason illustrates dangers in his well-known "Swiss cheese" model. (See figure 5.5.) According to Reason, defenses against accidents are like slices of Swiss cheese. These layers of protection include safety procedures; training programs; specialized hardware interlocks; monitors, alarms, and warnings; and various forms of containment systems.

Despite extensive precautions, according to this model, "holes" inevitably occur in the defensive screen. A gap may exist in a single protective system (such as a blind spot in your rearview mirror), or there may be systematic or idiosyncratic defensive weaknesses arising from a variety of human and technological factors. Some defensive holes are persistent, whereas others "move around" as a result of transient conditions such as lapses in attention or other aspects of human error, or intermittent bugs in sensors or systems, and variations arising from different operating modes.

Usually, the holes in the Swiss cheese don't line up, and thus one or more layers catch anything trying to get through the defenses. Under certain circumstances, however, the holes in the Swiss cheese do line up, and an accident results. Sometimes, multiple defensive failures that add up to an accident have a common origin or share common causes. Cost, production, and political pressures are perhaps the most frequent underlying cause of such correlated failures.

Reason's illustration reveals that many potentially dangerous conditions are ever-present. All they need to result in an accident is to be set loose over time by local circumstances. Even then, the accident may be checked by a defensive system, such as an alert supervisor, a precompletion diagnostic test, or some form of warning or shutdown system. Should those fail, there may be last-ditch defenses, such as the emergency procedures learned by pilots. In that way, multiple levels of defensive screens dramatically reduce the likelihood of an accident over a given period of time.

Nevertheless, eventually catastrophes *do* happen, often because the defensive system fails or is deliberately disabled in some manner. Of course, in those cases, rapid and effective response to an accident may be just as important as its prevention in the first place. In the instance of Hurricane Katrina, providing vital assistance—a process that could

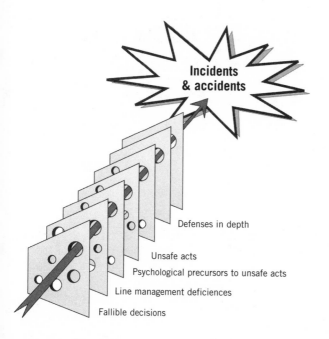

Figure 5.5 *James Reason's Swiss cheese safety model.*
Credit: *Courtesy Dr. Steve Shorrock, Department of Aviation, University of New South Wales. Adapted with permission.*

have begun well before the storm made landfall—was delayed by bureaucratic incompetence and politics. In the case of the *Columbia* space shuttle, it can be argued that while the triggering event was foam striking the spacecraft, the accident was actually caused by the ill-advised decision to return to earth as originally planned rather than determine the extent of the damage and take remedial action.

It should be clear from those examples that mechanical things aren't the only elements that can be misdesigned. All manner of human and organizational processes, such as information systems, rules for decision-making, training programs, and operating procedures, are subject to faulty design. Since a design mistake can occur anywhere—not just in those areas we often think of as designer's work—a flaw at any vulnerable point can contribute to an accident.

All the holes in James Reason's Swiss cheese lined up in the Hyatt disaster. While weaknesses in Gillum's structural engineering were at the root of the accident, it was the job of the engineering company to create a *process* that trapped slips, engineering errors, and oversights. Nevertheless, the motivation to save time and money is ever-present, and people will quite naturally look for more efficient ways of doing things. Without a rigorous, multilevel process for trapping hazards, the likelihood of an accident at some point is 100 percent.

CONCLUSION

One of our most pernicious myths is that human errors at the sharp end of an accident are usually responsible for the disaster. While it's true that some actions by operators inevitably occur in an accident's chain of events, they are usually just one of several causes. Design mistakes of many kinds are also "errors by humans," and these include high-level policy decisions; budgetary restrictions; training inadequacies; equipment procurement, installation, and maintenance practices; and measurement and reward systems. Such design errors are usually not labeled as the cause of an accident, whereas operator errors often are. We need to look to the whole scope of decisions, from those made just moments before an accident to those made years or decades beforehand in creating the technologies involved, to fully understand and prevent catastrophes.

Chernobyl's reactor, the Galaxy IV satellite, and the Hyatt Regency's skywalks were all design mistakes that waited for an appropriate situational trigger to set them loose to claim their victims. In the next chapter, we turn to another such mistake, one that claimed thousands of lives as a side effect of making them better.

CHAPTER 6

THE VIOXX DISASTER AND BP: THE SEDUCTION OF PROFITS

During the five years the popular painkiller Vioxx was on the market (1999 to 2004), more than one hundred million prescriptions for the drug were written in the United States alone. In that time, the drug caused well over a hundred thousand injuries or deaths. Using the metaphor employed by Dr. David Graham of the Food and Drug Administration (FDA) in his Senate testimony, those deaths were roughly equivalent to a fatal crash of a fully loaded Boeing 767 every week the drug was on the market.

How could that catastrophe have happened?

When Merck & Company withdrew its blockbuster drug from the market in September 2004, the company claimed it was for patient safety. It also said that the stroke and heart attack risks that had recently come to light were "unexpected." However, company documents produced in court and in congressional inquiries tell a different story, which revealed that as a result of early studies it sponsored, Merck long suspected the elevated cardiovascular risks of the drug—possibly as early as 1996–97—but had taken aggressive steps to prevent such damaging information from reaching the public.

In 1999, Merck conceived a study called VIGOR to showcase the new drug. It highlighted Vioxx's relatively low levels of gastrointestinal side effects compared with naproxen (Aleve, Anaprox), the traditional pain medication alternative. Indeed, a lower level of gastrointestinal side effects was the main selling point of Vioxx over its competitors. Ironically, Merck's own study provided damning proof of the company's negligence. Although participants in VIGOR included some with cardiac histories, the clinical trial required that no heart-attack-preventing aspirin be taken. This was done to maximize the expected differences in gastrointestinal complications between Vioxx and naproxen. Like other medicines in its class (known as nonsteroidal anti-inflammatory drugs, or NSAIDs), naproxen is a known stomach irritant. Avoiding stomach problems was Vioxx's raison d'être, and this advantage accounted for the painkiller's runaway success.

While tailoring a clinical trial to put a new drug in the best possible light was reasonable from a marketing standpoint, in this case the maneuver was medically misleading. Company e-mails reveal that Merck's own scientists realized that excluding aspirin from the clinical trial was unrealistic in light of the target market for the drug. That target market comprised many older patients with a history of heart disease who were also taking low-dose aspirin as a protection against heart attacks. The study's restrictions should have limited Merck's ability to generalize about a larger population.

In March 2000, the results of the VIGOR study showed that while Vioxx patients had half as many stomach problems as those taking naproxen, they also had many more blood-clot-related complications. Critically, the heart attack rate was four times as high as in the naproxen group, and would later turn out to be five times as high. Surprisingly, Merck's safety board for the study did not contain a cardiologist. Furthermore, in violation of Merck's own independence rules, the head of the board was paid by Merck and owned $70,000 worth of Merck stock. As Stanford's Dr. Gurkipal Singh would later say in his Senate testimony, "Clearly, the trade-off of 500 percent increase in the risk of heart attacks for a 50 percent reduction in stomach bleeds did not seem attractive—at least, not without a further discussion of data."

On March 9, 2000, Merck's head of research, Dr. Edward Scolnick, e-mailed others in the company that "cardiovascular events" were clearly present, and while incident rates were low, he said the results were "a shame," and noted that the problem was "mechanism based," that is, a characteristic of the drug's inherent effects in the body. In that e-mail, Scolnick made specific reference to the phenomenon identified in the 1996–97 study.

In spite of Scolnick's conclusions, Merck publicly claimed that there was "NO DIFFERENCE in the incidence of cardiovascular events" (emphasis in original). Instead, Merck rationalized that naproxen's beneficial anti-clotting effects were responsible for Vioxx's poor showing. These supposed beneficial effects of naproxen turned out to be wishful thinking. An FDA study later concluded that drugs like naproxen did not demonstrate a reduction of cardiovascular incidents as Merck had argued. The study also dramatically underscored the elevated risks of Vioxx in comparison with the other leading COX-2 inhibitor product, Pfizer's Celebrex.

Undeterred, the Merck VIGOR team published an article in the *New England Journal of Medicine* that hailed Vioxx's virtues, barely mentioning the adverse cardiac events they had found. Singh stated in his Senate testimony, "The VIGOR publication minimized the significance of heart attacks. While it prominently discussed the reduction of stomach bleeds in patients taking Vioxx, it did not mention that in spite of this, patients on Vioxx had more serious adverse events, and more hospitalizations than patients on Naproxen. The true rates for cardiovascular thrombotic adverse . . . hypertension and congestive heart failure—which were all higher in the Vioxx group—were not shown in the paper at all."

Just before publication, Merck researchers also secretly removed several adverse heart attack cases from the findings, later claiming that the data fell outside the preestablished (but highly unusual) study boundaries, and were not known to them prior to publication. To the contrary, court-produced e-mails later revealed that two of the study's three lead authors—Claire Bombardier, M.D.; Loren Laine, M.D.; and Alise Reicin, M.D.—knew of the troubling data. Merck's lies prompted a rash of ethical criticism and a rebuke by the editors of the journal: "Taken together, these inaccuracies and deletions call into question the integrity of the data on adverse cardiovascular events in this article."

As late as August 2004, after the FDA's drug safety office presented data showing that Vioxx at high doses tripled the risk of heart attack or sudden cardiac death, Merck continued to stonewall. The company issued a press release saying that it "strongly disagreed" with the FDA's analysis and claiming that "Merck stands behind the efficacy, overall safety and cardiovascular safety of Vioxx." With more and more data confirming Vioxx's greater risk, however, the company quietly informed the FDA on September 28, 2004, that it planned to voluntarily withdraw Vioxx from the market. It did so publicly two days later.

SHOOTING THE MESSENGER

During the years leading up to the withdrawal of Vioxx from the market, Merck had consistently put pressure on academic researchers to dissuade them from presenting adverse results about the drug or publishing unflattering views of Merck's handling of the situation. The drug company also successfully negotiated with the FDA to downplay the cardiovascular impacts on product labeling, a point to which we will return shortly.

In one egregious attempt to silence a critic, Merck pressured and then sued Professor Joan-Ramon Laporte of the Catalan Institute of Pharmacology in Barcelona to retract an accusatory 2002 article in the institute's drug information bulletin *Butlletí Groc*, which Laporte edits. The article, "So-Called Advantages of Celecoxib [Celebrex] and

Rofecoxib [Vioxx]: Scientific Fraud," not only summarized worrisome research and commentaries published in the British medical journals *The Lancet* and *BMJ* (the journal of the British Medical Association), but also raised questions about Merck's scientific ethics, particularly the willful selectivity of information presented to European drug authorities. A Spanish court ruled in Laporte's favor in 2004.

As the facts about Vioxx began to surface, even former boosters of the painkiller began to ask questions. Dr. Gurkipal Singh, the influential rheumatologist and medical researcher at Stanford Medical School, had been an early supporter who had been paid by Merck to educate other doctors about Vioxx's benefits. After the VIGOR results came to light, however, Singh found that he could not get satisfactory answers from Merck about elevated cardiovascular risks. Frustrated by the company's unwillingness to share data, he went on the offensive, accusing Merck of hiding information, even showing a cartoon of a figure representing Merck hiding under a blanket during his public lectures about the drug.

Eventually, Dr. Louis Sherwood, a Merck senior executive well known in academic medical circles, threatened retribution against both Singh and Dr. James Fries, his superior at Stanford. The doctors reported that Sherwood intimated that continued criticism of Vioxx would damage Singh's career and endanger Stanford's funding. Surprised by the heavy-handed tactics, Fries collected stories from colleagues at other universities who had also been intimidated by Sherwood and then wrote to Merck CEO Raymond Gilmartin, charging that the company had "crossed the line" in trying to silence its critics. The intimidation of Singh and Stanford stopped, although other Vioxx detractors were less fortunate.

Two days after a deposition by Merck critic, eminent cardiologist Dr. Eric Topol, was played in a court proceeding, he was told that he had lost his job as provost of the Cleveland Clinic, and that his position of chief academic officer of its medical school had been abolished. In his testimony, Topol had told a jury that Gilmartin had called the Cleveland Clinic Board of Trustees to complain about his "unjustified" criticism of Merck in articles he'd published in the *New York Times* and *New England Journal of Medicine*.

In the articles, Topol had written that Merck and the FDA had not taken timely action when legitimate questions about the link between Vioxx and cardiac problems emerged. In particular, the company did not initiate clinical trials to determine the risks in those patients with histories of cardiac problems as well as arthritis—a group that "may represent the largest segment of the population for whom rofecoxib [Vioxx] was prescribed." That is precisely the group about whom Merck's own scientists had been worried.

The death blow for Vioxx came in late September 2004. Merck informed the FDA on September 27 that one of its independent Data Safety Monitoring Boards, which monitor each specific clinical trial, had recommended that the long-term study of Vioxx called APPROVe be stopped early for safety reasons. It had been hoped that the study, which had focused on patients at risk for developing recurrent colon polyps, would identify a new application for Vioxx. Unexpectedly, however, the study showed an increased risk of cardiovascular events, including heart attack and stroke, in patients taking Vioxx compared with a placebo, particularly those who had been taking the drug for longer than eighteen months. By linking the withdrawal to a specific study and to long-term use, Merck would later claim to have seized the initiative as soon as the facts were known as well as reduced its legal liability from short-term-use patients who suffered adverse reactions.

Although Vioxx has been off the market since 2004, Merck has continued to take a beating over its effects. Initially, the company lost 30 percent of its stock market value—essentially ten years of growth. Compared with pre-withdrawal levels, Merck's stock price growth also remained below that of the S&P 500 index for more than three years, and the company has faced legal claims from nearly twenty-seven thousand people and on behalf of third-party payers such as insurance companies, labor union health plans, and state Medicare programs. Unlike individual suits that require proof that Vioxx caused patient harm, the institutional suits merely require proof that Merck continued to push the sale of the drug after it knew of Vioxx's increased risks.

After several years of fighting every individual case and winning many of them at massive expense, in November 2007 Merck announced a $4.85 billion settlement agreement with plaintiffs' lawyers. "Clinical trials prove that Vioxx raises the risk of heart attacks, but linking its use to any one person's problems is difficult, especially when the person had other risk factors like smoking," observed the *New York Times*. Despite the record size of the settlement, it is considered by many analysts to be a victory for the company and its obdurate legal strategy.

The complexities of legal burden of proof notwithstanding, if not for the courageous efforts of a small number of outsiders and whistle-blowers, it is likely that thousands more would have been killed or harmed by Vioxx. As one of Merck's critics said, each one of those injuries happened to a real person—someone's dad or mom, a person with friends and loved ones—not just a statistic, or a plaintiff in a lawsuit.

As one of America's best-managed and most trusted companies, why did Merck do what it did? The evidence strongly suggests that knowledge of Vioxx's health risks reached senior levels of the organization years before the drug was submitted for FDA approval in 1999. Furthermore, the zeal with which some Merck officials tried to silence medical experts who raised legitimate safety questions appears out of character for a company whose espoused values include scientific objectivity and concern for patients, backed up by a successful track record. While it is possible that this event was an anomaly, the sustained and widespread nature of the cover-up of Vioxx's risks over many years is reminiscent of other instances in which a company's obsession with its public image coupled with concerns about financial results overwhelmed all other considerations.

While the question of the dangers posed by COX-2 inhibitor drugs remains open, Vioxx appears in a class by itself for its risks to patients. Furthermore, Merck's behavior toward scientists who tried to get to the bottom of the hazards associated with the new drug raises questions about what happened to the company's traditional values of scientific integrity and patient safety, and how Merck's extensive protective mechanisms—such as the APPROVe Data Safety Monitoring Board that finally killed the drug—failed to do their job over eight years. How did such mechanisms lose their power, and why did no one rein in the most exuberant true believers who mercilessly attacked Vioxx critics?

An equally important question, however, is this: Why did Merck's external watchdog, the Food and Drug Administration, also fail to fulfill its role as protector of the public health? In our discussion of the *Columbia* case in chapter 1, we saw the dangers that arise when regulators and watchdog agencies develop financial and political ties to the entities they are supposed to be regulating and watching. In the Vioxx case, we see this phenomenon in full force again.

DO REGULATORS HAVE "CLIENTS"?

More than a century ago, the 1906 Food and Drug Act paved the way for the creation of the Food and Drug Administration. But it was not until 1937, when the reformulation of a commonly used sulfa drug killed over one hundred people, that the FDA was given the power to review new drugs for efficacy and safety prior to their release.

Before 1937, sulfanilamide was a drug that had been used to treat streptococcal infections. It had dramatic therapeutic benefits, and had been used safely in tablet and powder form for many years. In June 1937, a salesman for the S. E. Massengill Co. in Bristol, Tennessee, reported a demand for the drug in liquid form. The company's chief chemist and pharmacist, Harold Watkins, discovered that sulfanil-amide would dissolve in diethylene glycol. Massengill's laboratory tested the mixture for flavor, appearance, and fragrance, then manu-factured and shipped the product all over the country. Unfortunately, diethylene glycol is a poisonous substance found in antifreeze and paint, but Massengill had never tested its new elixir for toxicity. (The same chemical, mixed into government-manufactured cough syrup, killed 138 Panamanians in 2006, and set off a scare in 2007 when it was discovered in certain toothpastes imported from China.)

By the time FDA inspectors contacted Massengill, the company was already aware of the dangers posed by its new product. And while Massengill had sent a thousand telegrams to doctors and pharmacists around the country to recall the liquid sulfanilamide, the company requested only that the drugs be returned, failing to mention their tox-icity. In a race against time, and with a lot of dogged, manual detective work, virtually all the shipments and persons who had been prescribed the drug were located. Despite these heroics, 107 people died, many of them children. A more empowered FDA was born in the aftermath of that public health crisis. The enabling legislation was the Federal Food, Drug, and Cosmetic Act of 1938.

Arguably, the most celebrated success the FDA had with its new preapproval powers was Frances Oldham Kelsey's refusal to grant approval to thalidomide in 1960. Marketed in Europe, South America, and Africa as a safe over-the-counter sleeping pill and morning sick-ness medicine for pregnant women, thalidomide caused thousands of birth defects after it was introduced by the German drug manufacturer

Chemie Grünenthal in 1957. Kelsey, one of just four part-time physicians reviewing new drug applications to the FDA, thought that more tests were needed, and she resisted pressures from Richardson-Merrell, the drug's U.S. manufacturer, to permit its sale. Those pressures were particularly intense just before Christmas, since "that is when our best sales are," according to a company representative. (Since 1998, thalidomide has been available in the United States, but only for the treatment of skin lesions related to leprosy.)

Soon after a wave of deformed babies were born in Germany, Dr. Widukind Lenz determined that thalidomide was responsible. Among his own patients, Dr. Lenz discovered that half the mothers with deformed babies had taken thalidomide in the first trimester of pregnancy. Lenz warned the German manufacturer, Chemie Grünenthal, but the company disputed his findings. The German government withdrew the drug anyway, and other countries followed suit.

When the news about the birth defects caused by thalidomide overseas came to light in the United States, the public outcry was immediate. Kelsey was hailed on the front page of the *Washington Post* as the hero who prevented "the birth of hundreds or indeed thousands of armless and legless children." President John F. Kennedy awarded Kelsey America's highest civilian medal.

As a result of the thalidomide controversy, the Food, Drug, and Cosmetics Act Amendments of 1962 were passed unanimously by Congress. The reforms required "stricter limits on the testing and distribution of new drugs," and the amendments recognized for the first time that "effectiveness [should be] required to be established prior to marketing."

Kelsey's bold actions stand in sharp contrast with the FDA's timidity forty years later in the Vioxx case. "I think I always accepted the fact that one was going to get bullied and pressured by industry," Kelsey said. While she also believed that "it was understandable that the companies were very anxious to get their drugs approved," Richardson-Merrell appeared to be more than just anxious. Dr. Joseph Murray, the drug-maker's representative, made repeated phone calls and personal visits to her, and complained to her superiors that she was unreasonable and nitpicking, and was unnecessarily delaying the drug's approval. But Kelsey stuck to her guns, asking for more data, especially for answers to subtle questions about toxicity and risks to pregnant women.

In the wake of the thalidomide controversy, the FDA's approval requirements became more demanding over the years. Pointing to the fact that many new drugs were introduced in other countries with less stringent preapproval requirements, critics and drug company advocates complained that the agency was depriving U.S. patients of new medicines and increasing health care costs. In an attempt to address those criticisms, new legislation was passed in 1992 that permitted the FDA to collect "user fees" from drug-makers to offset the costs of bringing new drugs to market. With more resources and a measurement process that tracks new drug approval times, delays dropped from thirty to twelve months. Today, 60 percent of new drugs first come to market in the United States.

One key feature of the FDA's unusual funding arrangement is a requirement that the agency maintain its spending levels for drug approvals. (The 1992 levels were updated in 1997.) Although that provision seems a reasonable requirement on behalf of the drug companies to prevent earmarked payments from being diluted in the general funding pool, the rules ended up being subverted.

Congressional funding of the FDA did not keep up with the pace of new drug development or with inflation. The allocations did not even include provisions for staff pay raises. To maintain external funding under the agreement, the FDA raided other programs under its umbrella for money, increasingly concentrating on new drug approval to the exclusion of its other mandated activities. In 1992, the agency spent 53 percent of its drug center budget on new drug approvals; by 2003, that had risen to 79 percent.

Particularly hard hit by the funding squeeze was the agency's long-standing study of side effects and other aspects of drug safety for products already on the market. As was seen in the case of Vioxx, not only do some undesirable aspects of drug usage take time to develop, but the histories of many patients must also be analyzed to identify more complex health problems, such as drug-to-drug interactions. A robust postapproval program is therefore a necessary part of a comprehensive approach to drug safety, since faster approval increases the likelihood that low-probability or long-term usage risks will not show up during the preapproval process.

Exacerbating the consequences of the FDA's financial priorities have been a variety of organizational and cultural issues that undermine postmarketing safety investigations. On the FDA organization chart, the Office of Drug Safety (ODS) sits below the Office of New Drugs (OND), receiving only a fraction of its staff and funding. Furthermore, the ODS lacks any direct regulatory powers; it serves merely as a "consultant" to the OND within their joint parent organization, the Center for Drug Evaluation and Research (CDER).

Under the 1992 user fees legislation, the FDA has become responsible for meeting targets for new drug approval. While nearly a hundred safety officers of the CDER/OND are there to assure that approved drugs are safe as well as effective, the organization has a natural reluctance to correct mistakes or oversights in its approvals. Dr. David Graham, the associate director for science and medicine at the ODS—who would achieve notoriety as the FDA whistle-blower in the Vioxx case—testified before the Senate Finance Committee in November 2004, "When a serious safety issue arises post-marketing, [the Office of New Drugs'] immediate reaction is almost always one of denial, rejection and heat. They approved the drug, so there can't possibly be anything wrong with it. The same group that approved the drug is also responsible for taking regulatory action against it postmarketing. This is an inherent conflict of interest."

Professional and methodological differences between the ODS and the OND further complicate postmarketing safety investigations. However, it may be the OND's interpretation of its mission that creates the most conflict. The Office of New Drugs sees the pharmaceutical companies—known as drug "sponsors"—as its *clients*, a perspective that encourages it to please rather than control the drugmakers. As you can imagine, taking action against a drug like Vioxx, which earned nearly $7 million a day, is a not a good way to please a "client."

The urge to please one's client also affects the ODS, which, as a consultant to the OND, experiences strong pressure to stay on the client's good side. According to Dr. Graham, if the new drug reviewing division is the "single greatest obstacle" to protecting the public, a close second is "an ODS management that sees its mission as pleasing the Office of New Drugs."

While Dr. Graham did fulfill a vital role as guardian of the public health, like Frances Oldham Kelsey did in the 1960s, it is emblematic of changes in the approval process since the 1960s that Graham's outspoken advocacy came only after a harmful drug was on the market, while Kelsey had been able to exert her influence before the harm was done. It seems that the speed-up in the drug approval process may have gone too far—and changes to postapproval drug evaluations not far enough.

While the exact nature of the FDA's fiscal, organizational, and cultural problems continues to be hotly debated, it is hard to dispute the relationship between the shrinking funds of the ODS and its mandated task of monitoring postmarketing drug safety. In the Vioxx case, the early warnings took longer to confirm than necessary, according to Dr.

Graham, who testified that between twenty-six thousand and fifty-five thousand Americans needlessly lost their lives as a result of the delay.

In 2002—eighteen months after the full VIGOR results were made available to FDA—the agency finally negotiated a modest relabeling with Merck that identified the heart attack risk with high doses of Vioxx. However, the change was not made on the package's warnings label, which would have sent a strong message to doctors and consumers. Nor did the FDA ban the high-dose formulation, which dramatically increased the risks. According to Graham, "FDA's label change had absolutely no effect on how often high-dose Vioxx was prescribed." Dr. Sidney Wolfe, director of Public Citizens Health Research Group, broadened this criticism of FDA's labeling practices: "For most [drugs] eventually taken off the market—there was a futile, dangerous interval before withdrawal during which there were attempts, through labeling changes, to solve a problem of an unacceptably dangerous drug, mainly ones for which there were safer alternatives."

Graham's and Wolfe's comments mirror the findings of three surveys of FDA employees performed by the Public Citizens Health Research Group, the FDA itself, and the Inspector General's Office. The conclusion from these surveys is that within the current FDA, the expression of scientific opinions is repressed, reports are censored, and recommendations are ignored or overruled by senior level, pro-industry administrators.

Two months after Vioxx was withdrawn, in December 2004, a team of Swiss scientists commented in a study published in one of Britain's most prestigious medical journals, *The Lancet*: "Our findings indicate that Vioxx should have been withdrawn several years earlier. . . . The reason why manufacturer and drug licensing authorities did not continuously monitor and summarize the accumulating evidence needs to be clarified." In a scathing editorial, *The Lancet*'s editor-in-chief,

Dr. Richard Horton, wrote: "With Vioxx, Merck and the FDA acted out of ruthless, short-sighted, and irresponsible self-interest." It seems clear that many people feel that Vioxx should never have been approved, and probably would not have been sanctioned if FDA had continued in the spirit of Frances Kelsey.

While we may not be surprised that company scientists yield to corporate pressures placed on them, it is harder to forgive the passivity of FDA policy-makers. Vioxx was approved on a fast-track basis despite the availability of many existing arthritis pain medicines. Pfizer's Celebrex, a COX-2 inhibitor like Vioxx, had been approved six months before, eliminating any *medical* urgency to rush to judgment on the new COX-2 drug (although, no doubt, increasing Merck's marketing urgency). Since the pharmaceutical industry wields such power over elected officials in Washington, D.C., one interpretation of events is that the FDA's actions on approval and safety are politically motivated. As reported in the *Washington Post*, "Drug companies spent more on lobbying than any other industry between 1998 and 2005— $900 million, according to the nonpartisan Center for Responsive Politics. They donated a total of $89.9 million in the same period to federal candidates and party committees, nearly three-quarters of it to Republicans." Senator Charles E. Grassley (R-Iowa), a strong advocate of FDA reform, commented, "You can hardly swing a cat by the tail in Washington without hitting a pharmaceutical lobbyist."

WHY WEREN'T THERE MORE WHISTLE-BLOWERS?

Neither Merck nor the FDA reacted objectively to the growing evidence of the dangers presented by Vioxx. Rather, they behaved in the manner characteristic of people who—as Dr. Singh's cartoon suggested—have something to hide. A benign interpretation of this behavior is that it was an overzealous reaction to being attacked by individuals who were unjustly impugning Merck's product and OND's judgment. Another explanation is that both organizations engaged in *whistle-blower retaliation*, the deliberate and orchestrated intimidation and attempted punishment of individuals seeking to bring potentially embarrassing and damaging information to light.

Unfortunately, as we have seen, individuals who go against the grain of hierarchical organizations are often severely punished when they try to take their dissent beyond narrow channels. The point at which dissent becomes unacceptable varies from one setting to another, but it usually involves external publicity or regulatory notification. Within organizations, it is almost always considered disloyal not to keep quiet when told (or even "hinted at") to do so. Outspoken employees will often be pressured by their bosses, criticized by their peers, and excluded from forums where their contrary opinions might be publicly aired.

Even in cases where there are clear ethical violations or outright fraud, the whistle-blower is often subjected to greater punishment than the wrongdoer. A classic piece of research has documented how dedicated whistle-blowers—those who indomitably persist in their attempts to bring institutional wrongdoing to light—are overwhelmingly punished by their organizations. One study shows 60 percent are fired and another 20 percent have their responsibilities changed or are otherwise harassed. In a second study of scientific misconduct, the most frequent consequences for whistle-blowers are strong pressures to drop their allegations, and counterallegations—a common harassment tactic that puts the accuser on the defensive. Denials of salary increases, promotion, and research opportunities are also common punishments. From these studies and many anecdotal stories, Singh's, Topol's, LaPorte's, and Graham's experiences are easily seen as the rule rather than as the exception.

Given the strong disincentives facing potential whistle-blowers, it's not surprising that there weren't more of them in the Vioxx case.

Nonetheless, thousands of lives were at stake. It is, therefore, not unreasonable to ask why more people who saw the risks did not speak up.

As explained in chapter 1, our minds possess powerful mechanisms for rationalization that allow us to reconcile selfish behavior with an altruistic self-image. In fact, as examined in chapter 2, a good deal of evidence exists to indicate these mechanisms are hardwired into us through evolution. Ancient programming encourages us to protect ourselves and concoct sophisticated stories to justify what we have done.

As a result, when faced with many high-stakes "greater good" dilemmas in the modern world, people's judgment doesn't always produce the outcomes we might hope for. Rather than recognizing that personal sacrifices are a fair exchange for avoiding collective disaster, many people choose to be bystanders no matter what the consequences might be for others. We observed this in the *Challenger* and *Columbia* accidents and other cases. It is a testament to the power of self-interest, fear of retaliation, and rationalizations that while many inside Merck apparently knew of Vioxx's potential for heart attacks and strokes, no one publicly came forward.

THE BRITISH PETROLEUM TEXAS CITY REFINERY FIRE

Unfortunately, the pattern of management that opts for short-term over long-term benefits in the face of serious dangers is more common than we'd like to think. One of the most serious industrial accidents in U.S. history occurred on March 23, 2005, at the British Petroleum refinery in Texas City, Texas. During a dangerous start-up procedure of an isomerization unit that produces highly flammable gasoline-enhancing chemicals, an inadvertent overfilling of the unit let the highly volatile chemicals escape. They formed an explosive vapor cloud that then ignited, causing two huge explosions and a fire that consumed an employee construction trailer just forty yards away.

Fifteen people died and 180 were injured. Many of the same factors that facilitated the Vioxx disaster were in evidence at BP's refinery.

Initially, after the deadly explosion, BP officials accused workers of being negligent by violating procedures and not sounding an evacuation alarm. Six of those workers were fired as a result. The company then dodged responsibility for locating its trailers dangerously near the isomerization unit by insisting its procedures could not have anticipated multiple failures by personnel that could result in a massive explosion.

As the story unfolded, however, facts came to light that indicated this refinery was chronically prone to accidents and deaths: twenty-three workers had died during the previous thirty years, approximately one every eighteen months, four since BP took over the refinery as part of the Amoco acquisition in 1998.

Also putting the lie to BP's public statements, the trailer's close proximity to a volatile unit violated industry guidelines as well as BP's own siting rules, which required trailers to be at least 350 feet from such a unit. Those requirements were put into place after a similar accident occurred at a different BP refinery in 1995. Documents released by BP under court order showed that the company's management ignored questions by union representatives about the location of that particular trailer. A BP-commissioned safety survey also revealed that employees considered "making money" to be the number one priority of the company while "people" came in dead last on the list.

Perhaps the most damning condemnation of BP was the known danger associated with the overflow handling of the isomerization unit itself. As examined in the previous chapter, design mistakes are often critical in accidents. Although the unit had been scheduled for upgrading, financial pressures prevented the redesign despite a long history of problems. Flammable materials had escaped its vent stack at least four times previous to 1995, and since 2000, thirteen out of sixteen restarts had been abnormal with either dangerously high liquid levels or high pressures. Yet, despite those past problems and the obvious risks from an overflow of the unit's explosive contents, gauges that measured the quantity of materials were faulty, key valves did not work, and motor vehicles that could—and almost certainly did— provide an explosive spark were allowed to be operated nearby.

The engineering of the isomerization unit, the rules for the siting of trailers, and the safety and follow-up practices associated with restarts are all design issues. Design issues are the responsibility of the management, not of the workers. Yet in its own follow-up report, released eight months after the accident, BP management barely acknowledged its role in the disaster with this evasive statement:

Over the years the working environment had eroded to one charac- terized by resistance to change, and lacking trust, motivation and a sense of purpose. Rules were not consistently followed, rigor was lack- ing and individuals felt disempowered from suggesting or initiating improvements.

BP did not, or perhaps could not, own up to knowing what was going on before the fact:

Given the poor communication and performance management process, there was neither adequate early warning system of prob- lems, nor any independent means of understanding the deteriorating standards in the plant.

Contradicting this official view, both the employee safety survey and an internal safety business plan from early 2005 highlighted sig- nificant safety issues. In fact, the safety report predicted that an accident resulting in the loss of life was a serious short-term risk.

And so it was, three months later.

* * *

In this book, no accident represents as many potentially avoidable deaths and injuries as Vioxx. It is, conceivably, on the scale of the U.S. deaths from the Vietnam War. There are also few instances where a responsible organization tried to silence its critics with such ruthlessness, or so resolutely maintained its innocence in the face of grievous harm.

In comparison, the accident at BP's Texas City refinery seems rather modest, although we should not let simple comparisons fool us into treating it lightly. BP ignored the danger signs for years, just as Amoco had done before them. And people died at Texas City with distressing regularity, although not in large numbers. That, of course, made no difference to the bereaved, nor should it to us.

In the next chapter, we will deal with a different kind of accident. One that was deeply embarrassing to the U.S. government, as well as one that should not have happened. What is most interesting—and the issue upon which we focus—is how it could have occurred at all, since every imaginable human, organizational, and technical precaution would appear to have been taken.

CHAPTER 7

WHEN ALL THE BACKUPS FAILED: HOW AMERICAN F-15S ACCIDENTALLY SHOT DOWN TWO U.S. ARMY BLACK HAWKS

On April 14, 1994, in northern Iraq following the first Persian Gulf War, two U.S. Army Black Hawk helicopters and their crews were transporting American, British, French, and Turkish military officers, as well as some Kurdish representatives and one American political adviser. At the same time, a U.S. Air Force Airborne Warning and Control Systems (AWACS) aircraft was flying over Turkey to monitor for enemy or hostile aircraft in violation of the no-fly zone imposed on northern Iraq. The pilots of two U.S. F-15 fighters that were also patrolling the area misidentified the Black Hawks as Iraqi Hind helicopters and shot them down, killing all twenty-six people aboard.

While such tragic incidents of friendly fire are always a risk when a large military presence is concentrated in one area, this disaster could have had catastrophic international consequences. How could such an egregious error have occurred? To answer that question, the set of causal factors we've already examined must be dramatically expanded.

THE ACCIDENT

On the morning of the tragedy, the AWACS was, as usual, the first air-craft aloft. All but one member of a new AWACS crew had served with Operation Provide Comfort (OPC), the humanitarian mission in which the Black Hawks were also participating, but this was their first mission together. They were eager to get started. The AWACS aircraft, a modified Boeing 707, departed Incirlik, Turkey, a few minutes early at 7:36 A.M. and flew a wake-up orbit to warm up and safety-check the aircraft's equipment. AWACS then proceeded to its station, a narrow track of secure Turkish airspace north of the Iraqi border. The AWACS was fully operational by 8:45 A.M.

April 14 was to have been a special day for the detachment of army UH-60 Black Hawk helicopters designated Eagle Flight. They were scheduled to fly a senior group of VIPs deep into the no-fly zone (also known as the Tactical Area of Responsibility, or TAOR) to meet with Kurdish leaders. They requested takeoff clearance at 8:15 A.M. from their base near Diyarbakir, Turkey, and departed seven minutes later with their Turkish liaison officers on board, as required.

Turkey's role in OPC operations was complex and highly sensitive. It had veto rights over every air operation (and, even after the shoot-down of the Black Hawks, the Turkish officials tried to dictate search and rescue operations). To complicate matters, while OPC flights were trying to protect the Kurds from Iraqi attacks, Turkish aircraft were flying Special Operations into the no-fly zone to bomb and strafe Kurdish villages. The Turks had long been concerned that a push for Kurdish independence threatened their territorial sovereignty because of the large number of Kurds that live in Turkey.

The two U.S. Air Force F-15 pilots, designated Tiger 01 and Tiger 02, began their mission briefing at 7:35 A.M. The primary purpose of this first flight in the morning was to "sanitize" the no-fly zone to make it safe for the AWACS to move south from Turkey over potentially hostile territory. During the tactical section of their briefing, the two pilots performed a line-by-line review of the Air Tasking Order, which contained a list of the more than fifty OPC aircraft scheduled to fly inside the TAOR that day. In addition, Tiger 01, the lead pilot, provided an overview of the three target scenarios: a high fast flier, a medium or low fast flier, and a low slow helicopter. The two pilots also reviewed radar sweep procedures and other details of the mission. The tactical briefing ended at 8:20 A.M. After proceeding to their aircraft, the F-15 pilots started their engines at 9:00 A.M. and checked in with the mission director on the ground for any last-minute changes. There were none. After arming their missiles and checking their aircraft IFF system ("identify friend or foe"), the pilots took off for the no-fly zone on schedule at 9:35 A.M.

Just after takeoff, the F-15s checked their IFF again, testing each of its four modes by using each other as the target. They then switched their radios to the en route frequency, checked in with AWACS to tell them that their flight status was as specified on the Air Tasking Order. Halfway between their first and second checkpoints en route to the TAOR, the pilots performed a three-way radio check with AWACS, using the frequency-hopping antijamming capabilities of their sophisticated HAVE QUICK II radios.

Just before entering the TAOR, the F-15s checked in with the Airborne Command Element—known as ACE—their mission boss in the chain of command, who was aboard AWACS. He had no additional information for them. After turning on all their combat systems (except the master arm switch, activated right before an engagement with hostile aircraft), they switched their IFF Mode I code from 43, the one designated for peacetime flights in Turkey on that day, to 52, that day's Mode I code for the TAOR. The F-15s crossed the Iraqi border right on schedule at 10:20 A.M.

In the meantime, the two Eagle Flight Black Hawks had crossed the border into Iraq at 9:35 A.M. and immediately descended into Zakhu, the Military Command Center (MCC) forward base. After landing, conducting a quick briefing, and loading up with eighteen VIP passengers, including the Turkish and U.S. MCC co-commanders, the helicopters took off at 9:54 for the town of Irbil, far to the east and south of Zakhu, near the southern boundary of the no-fly zone, deep into Iraqi airspace.

The route from Zakhu to Irbil overflew heavily mountainous terrain. Twenty minutes after leaving Zakhu, the Black Hawks entered a deep valley and dropped off the AWACS's radar screen due to the rough terrain that hid them from the AWACS's powerful radar.

At 10:20 A.M., just as the F-15s entered the TAOR as the official first flight of the day to begin their sanitizing sweep of the airspace according to the Air Tasking Order, the helicopters were already well within the no-fly zone. The Black Hawks were flying at 130 knots, two hundred feet above ground level, in a straight line along a small river valley, with seven-thousand-foot-high mountains on either side.

At 10:22 A.M., Tiger 01, the lead F-15, picked up the Black Hawks on his search radar. He confirmed their speed and heading, reported his contact to the AWACS, and initiated an IFF query. His IFF Mode I check for April 14's code 52 received no positive response. He then switched the IFF interrogator to automatic mode, and tried again on Mode IV, the setting that should indicate any friendly aircraft, even if its IFF was not "squawking" the day's correct TAOR-specific encrypted code. This time, the symbol on his screen changed briefly to "friendly," but then returned to "unidentified." Tiger 01 believed that there were bugs in the F-15's IFF system; thus a transient friendly response was a known condition that did not preclude the presence of hostile aircraft. As a result, he assumed the helicopters were, in fact, hostile.

When Tiger 01 checked in with the AWACS, he was told that the location he specified for the helicopters was "clean" of any aircraft.

However, one minute later, the AWACS began to receive intermittent friendly IFF signals from the same location, but that fact was not relayed to the F-15s.

At 10:25 A.M., Tiger 02, the F-15 flight wingman, confirmed the location, altitude, and heading of the low slow target. This time, AWACS reported "hits there," indicating radar returns. However, AWACS did not report the intermittent friendly IFF returns they were receiving at 10:25 or the consistent friendly identification that appeared on their scopes one minute later.

All the details of the ensuing disaster were captured on the AWACS data tapes and by a conventional video recording on one of the AWACS display screens. However, neither of the F-15 pilots turned on their heads-up-display recording system to create a record of their view of the incident. Furthermore, there were discrepancies between the pilots' incident reports, recorded immediately after the accident, and their later testimony.

According to the rules of engagement, fighter pilots must confirm their electronic identification of unfriendly aircraft with a visual identification, or VID. Descending from twenty-seven thousand feet, Tiger 01 performed a second IFF check, again getting no positive response in either Mode I or Mode IV. By 10:26 A.M., Tiger 01 had closed the distance-to-target to seven nautical miles, but still couldn't see the camouflaged Black Hawks against the rugged green terrain. At five miles, he finally spotted the Black Hawks on the Target Designator box of his heads-up display. He called AWACS: "Tiger 01 is tally, one helicopter." At the same time, the en route controller aboard AWACS initiated an "unknown, pending, unevaluated" track in the area of the helicopter's radar and IFF returns, but he said nothing to the pilots.

To make his visual identification, Tiger 01 flew rapidly past his target at 450 knots, passing above and to the left at a distance of approximately 1,200 feet (two-tenths of a mile). After the pass, when he pulled up to circle around the helicopter, he spotted a second helicopter flying in trail position behind.

At 10:28, Tiger 01 reported: "VID Hind—correction, Hip . . . no Hind." *Hip* and *Hind* are NATO designations for two different Soviet-made helicopters flown by the Iraqis as well as some U.S. allies. (See figure 7.1.)

As briefed that day for low slow intercepts, Tiger 02 put some distance between himself and the lead F-15, spotted the two helicopters on radar, and initiated an IFF interrogation. As expected, the lead F-15 squawked friendly, but the helicopters remained unidentified by IFF and were thus assumed to be hostile. Tiger 01 reported, "ID Hind, Tally

Figure 7.1 *Front and side views of U.S. Army Black Hawks and Soviet Hind helicopters. The Black Hawks appear darker and to the right in each photo.*
Credit: U.S. Air Force photo. Obtained under Freedom of Information Act by Joan L. Piper.

two, lead trail . . . ," and AWACS responded with "Copy Hinds." In the same transmission, Tiger 01 asked his wingman to "confirm Hinds."

Tiger 02 initiated his confirming VID, passed the two helicopters at a distance of 1,500 to 2,000 feet, about one-third of a mile, and to their right. He called in "Tally two." In later testimony, the second pilot stated that he was confirming two helicopters, not two Hinds.

Tiger 02's testimony would later prove to be inconsistent. Initially, he reported events in the sequence described above; later, he reversed the order of events such that Tiger 01's subsequent call of "engaged" (described immediately below) preceded his report of the helicopters. Various analysts have attributed this reversal to self-protection during his court-martial: He could not have been derelict in his duty to properly identify the helicopters if Tiger 01 had already announced his intention to shoot them down.

At the time, though, the F-15s pulled up and flew around to the northwest, the opposite direction the Black Hawks were flying. At a distance of ten nautical miles (eighty seconds' flying time at 450 knots), they turned to point back toward their targets. Tiger 01 called, "Cougar [the AWACS call sign], Tiger 02 has tallied two Hinds, engaged." This was the signal that the F-15s were preparing to shoot down the helicopters.

The lead pilot directed his wingman to "arm hot," clearing the second F-15 to shoot as long as the rules of engagement were met. The lead then called, "Tiger 01 is in hot," indicating that he had armed his missiles. Before shooting the trailing helicopter, however, he performed one final IFF Mode I check as he has been trained to do, and received no response, the same as before. Then, from a range of about four miles, Tiger 01 released an advanced radar guided missile (AMRAAM), which reached and destroyed the target in seven seconds.

The lead helicopter then made an evasive hard left turn. Tiger 02 followed, closed to within two miles, and destroyed the second helicopter using a heat-seeking Sidewinder missile.

By 10:30 A.M., eight minutes after first contact, the engagement was over. All twenty-six people on board the two Black Hawks were dead.

ROUND UP THE USUAL SUSPECTS

A logical place to start an analysis of that disaster is with the F-15 pilots. After all, they were closest to the action. As previously indicated, this presumes that those closest to the accident are closest to its causes, and possibly at fault. Although the pilots were ultimately the people who pulled the trigger and doubtless made errors in judgment and violated a number of procedural rules, the conditions that gave rise to the shoot-down were complex. Tragic mistakes like this can't be understood through a narrow focus, especially one that concentrates solely on the F-15 pilots.

In his comprehensive analysis of the shoot-down, former army officer and now Harvard Business School professor Scott Snook explores individual, small-group, and organizational contributions to the tragedy, but finds that even these three perspectives—when viewed separately—do not provide sufficient explanation. Similar to previous accidents, as well as to occurrences in many different complex systems, this tragedy graphically illustrates that cause and effect are often separated in time and space, and only by examining events from a systemic perspective can one begin to understand what happened and why.

To understand why and how this disaster occurred, it is essential to unravel the circumstances that brought the air force F-15s and army Black Hawk helicopters together in a high-risk way, as well as the larger conditions that led to the administrative, technical, aircraft recognition, and corrective-action failures that did not prevent the engagement in the first place or terminate it before it ended in misfortune.

Equally important, rather than giving in to one's natural reaction to the needless loss of life, it is imperative to understand that virtually identical conditions produced more than 1,100 days of accident-free operations, as well as the deaths of twenty-six people in a chain of events lasting just eight minutes. As we have seen, it is in the nature of complex systems to produce exactly this type of counterintuitive behavior. Latent conditions in technology and organization can exist for a significant time, waiting for circumstances to line up that create a calamitous accident. While many actions were taken that contributed to the shoot-down, and a number of them violated rules and procedures, a systemic perspective is essential to shed light on the complex interplay of actions and how the loss might have been prevented.

ANALYSIS OF THE ACCIDENT

One of the questions that disturbs people when they first learn about this case is, "Why did the pilots act so quickly?" That is a sensible concern, considering that the elapsed time from first contact to the destruction of the Black Hawks was only eight minutes. To understand the pace of this incident, one must recognize that F-15 pilots flying at over five hundred miles per hour do not exist in ordinary time. In aerial combat, the specific warfare for which the F-15 air superiority fighter was designed and its pilots trained, fractions of a second can, and often do, make the difference between success and failure, life and death. Taking rapid, decisive action concerning the application of lethal force within specific rules of engagement is what fighter pilots are trained to do. Equally important, encountering hostile helicopters would be seen as an opportunity for real air-to-air combat—very rare for peacetime pilots.

Adding to the pilots' urgency was the rivalry between the OPC's F-15 and F-16 squadrons. F-16s would enter the TAOR within fifteen minutes of the F-15s, and they were better equipped and trained for low-level helicopter pursuit. A number of incident evaluators believe that this competitiveness may have contributed to the pressure that the F-15 pilots felt to see what they wanted to see and to proceed with the engagement once the helicopters had been identified as hostile. Of course, it is impossible to know precisely how much any indirect factor may have actually contributed to the misidentification or to the pace of the engagement. Equally important, the pilots' legal position during their testimony might certainly have influenced their retrospective statements.

The F-15 squadron had also experienced a number of flight discipline problems, and it would be fair to characterize its pilots as opinionated and aggressive. On top of this, the Combined Task Force commander was an active F-16 pilot, and he based a lot of his information about operations on personal experience, assuming that F-15 operations would be similar. Similar, yes; exactly the same, no.

In considering the pilots' states of mind, it is useful to recognize that the pilot of a single-seat F-15C is often very busy. He simultaneously flies the aircraft, operates its radar, defensive, and weapons systems, coordinates with at least one other pilot, and receives support information from AWACS and instructions from command. Especially when a potentially hostile target has been identified, there is an unavoidable tension between the pace with which actions need to be taken and the information-processing limitations of the pilot. In addition, under combat conditions, the pilot's physiological state is altered by adrenaline and stress. That causes perceptual changes, including his sense of the passage of time.

According to the rules of engagement, pilots were required to perform a visual identification of suspected hostile aircraft. To accomplish that, the pilot has to get as close as possible to the target without hitting it, getting shot, or crashing into adjacent terrain. In this case, a crash was a distinct risk, since the helicopters were flying very close to the ground within a narrow valley with mountains on both sides. F-15 pilots, unlike F-16 pilots, primarily flew high-altitude missions, and were not expert in low-altitude flying.

After informing AWACS, the lead F-15 pilot made his visual identification at 450 knots at a distance from the target of two-tenths of a mile, more than the length of three football fields. Nevertheless, by observing the helicopters' physical characteristics, the pilot felt confident that they were Russian-made, although he was unclear of its official designation as either a Hip or a Hind. He checked this fact using a lap-board aircraft recognition "goodie book" during the time he looped his aircraft around to come in behind the helicopters for the next phase of the intercept. However, in evaluating his reference pictures, he was not actually looking at the target aircraft, since he was flying away from them.

Snook devotes considerable diagnostic effort to understanding the recognition mistake made by the pilots. His analysis comes down to three issues:

1. The high-speed visual pass at significant distance and under unfamiliar, close-to-the-ground flying conditions, viewing dark-green camouflaged targets flying over similarly colored mountainous terrain, generated ambiguous visual data.

Since the pilots lacked the specific training that might have allowed them to differentiate between Iraqi and U.S. camouflage paint-work and other telltale differentiating signs, the strong expectations set by the situation coupled with ambiguous visual "confirming" data encouraged both pilots to "see what they expected to see," not what was actually there. This discrepancy is explained by sociologist Karl Weick:

> The costs of being indecisive frequently outweigh the costs of being wrong. This means that sensemaking will tend to be schema-driven rather than evidence-driven, which is what happens when people resolve speed–accuracy trade-offs in favor of speed. Time pressure encourages people to seek confirmation of expectancies, to cling to their initial hypotheses.

2. The Black Hawks had been fitted with external fuel tanks that changed their appearance enough to more closely resemble the Soviet Hind helicopter than the conventional Black Hawks to which the pilots had been exposed in training.

3. The backup of a second confirmation pass by Tiger02 did not work as expected. Tiger02 later said that he "trusted" his flight leader and did not second-guess his judgment.

The relationship between the lead pilot and his wingman represented a highly unusual rank inversion. In one of the military's rare cases where a mission-related role takes precedence over a formal rank, the lead pilot was junior by several grades and experience to his wingman, as well as his direct subordinate. Despite this, during the mission, the wingman was subordinate to the lead, and this inviolable relationship was unlikely to be questioned by either officer during the engagement. Under any other circumstances, the senior and more experienced military officer would have been responsible and called the shots.

Tiger 02's visual identification at greater distance than that of Tiger 01 gathered no disconfirming information, and this was sufficient in this situation to serve as confirmation. This is a failure of social redundancy (as examined in chapter 5), and is one of a number of instances in the case in which checks of one person by another did not work as expected, because the redundant party did not provide a truly independent judgment.

The investigation made a considerable point of the failure of Tiger 02 to be explicit about what he saw and did not see. As a result, this case has since been used as an example of poor combat communications in pilot training. Nevertheless, the powerful role of context and expectations in shaping events still stands, as does the failure of redundancy that arose from those expectations.

There can be no doubt, however, that the F-15 pilots proceeded quickly from recognition to engagement, especially since slow-flying helicopters posed no immediate threat to them or to OPC aircraft. Why they did so remains unanswered.

RADIO PROBLEMS

Because of the inherent risks, when Operation Provide Comfort was first planned, procedures and technology were employed to ensure that friendly aircraft would be able to fly safely in the no-fly zone while Iraqi aircraft would be quickly identified and shot down. Those methods included detailed flight scheduling coordination, IFF radar, clearly defined rules of engagement, and the AWACS coverage. As we shall see, all these systems possessed technical or procedural design flaws before the accident ever occurred.

In the post-accident investigation, the reasons the Black Hawks did not properly respond to the interrogation modes used by the F-15s were inconclusive. The F-15 IFF equipment was found to be operating properly and should have indicated that the helicopters were friendly even if they were not set to the correct Mode I setting. In fact, one of the interrogation modes used a separately set encryption key. Since the Black Hawks' equipment was destroyed in the shoot-down, however, it was impossible to determine whether that was the source of the problem.

Army helicopters and air force F-15s characteristically used different radio frequencies within the no-fly zone and used incompatible radio equipment as a result of separate equipment procurement practices for the two services.

Modern military radios operate on a number of different frequency bands. They can use both AM and FM modulation and employ various security capabilities. Encryption secures the message itself, anti-jamming prevents deliberate or inadvertent disruption of transmissions, and anti-direction-finding prevents disclosure of the location of the sender. Encryption is implemented through software loaded into the radio's firmware and by mission-specific keys that were changed each day for each region in which the aircraft operated.

The remaining security features are implemented using "frequency hopping," a technique in which the radio skips in a pseudo-random way among a number of radio channels. Frequency hopping also requires loading special information, including the "hop sets" to be used, the keys that drive the hop sequence, and the exact time of day (to synchronize the hopping among different radios).

In this case, the primary radios in the army helicopters and the air force F-15 did not operate on the same frequency bands. One of the helicopters did possess HAVE QUICK II capabilities, but the Combined Force Air Component (CFAC) of Operation Provide Comfort had decided not to implement cryptographic procedures to support Eagle Flight, because not all their radios were so equipped. Consequently, although the hardware was compatible, the radio was effectively useless in HAVE QUICK mode, since it lacked the daily hop sets, cryptographic keys, and GPS-based time codes. Thus, the helicopters and F-15s could not monitor each other's communications or contact each other directly. Tragically, while the F-15s' radios were capable of communicating with the Black Hawks' simpler radios, their normal procedures did not require that they do so, and no such communications were attempted.

In summary, from the F-15s' perspective, the flight of two army Black Hawks did not exist. That is, according to the Air Tasking Order schedule, friendly helicopters were not supposed to be in the TAOR at all, let alone prior to their first flight sanitizing sweep. The AWACS also did not tell the F-15s of any friendly aircraft when they checked in upon entering the TAOR, or even after the targets had been picked up on the F-15s' radar. Furthermore, when the targets were IFF-interrogated by the F-15s, they did not "squawk friendly." With all these factors considered together, it is no surprise that Tiger 01 and Tiger 02 believed that the blips they saw on their radar represented hostile aircraft.

AWACS: PROVIDING NEITHER "WARNING" NOR "CONTROL"

A close-up examination of this accident suggests that *Airborne Warning and Control System* is a misleading name for this otherwise invaluable set of tactical support capabilities. While there may be many questions one might pose about the causes of the accident, the most nagging may be, "Why didn't the people aboard AWACS, who had all the necessary information, do anything to stop the incident?"

While the organizational-level issues that separated the army's helicopter flights from an air force–dominated operation are understandable to anyone who has worked in a large enterprise—or even the military—as are a number of the circumstances leading to the pilots' tragic helicopter recognition error under conditions of stress, ambiguity, and possible motives to rush to judgment, it is less obvious how an AWACS crew of nineteen people with sophisticated technology and experience failed to keep track of just two helicopters and two F-15s, and inform the relevant parties of what was going on. Indeed, what happened aboard the AWACS is the key to this case as well as a source of insight that can be transferred to other potential disaster settings.

The operational environment aboard an AWACS, a modified Boeing 707, is a noisy one. Crew members use internal radio networks to talk with one another, and interdependent crew members are given side-by-side consoles to facilitate face-to-face interaction. In particular, the mission commander, senior director, and airborne command element have adjacent consoles, as do the members of the Surveillance and Weapons sections.

The Surveillance Section is primarily responsible for tracking unidentified aircraft. The four members of the Weapons Section are responsible for the activities of friendly aircraft. The enroute controller is responsible for TAOR entry, exit, and IFF identification; the TAOR controller is responsible for threat warning and tactical coordination within the no-fly zone; and the refueling controller coordinates that very important task. Unfortunately, on the day of the accident, the enroute controller's regular console was out of order; thus, he had to be placed at a spare console at some distance and facing away from other Weapons Section crew members.

The consequences of such a change in seating position are subtle. It is easy to see that physical proximity might have allowed a more casual, off-the-radio-net interaction between the enroute and TAOR controllers, who would normally be sitting next to each other instead of some distance apart. In an environment where people cannot easily move around, several feet of distance may be enough disincentive to prevent such an interaction, and informal communication may have been particularly critical on this first day the crew was flying together.

The accident investigation board found that it had become routine for AWACS crews to receive real-time information from helicopter crews and disseminate this information to aircraft in the area, a responsibility typically reinforced by on-site AWACS instructors. However, with only three mission hours together, and no specific instructions or training on this obviously important responsibility, the AWACS crew did not pick up this critical informal task. Furthermore, with the enroute controller physically separated from the TAOR controller, informal communication (such as pointing at the screen and asking a question) would have been impossible.

Just as the pilots' expectations shaped what they thought they saw, expectations aboard AWACS had a similar effect. Unlike the F-15s, AWACS knew that there were friendly helicopters in the TAOR that morning, although they did not know their mission in advance. During the investigation, the enroute controller stated that he thought the friendly helicopters had landed when he created a new track in the vicinity of the radar returns at 10:27 A.M. That is a plausible explanation, especially since most helicopter flights ferried personnel to and from the MCC base at Zakhu. However, the reasons that no one mentioned the possible presence of friendly helicopters remains, in the end, unanswered.

HIGH STATUS OF FIGHTER PILOTS

There were other even more subtle factors involved. It should come as no surprise that the organizational culture of the U.S. Air Force is dominated by pilots, and that fighter pilots who fly the fastest planes have the highest status of all.

Fighter pilots were clearly the elite of the air force for more reasons than simply their prestige. General M. McPeak, then chief of staff of the air force, was a consummate fighter pilot and had placed a number of other fighter pilots in senior positions. Joan L. Piper, mother of Laura Piper, one of the Black Hawk casualties, charges in her book *A Chain of Events* that McPeak manipulated the investigative and legal process, and thwarted a Senate committee investigation to prevent the fighter pilots from bearing responsibility.

In investigating that charge, the GAO did not find interference with the legal process, but they did not have subpoena power in their inquiry. The air force refused to comply with subpoenas of the U.S. Senate, in its separate probe. That was unusual in itself, and it resulted in truncating the Senate investigation without the release of findings.

Given the high status of fighter pilots in the air force, "ordinary mortals," such as AWACS technicians, might well feel that it is not their place to question them in the midst of a mission, or to second-guess their judgment in the identification of target aircraft. It is also sensible from an AWACS crew member's perspective to believe that seeing an aircraft through one's canopy is a pretty reliable way to confirm its identity, and they would have no way of knowing the quality of the look a pilot actually got.

Air force norms also dictate that "eyeballs trump technology," so the informal organization certainly would have shifted the burden of responsibility to the pilots once the visual identification was made.

We must also appreciate that ongoing organizational friction between the F-15 fighter squadron and AWACS leadership over the independence of flights might have affected communications. Fighter pilots strongly value being able to call the shots in the fulfillment of their mission, while AWACS command seeks greater managerial control over the airspace. Since the pilots have more status and clout, one can see that an AWACS technician might hold back somewhat before raising an issue, particularly in the middle of an intercept, and especially on the first day of a new rotation. Certainly, allowing high-status persons in any organization to bend the rules—especially if you know that the issue is sensitive—is not restricted to the military.

Further contributing to the AWACS tendency not to query the F-15 pilots' actions was a strong OPC radio communications norm called "min comm." Beyond its literal meaning to keep communications to the minimum by using as few words as possible, and by employing brevity-oriented words with defined meanings (such as *tally* to report a number, as in "ID Hinds, tally two"), it was expected that AWACS personnel would not even try to convey unnecessary information to pilots, especially things that they were already supposed to know. While the brevity norm is clearly efficient when everything is as it should be, it also has the potential to impede sorting out an ambiguous situation that might be better served by more conventional two-way conversation. Many people fall into the trap of not asking "dumb questions" when they really ought to just ask them.

INADEQUATE PREPARATION AND TRAINING

Beyond those issues, several other factors inhibited AWACS crew members' ability to use what information that they did have to avert the tragedy. In particular, while the AWACS crew consisted of experienced personnel and leaders, this was their first actual mission flying together. Clearly, any group operating as a unit for the first time is likely to have a learning curve, especially related to interdependencies among separate roles, responsibilities for which they had not been trained, and judgments that contravened organizational norms or formal protocols, such as the Air Tasking Order.

Of course, the importance of that kind of teamwork is recognized by AWACS command, and standard provisions existed to prepare the crew for their work together. Potentially the most powerful tool in the preparatory arsenal is a "mission simulator," which, with the right software, is capable of exposing the entire crew to virtually identical conditions to those they will encounter in the field. Simulators are invaluable training tools because they can provide far more preparation for unusual events than people are likely to get in most real-life situations.

Unfortunately, three significant problems impeded the full use of that tool. First, the entire crew was not available for the simulation; most important, only one leader was available. Second, the crew's second simulator run was canceled because of a competing exercise. Third, the simulator programming was inconsistent with the actual situation. Significantly, it lacked helicopter-tracking scenarios, it did not employ the same rules of engagement, and it certainly did not include the critical "informal" responsibility to act as a relay station for Eagle Flight information beyond that on the Air Tasking Order. The most important aspects of AWACS's potential role in the prevention of this accident were therefore missing from the crew's pre-mission training, thus making it necessary for the crew to learn the old-fashioned way—by direct instruction and trial and error.

During the accident investigation, it emerged that preparing new simulator programming was considered too expensive, and it also came to light that there was even a shortage of conventional training materials, such as manuals. As we have seen in many cases, financial pressures are often responsible for increasing the likelihood of many different kinds of disasters.

In addition, a rash of early retirements had occurred in the air force as a result of defense spending cutbacks associated with the "peace dividend" after the end of the Cold War. That attrition had the effect of promoting to senior positions personnel who might otherwise have been passed over or allowed to mature further in junior positions. Evidence suggests that this AWACS crew had inconsistent performance records. While a first-class crew might have overcome the various obstacles described, this crew was uneven in ability, and appears not to have had the right stuff to do so.

Many of the problems listed might also have been overcome had the direct leadership onboard the AWACS been strong and effective. It was not. Even so, institutional reliance on exceptional midlevel leadership to overcome systemic organizational weaknesses is a risky proposition. Most leaders, like most people, will be average at what they do. In this case, the onboard leaders relied on formal role definitions and put very little of themselves into the definition of the team and the mission. While increasing comfort with their team, and the team's interactions with one another, might have overcome initial weaknesses in personnel and leadership skills over time, during the first few hours of the first day of the first mission, there was no time for leaders to settle into their roles or for the stronger team members to pick up whatever slack there was.

A further complicating factor was the presence of an unusual form of leadership redundancy. Six instructor or staff personnel, part of the permanent Incirlik detachment, were on board to act as experts to help the crew answer questions. Ironically, they may have created a false sense of security if the new crew assumed that the experts would intervene if something needed correction. As it turned out, a number of these shadow crew members were not actively monitoring the activities of the controllers. In fact, one was taking a nap during the incident, and that behavior may have reinforced the lackadaisical attitude on board. Here is another case of a failure of social redundancy to perform as organizational designers might have expected.

BEYOND THE CHAIN OF EVENTS

In this case, there is a strong and quite natural tendency to focus on those individual factors—however small—that might have prevented the tragedy. Since the formal accident investigations inventoried well over a hundred items that had gone wrong, there are plenty of candidates to choose from, and one might argue that almost any of them might have made the difference and prevented the deaths of twenty-six people. As true as that might be, the unlikely combinations of events that seem to typify this type of accident actually, in fact, define them. Chasing the details in system accidents is not the best way to understand how they came about or to develop strategies to prevent future catastrophes.

One important lesson is that prior to the shoot-down, there were at least two serious near misses that could have precipitated corrective action had they been heeded as signs of uncontrolled risks. Seven months before the shoot-down of the two Black Hawks, F-111 fighter planes targeted two Black Hawks that were on the ground inspecting an airfield inside the TAOR. In much the same way as in the later incident, AWACS did not provide warning to the fighters, and there was no direct radio contact between the fighters and the helicopters. Fortunately, at the last minute, the fighter pilots recognized the Black Hawks just as they were lining up for their attack run. In another incident, the ACE aboard AWACS intervened when helicopters were spotted, although it took ten minutes to verify that they were friendly, an eternity in air-to-air combat.

While it is certainly true that the F-15 pilots could have been more restrained in initiating the engagement (and likely would have been if they had checked in with the ACE as they were obligated to do under the rules of engagement), most of the protective failures that seem so obvious in hindsight actually flow from the single cause of mixing helicopters and fighters in the same combat airspace without adequate protections. This major contributor is not a failure of implementation or human errors; it is a failure of basic design. Just like Chernobyl. Just like *Challenger*. Just like the Hyatt Tea Dance tragedy.

At the same time, there are important lessons in the details of the accident about the specific failure of various defensive systems. Putting aside the state of mind of the F-15 pilots after their IFF radars failed to identify the helicopters as friendly, which would have tended to reinforce the erroneous perspective they already had from the Air Tasking Order and their conversations with mission superiors, we might wish to examine the specific visual identification mistakes made by the pilots that finalized their fatal recognition error.

Most of the pilots' recognition training had been devoted to fixed-wing aircraft rather than to helicopters, and it appears that they did not know basic helicopter distinctions such as paintwork and the appearance-altering impact of the Black Hawks' external fuel tanks. Furthermore, insufficient attempts had been made by OPC Command to visually distinguish U.S. Army helicopters from others in the region (a defensive step that was finally implemented after the shoot-down). In the absence of such training and aids to simplify recognition, the pilots were much more likely to make mistakes.

It is also clear that the visual identification made by the pilots was from too great a distance to definitively confirm the type and nationality of the helicopters. This uncertain ID has led some critics to consider the pilots "single-incident rogues" who abandoned their prime mission to go out of their way to shoot down two helicopters that represented no serious threat. Given the specific combat conditions, however, their mistake was somewhat understandable, although no less tragic. While other defensive systems, especially aboard AWACS and within the pilots' chain of command, should have trapped the hazard before it escaped, those systems were clearly compromised. In short, all the backups failed, the holes lined up, and twenty-six people died.

Officially, many applicable rules and procedures were violated by the AWACS's crew. However, it is arguable that many of those violations had become standard operating procedure, or simply the ordinary mistakes and slips of attention made by average personnel. The official plan that was supposed to provide safety had become seriously degraded. Since AWACS's Command, not local crews, was responsible for crew and leadership selection, training, safety procedures, and discipline, AWACS's failures during this mission actually represents design, implementation, and management failures at command level. We can also apportion some responsibility to the procurement and operational decisions that led to radio communications incompatibility, maintenance lapses (or possibly a design fault) that led to the IFF failure, and to the cutbacks in mission training that had allowed both pilots and their onboard commander to forget critical details of the rules of engagement that might well have averted this tragedy.

In summary, scarcity of resources, considerable organizational change, and a long period of safe operations created an organizational mind-set that assumed restricting resources would not have serious consequences. In response, the military cut staff levels and quality, training time and resources, and spending on technology and operational support. Furthermore, as the organization settled into a routine in a context of diminished external threat, internal squabbling increased and mission discipline slipped. Over time, the organization drifted from higher to lower efficacy, although it is doubtful that many people noticed the differences, despite warning signs. In the absence of a crisis, the increase in latent risk was not obvious, and thus became easy to ignore, especially under conditions of resource scarcity.

Of course, the pilots were the ones who pulled the triggers and who must bear ultimate responsibility for the recognition mistake and irreversible judgments that defined this tragedy. At the same time, there were many other contributors, and there could have been many steps by many different people to avoid the catastrophe. The helicopters were not supposed to be in the no-fly zone before the F-15s, their electronic friend-or-foe system did not work reliably, the pilots were inadequately trained in helicopter recognition, the AWACS crew were unaware of their helicopter management role, the fighters had no means for secure direct radio contact with the friendly helicopters, and their own onboard commander and staff experts failed to inform them of the helicopters' presence or told them to stop while they figured out who the helicopters were and what they were doing there.

When this highly unlikely—and many would have said impossible—set of conditions coalesced, the hazard "escaped" and twenty-six people died, many of them the tragic victims of the first high-tech AMRAAM missile ever fired in combat.

As we have already seen and will see again, the key to avoiding such accidents is understanding that they are not impossible after all.

CHAPTER 8

BUTTERFLY WINGS AND STONE HEADS: HOW COMPLEXITY INFLUENCES CATASTROPHE IN POLICY DECISIONS

The words *catastrophe* and *disaster* are so often used in connection with human activity that they suggest split-second decisions gone wrong—big, massive miscalculations: the writ-large equivalent of dropping a glass and watching it shatter into thousands of pieces on the floor.

Certainly many of the cases we've examined contain such shattering moments. By now, though, readers should have begun to look deeper and farther back for the roots of accidents, not just right before the sharp edge when they occur.

This chapter will examine how policy disasters can result from decisions that the people involved probably wouldn't recognize as fatal mistakes, even with the benefits of hindsight. When cause and effect are looped together—so that more of the effect inexorably creates more of the cause—very small distinctions at the outset of a complex social and technical process can create massive distinctions (and, as we shall see in the case of Easter Island, extinctions) down the road. When cause and effect are mutually interdependent, results are often unexpected—not to mention often unintended and undesired—to the dismay of unsuspecting policy-makers and citizens alike.

BUTTERFLY WINGS

The idea that small differences can lead to major consequences down the road and at a distance is often called the *butterfly effect*. It is among the few concepts from complexity science that is widely known to the general public. Anyone who has seen Steven Spielberg's *Jurassic Park* may remember actor Jeff Goldblum's flirtatious explanation of this phenomenon to a bemused Laura Dern as they bounced along in a jeep on their way to meet a hungry *Tyrannosaurus*. When the MIT meteorologist Edward Lorenz stumbled on the butterfly effect in 1961, the moment was probably less entertaining than in Spielberg's movie, but it was far more important in the larger scheme of things.

Lorenz had built a mathematical weather simulator using an unusual vacuum tube computer called a Royal McBee. His simple twelve-equation weather model possessed many real-life characteristics, including the capacity to not quite repeat itself. Lorenz's breakthrough occurred when he restarted a particular computer run in midsequence, using the three-digit numbers from his printout as a starting point rather than the complete six-digit numbers the model actually used to store internal data. To his surprise, even though his new starting point was different in only the fourth decimal place, the model did not, as he expected, reproduce the earlier results with only minor changes. Rather, the second computer run diverged dramatically from the earlier results. It was as if Lorenz had entered completely different starting conditions.

The principle that small differences create small changes is a fundamental one in classical science, as it is in ordinary life. For example, we do not assume that if we slightly increase our driving speed on the way to work from one day to the next that we will end up at a different destination. Rather, it just takes us less time to get there. We assume—because it appears to be true in so many cases—that life is relatively immune to small differences, and small variations have small, proportional consequences. Lorenz's weather model, in contrast, showed him something different: Small differences in initial conditions can sometimes create weather so different down the road that the actual starting point appears totally irrelevant. How could his model have behaved so differently from the way that everyone assumed it would? The answer requires a brief detour into the history of science.

One of the greatest innovations of the last three hundred years is the mathematics of differential equations. They have made many classical problems in physics, electrical circuits, mechanics, and fluid dynamics amenable to exact solution. Differential equations represent a mathematical power tool for solving many classes of problems, and it is hard to overstate either their importance to science or their contribution to our lives.

But the mental trap created by these extraordinary equations was that they had limitations, albeit unknown ones. Nonlinearities, such as those introduced by some systems with feedback, create equations that sometimes cannot be solved in the usual way. Since mathematics, like all forms of science, has areas that are known and areas that are unknown, the conceptually rugged territory of nonlinear mathematics remained mostly unexplored.

Deprived of a direct path to being solved, many nonlinear problems had to be simplified by making assumptions about their problematic elements. While that simplification made the problems more tractable, and even produced solutions that were good enough to solve real-world problems under a variety of conditions, eliminating the nonlinearities obscured precisely the type of phenomena that

Lorenz and other chaos-hunters would soon discover. Without realizing it, by simplifying things in order to make equations solvable, scientists had inadvertently thrown out some of the most interesting and important results. Chaos was still there, of course, but by removing the troubling nonlinearities from the equations, it passed unnoticed through the scientists' mathematical sieve.

Once deterministic chaos was discovered, scientists found that it occurred in many systems, even the simplest ones. In addition to the chaos that occurs in mathematical models such as Lorenz's weather simulator or the Mandlebrot set (that often shows up in the brightly false-colored posters that decorate many college dorm walls), chaotic behavior is seen in electrical circuits, lasers, chemical reactions, fluid flows, and mechanical devices. In the natural world, deterministic chaos manifests itself in the behavior of certain planetary moons, changes in the magnetic field of celestial bodies, ecosystem population changes, and molecular vibrations, among other phenomena.

In failing to understand the distortions introduced by their simplifications, classical science had fallen into a common pitfall: getting trapped by one's explanatory paradigm rather than recognizing that it is just a *model* of a more complex reality. Just as earlier generations of scientists believed in perfect circles as the basis for planetary orbits or that breathing "bad air" was the cause of malaria, most scientists since Newton believed that the universe could safely be explained by the tools at hand. This was not so much arrogance as a manifestation of a larger belief system that would eventually be overturned by a new scientific paradigm consisting of general relativity, quantum mechanics, and complexity theory. But, as Kuhn argued in *The Structure of Scientific Revolutions*, ignoring implications that do not fit one's worldview and mental model of a situation is a very natural thing to do, albeit risky. As we will see, that tendency is not restricted to scientists.

SCHELLING'S NEIGHBORHOOD

One of the researchers who first applied concepts of feedback and nonlinearity (but not chaos, per se) to human behavior was the economist and Nobel laureate Thomas Schelling. In his gem of a book *Micromotives and Macrobehavior* (1978), he examines ways in which "local" decision-making can unintentionally lead to policy consequences at considerable variance with the intentions and best interests of the decision-makers.

One of Schelling's most important insights came from modeling how segregation arises in neighborhoods. It is widely believed that segregation in housing (or even in other types of groupings, such as distributions of men and women at a party) arises from conscious intent. In other words, some people desire greater homogeneity and thus create neighborhoods that reflect their preferences in a simple and direct causal manner.

Schelling showed that while people's desires for exclusivity are important, segregation may be an "emergent phenomenon," even when each individual's desire may be largely nonsegregationist. In other words, the wider society may be considerably more segregated than the preferences of its individual citizens. If that is true, segregation in housing patterns and in other social spheres may not necessarily be anyone's fault, and bigotry is not the only reason it exists.

In his early experiments, Schelling used a pencil and paper or sets of coins to represent the races of the incumbents in a simplified artificial world. Now, of course, we use computers. My example uses a computer model developed by Uri Wilensky of Northwestern University. Wilensky has been extending the simulation work by Mitchell Resnick of the MIT Media Lab. (For information on how to run these models, go to our Web site at www.flirtingwithdisaster.net.)

The picture shown in figure 8.1 is a screen shot of a simple computer-based world inhabited by gray and black "turtles." These

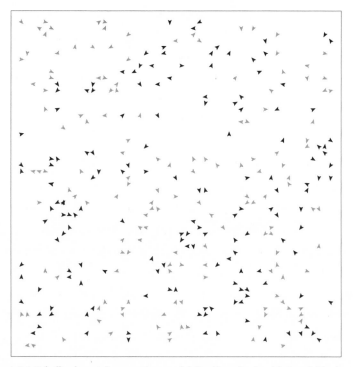

Figure 8.1 *Schelling's racial segregation model. Replicated using NetLogo's Turtles and Frogs simulation. This picture shows a low population density example at the start of the simulation.* Credit: Plot produced by NetLogo and Mathematica.

turtles are software-based entities that behave according to a particular set of rules described in an extension of the Logo computer language originally developed by MIT's Seymour Papert. Logo-based software programs are widely used as educational tools. In the case shown here, there are three hundred turtles, half of each color, in a world that has a total turtle-carrying capacity of 2,500.

When each simulation round begins, the turtles are randomly distributed. This means that approximately half the turtles adjacent to any given turtle are the same color while half are the contrasting color. For each simulation run, the experimenter sets all the turtle's similarity requirements—their preference for neighbors that are like them. This is an important variable in the model and, in the first example, the preference is set moderately low at 30 percent. This means that each turtle will be "happy" if its neighbors consist of 30 percent or more like them (that is, black or gray) and 70 percent or less different from them.

It is important to think about what being "like me" means in human terms. For some people, this might mean race; for others, it could be religion; for still others, having children of a similar age. Of course, the model represented here is a far cry from the real world (as part of this model's setup, all the computer-based turtles are programmed to have the same similarity requirements, for example), but it is nevertheless capable of encouraging important insights.

When a given turtle finds itself with less than the desired proportion of like-me neighbors, it jumps randomly to another position. (In the model, the world wraps around like a map of the earth so that turtles that jump off one side of the world come back on the opposite side.) According to the rules built into the programming, turtles cannot land on each other; nor will they remain where they land if the new location does not meet the simulation's similarity requirements for the run.

Eventually, the turtle-hopping settles down, although this can take some time if the turtle density and similarity requirements are high. The plot shown in figure 8.2 displays the relationship between the average degree of similarity over the course of five typical simulations with varying numbers of total turtles but a constant (though modest) desired similarity level of 30 percent.

The plot shows several surprising results. First, all the final similarity figures are much higher than the minimum required similarity level of 30 percent—more than twice as high, in fact. Second, there is a distinct relationship between the final level of overall similarity and the population density. When desired similarity is constant, lower population density is associated with *higher* final segregation. To put it in more conventional terms, in Schelling's world, "rural" environments

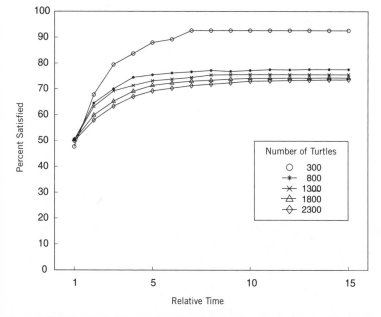

Figure 8.2 *Turtle similarity over time. Plot showing the average degree of similarity of all turtles for a number of different turtle densities. The number of turtles in a world with a capacity of 2,500 is varied from 300 to 2,300.* Credit: Plot produced by NetLogo and Mathematica.

will tend to be more highly segregated when the desired degree of similarity is held constant.

These results were somewhat controversial three decades ago when Schelling first presented them. Many people believed that individual racial tolerance was the only determining factor of segregation. Although this simple simulation does not replicate real-world dynamics, it does raise some perplexing questions about the causes of segregation, particularly the unexpectedly powerful influence of modest preferences in rural settings.

Further analysis unveils a more complete picture. Figure 8.3 shows the impact of turtle density for high and low desired-similarity simulation runs. Higher densities—the big cities in turtle land—always depress the final similarity obtained for a given desired similarity; there

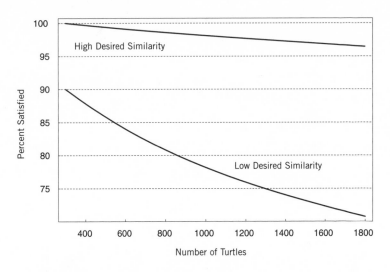

Figure 8.3 *Impact of varying turtle density on final similarity for low and high desired similarity runs.* Credit: Plot produced by NetLogo and Mathematica.

are fewer places to move when things are crowded. Nevertheless, the resulting segregation is still much higher when desired similarity is high, irrespective of the density. It is also clear that when desired similarity is high, population density makes very little difference, while when desired similarity is low, population density has a large (inverse) impact.

Translating this simple model into real-world terms, it would tell us that when turtles (or people) are strongly prejudiced, they create an exclusive world whether they live in the city or the country, but when they have only modest like-me preferences, population density has a generally linear impact on the resulting overall degree of segregation in the community by reducing the resulting degree of segregation as population density rises.

Viewed the other way around, in figure 8.4, when density is low—the rural setting in turtle-land—desired similarity makes relatively little difference. The end-state similarity (when all the computer-based turtles are happy) starts high at 90 percent and rises to 100 percent, as high as it can go. In contrast, when population density is high,

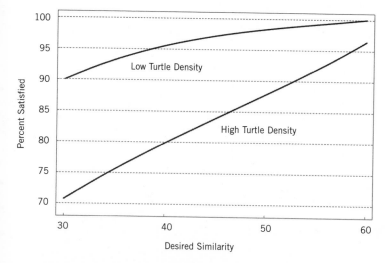

Figure 8.4 *Impact of varying desired similarity in low and high turtle density environments. Credit: Plot produced by NetLogo and Mathematica.*

similarity preferences have a relatively greater impact. Nevertheless, the average end-state similarity starts out at more than twice the nominal desired similarity percentage and rises more or less linearly as the desired similarity for all turtles increases.

Finally, an interesting picture emerges when both density and desired similarity are high. The steady-state world is shown in figure 8.5. Although the picture appears as designed as an elegant garden, the contours between groups of turtles are merely an emergent property of the iterative process that continues until all the turtles are happy. Such intricate patterns are characteristic of many iterative processes in nature, and in earlier times they were attributed to deliberate intervention by the gods. Of course, sometimes complexity is the result of willful intent, but often it simply emerges as people go about making what appears to them to be rational decisions. Often, this works out okay, but sometimes—as we will see in the next two examples—the complexity that emerges from a large collection of apparently rational choices is a recipe for disaster.

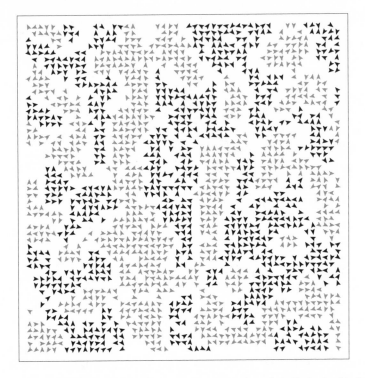

Figure 8.5 *Final state with 1,800 turtles and 60 percent desired similarity. In this dense world, 96.4 percent final similarity satisfies all turtles. Notice the planned appearance of the boundaries, although they are strictly an emergent property of the simulation, unplanned and without willful intent.* Credit: *Plot produced by NetLogo and Mathematica.*

ROBIN HOOD

While almost every segregated city and neighborhood—not to mention high school cafeteria—could serve as a real-life illustration of the complex dynamics Schelling identified, we'll next use an illustration from a completely different field—public school finance. Though there aren't many bona fide school finance disasters, the way there are space shuttle and hurricane disasters, this one deserves the label. The "Robin Hood" debacle cost Texas taxpayers an estimated $81 billion in depreciated real assets—the value of their homes. This makes it one of the largest financial disasters in history—about half the size of the savings and loan crisis of the mid-1980s. Note, however, that it was not one in which the federal government, and ultimately American taxpayers, picked up the tab. Texas homeowners were on the hook all by themselves.

In the United States, public education is the responsibility of each state, and 95 percent of it is funded by local property taxes. This means that the tax base available for education is directly proportional to the property wealth of the taxpayers. As a result, rich districts generally have more money to spend on schooling than do poor ones.

To redress this violation of the spirit of public education, most states shift money from the rich to the poor by using various forms of taxation to raise money, and grants and subsidies to redistribute it. The mechanics of this process (that is, the specific formulas used to calculate how much is paid or received by whom) is an important issue in the design of public policy, and a political one as well.

Like any tax or subsidy, financial redistribution changes consumption patterns because it make goods and services more expensive for some and less expensive for others. One controversial example is high mobile telephone roaming charges in Europe. While naturally protested by the relatively small percent of the population that carry their mobile phones between countries, the revenues from high roaming charges are claimed to lower mobile phone costs for the rest of the population, thereby making them more accessible to the less affluent.

In school finance, property values change because the costs and benefits that result from the redistribution plan are incorporated by buyers and sellers into home valuations and purchasing decisions. This affects property values both within a given district and between districts, since people relocate. In a district whose property owners pay a tax surcharge for which they will not receive a benefit, property values fall, while property values in districts that benefit from the transfer payment will rise because residents and prospective home buyers in that area get services they don't have to pay for.

Since the cash flows of redistribution are based on property values, and property values are themselves influenced by the effects of redistribution, school finance is a dynamic system. That is, it contains feedback loops. Delays occur because it takes awhile for the effects to be felt, and not all changes occur at the same rate. Despite that logic, in the Robin Hood case the lawmakers who designed the specifics of the program did not understand its dynamics. In particular, they did not understand that the net effects of their distribution plan could not be simply extrapolated from its initial values without understanding how the system as a whole would adapt over time, particularly how the behavior of home owners, state legislators, and local district officials would respond to changing housing prices both within and between districts.

Here's how Robin Hood worked. For each district in Texas, the state divided the total assessed property value by the number of pupils, making allowances for learning disabilities, limited English proficiency, and other similar factors that create special needs requiring additional resources. The state then compared this number with a "confiscation threshold," originally $340,000. Each local district retained the property taxes below the threshold, but all the money collected on the property value above the threshold went into state coffers.

Since property values above the threshold do not contribute to local benefits, property values will fall. Using a standard mortgage calculation, we find that about $11,000 of home value was destroyed for each $1,000 per year in taxes paid for which no benefits accrued to the homeowner, assuming a twenty-year mortgage and 7 percent interest. As a result, in the state's most affluent districts, property value per pupil fell during the 1990s, which was otherwise a period of significant income growth during which property values would normally rise.

As the property values fell in the affluent areas, the state lowered the confiscation threshold to make up the money it needed to fund the poorer districts. Naturally, that depressed housing prices even more in the affluent areas. To make matters worse, as housing prices and the confiscation threshold both fell, the affluent communities found themselves with less money to fund their local needs, so they responded by increasing the property tax rates to make up their local deficits. Of course, that deepened the death spiral.

The final turn of the wheel came as people moved out of the higher-priced areas to escape the creeping taxation. Their flight accelerated demand for housing and increased housing prices in areas that had been below the threshold, and the combination of lowering thresholds and rising housing values in these previously "confiscation safe" neighborhoods caused the middle-market districts to become trapped in a destructive spiral of their own.

Since Robin Hood's designers did not understand the dynamics they had built into the system, it should come as no surprise that they made these errors. Over the decade that Robin Hood was in effect, $81 billion in property wealth eroded, or $27,000 per pupil. To understand what that means in real terms, if the eroded value had been captured as real assets, the wealth would fund an income stream large enough to bring the entire school system to the level of Texas's wealthiest districts, approximately $1,350 per pupil per annum. It is sadly ironic that through faulty design, Texas's lawmakers managed to destroy as much value as they might ever have hoped to create.

To be fair, the constraints of school finance in Texas are severe. A statewide property tax that is successfully used elsewhere for educational finance is specifically forbidden by the Texas constitution, causing various earlier redistribution schemes to be found unconstitutional. Nevertheless, the difficulty of a problem is no excuse for a disastrous solution. It seems highly likely that a majority of Texas voters would not have supported either Robin Hood or its legislative advocates if they had known what it was going to do to the value of their homes.

As we have just seen, a failure to understand the dynamics we are talking about in this chapter—how effects can amplify causes, which can go on to amplify effects even more—led to one of the worst financial disasters in American history. Because we have had the mathematical and computer-based tools to model and predict such outcomes since the 1960s, there was no technical reason for the mistake. But state decision-makers were trapped in a static view of cause and effect, and did not realize that this kind of modeling was necessary. Instead of prototyping their ideas in software to help anticipate the likely outcomes, they resorted to simple models of cause and effect in the creation of what became a tragic experiment using large amounts of money that belonged to the citizens of Texas.

EASTER ISLAND

Easter Island is the most remote inhabited place on earth, located in the South Pacific Ocean, 2,200 miles west of Chile and 1,300 miles east of the Pitcairn Islands from which Easter Island's original colonists probably came. The island was given its common name when it was discovered by Dutch explorers on Easter Sunday in 1722. To the native population, it was Rapa Nui, which means "Big Rapa."

For many years, the dominant theory of the origins of Easter Islanders was that they came from South America. However, contemporary DNA analysis of the skeletons of early inhabitants has shown that they bear the unique genetic marker of the Polynesian people. We now know that Rapa Nui was settled by Polynesian explorers about A.D. 900, perhaps a hundred years before other Polynesians arrived in Hawaii. The Polynesians were arguably the most accomplished seafaring people in history, taking their oceangoing canoes on long and perilous voyages, and leaving their mark on 350 islands throughout the South Pacific—essentially every habitable piece of land in this vast expanse of ocean. When they came to Easter Island on a journey that probably took two to three weeks beyond the sight of land, they came to stay, bringing bananas, taro, sweet potato, sugarcane, paper mulberry, and chickens.

Despite the island's many resources—rich volcanic soil, lush and diverse forests, and the most extensive population of sea- and land birds in the South Pacific—it was not ideal for its new inhabitants. Farther from the equator, and colder, windier, and drier than other Polynesian habitats, Easter Island was subtropical, like parts of Florida, and its forests, vegetation, and crops grew more slowly than on warmer and wetter islands. The climate supported a different mixture of crops than the settlers' homeland, and there were fewer species of fish—perhaps a tenth as many as on Fiji, which boasts more than a thousand. Coastal fishing was also less plentiful on Easter, since the seabed dropped off rapidly to the deep ocean. Though rich in many ways, Easter's ecosystem would turn out to be quite fragile.

Easter Island was also different from other Polynesian-settled islands economically and socially. Dogs, pigs, and some common tropical crops were absent, despite being plentiful elsewhere in Polynesia, and the trading patterns that tied other island colonies together do not appear to have included Easter. Tools made from Easter's distinctive stone were never found on other islands, and goods from other locales are not found on the island. For nearly a millennium, Easter Island rose and fell on its own, more than a thousand miles from another flourishing society.

While the origin of Easter Island's inhabitants was a great mystery for many years, other puzzles were even greater. Part of the long-term fascination with Easter Island derives from the giant stone statues, or *moai*, found there. The moai were created by its earliest inhabitants. (See figure 8.6.) How did these ancient people quarry, carve, and transport such giant totems, and why did they do so?

The final mystery is what caused Easter's flourishing civilization to disappear a century before the first Dutch explorers landed there in

Figure 8.6 *Moai from Easter Island. Credit: Getty Images.*

1722. It turns out the two questions are intertwined, and both are related to the topics we've examined in this chapter. They serve as an extraordinary example of a dynamic system, and the unexpected nature of any such system's many interdependencies.

When the first Dutch arrived at Easter Island, they could not imagine how its people settled there. The watercraft the European visitors found consisted of a few leaky canoes that would have been completely unsuitable for ocean travel. They were also mystified how the islanders could have transported and erected the enormous stone statues that greeted them. Such work would require tall trees, long ropes, and many strong men as well as the food to feed them. Easter appeared to have had none of those things. Its tallest tree—if you could call it that—was a large bush only seven feet tall, the population was modest and frail, and there appeared to be no organized agriculture.

In contrast, however, we know from archeological studies that during Easter Island's heyday several centuries earlier, it was the proverbial island paradise, rich in birds and fish. The palm trees that covered the island then served as habitat to the former, and provided the wood for the strong oceanworthy canoes needed to catch the large fish that were a staple of the islanders' diet. As in many tropical islands, tree root systems also held the soil in place, and the trees themselves served as wind blocks. Easter Island even featured the world's biggest species of palm tree, as well as other trees rich in fruit, hardwood, and bark for rope and clothing. Trees were used for fishermen's canoes, for building and thatching houses, for making harpoons and fishhooks, and as nesting places for birds.

Easter Island was once divided into eleven regions—like wedges of a pie—each the domain of a single clan led by a local chief. However, easy overland travel combined with Easter's uneven but complementary resource distribution encouraged integration of the clans, including unified governance by a single high chief. In that arrangement, islanders shared access to the best beaches from which to launch canoes, utilized common stone quarries, and permitted interclan hunting for land and seabirds.

As in other Polynesian societies, clans competed intensely despite Easter's cooperative spirit. However, since Easter's remoteness precluded interisland trading or raiding, competition took the form of the construction of massive stone platforms (called *ahu*) and *moai*. The giant statues were related to Polynesian ancestor worship, and were known in the local language as "the living face of our ancestors." The statues were therefore believed to be the Easter Islanders' gods, the protectors of their island.

Unfortunately, building the statues became an islandwide obsession, with tribal chiefs competing with one another in terms of the size and complexity of the artifacts. Some of the largest completed statues weigh eighty tons, twice as much as the largest monoliths at Stonehenge, and one unfinished statue was estimated at four hundred tons.

Naturally, each massive statue had to be transported from the quarry site to its final position, and that endeavor was the proximate cause of the destruction of Easter Island. The inhabitants used palm trees to create the logs, ropes, and sleds to move the statues, and they cut the trees down to make a network of roads to transport them. Eventually, the island was stripped of all its trees.

Without trees, everything made from them disappeared, as did the benefits of the bird populations. Without timber and rope, there would have been no more statues transported or erected, no more seagoing fishing canoes, no fruit, and no fires to keep warm in the winter. Without trees, there would be less rain (since scientists now know that tree growth and rainfall are mutually interdependent), and Easter's soil eroded from the loss of the tree root systems, unrestrained wind, and greater water runoff. Crop yields must have tumbled, and with them the political stability that stemmed from the chiefs' ability to deliver on their promises of bountiful harvests.

Plunged from plenty to scarcity by a complex interplay of forces they could not have understood, the Easter Islanders made weapons and turned on one another in a cannibalistic fight to the death for what little their devastated island could still provide—speeding up the very trampling forces leading to the islanders' decline.

In telling the Easter Island story, we must remember that for hundreds of years the cause of its destruction remained a mystery. In fact, until one connects the destructive power of a societal religious obsession with the consumption of an essential natural resource and the resulting changes to the local ecology, it was nearly impossible to understand how the Easter Islanders could not have recognized their self-destruction and taken steps to prevent it. Then, as now, it was difficult to imagine that thousands of effects, interlinked by complex feedback loops, could result from the abrupt end of just one natural resource. It would have been impossible to conceive that one day an islander would cut down the very last tree and, with that act, one thousand years of civilization would collapse soon thereafter.

This unintended consequence of a friendly competitive obsession must have shocked the Easter Islanders, who surely could not have imagined what they were doing to themselves. Easter Island's collapse illustrates the difficulty with making decisions when consequences are both indirect and ranging far in the future. Many consider it a real-life allegory for today's ecological problems that also require current sacrifices based on an understanding of complex, indirect consequences.

As subtle as such societal risks can be, some societies manage to avoid them. Japan may be the most visible example. When the Tokugawa Shogunate united the country in the 1600s after 150 years of civil war, a long period of prosperity ensued. Peacetime caused great devastation to Japan's forests, as raw materials were needed for construction, fertilizer, and fuel for the expanding and ever-prosperous population. Recognizing their impact, Japan's leaders took action on both the demand and supply parts of the problem.

They shifted to coal rather than wood for heating, increased the efficiency of stoves and heaters, and adopted more timber-efficient construction methods. At the same time, they developed a series of plantation forests to increase wood production. Today, continuing that long-term outlook, despite having the world's highest population densities for a large developed country, Japan is still more than 70 percent forested.

INTERDEPENDENCE AND ACCIDENTS

In many real-world problems, important phenomena are interconnected, just as they were in Easter Island. Energy conservation, for example, would not only reduce dependence on imported oil, but it would also save consumers money and cut urban air pollution, acid rain, greenhouse gases, the production of radioactive wastes, trade deficits, and long-term defense costs in the Persian Gulf. These activities are themselves connected to others, a phenomenon called *higher order effects*, the intensity of which are nearly impossible to guess by intuition alone.

The story of Easter Island shows that many important dynamics take a long time to have a visible effect. While the ultimate deforestation of Easter Island was inevitable when the rate of tree consumption exceeded that of regrowth, the problem occurred long before anyone probably noticed. While conservation might have helped—if indeed there was awareness of the need for it—deforestation was accelerated by secondary effects such as the impact of erosion and the growing rat population's damage to the palm nuts essential for replanting. (Rats were not native to Easter Island; they came as stowaways on the original settlers' canoes.) These effects exacerbated the already significant differences between Easter and other Polynesian islands. Its drier and colder climate, combined with ever-fewer trees, created a lower forest resiliency than warmer, wetter tropical islands. As a result, Easter Island provides a unique example of total human-driven deforestation.

In complex systems, timing can sometimes dramatically accelerate, so that gradual buildups quickly give way to brutally swift transformations. At some point on Easter Island, there were insufficient trees to meet all the inhabitants' needs. That lack forced the society to allocate scarce resources, perhaps for the first time. Facing the choice between the short-term requirements of statue-building versus the long-term needs of the clan would not have been an easy decision. The evidence suggests that priorities continued as before. As a result, Easter Island society peaked and crashed within a relatively short time. As the society collapsed, the clans first toppled one another's statues and, soon after, their chiefs.

Cycles are another phenomenon generated by complex systems. We know from general systems theory that business and commodity cycles often arise from system structure, not necessarily from exogenous factors or individual triggering events. Delays in the corrective feedback loops that exist within real-world systems give rise to real estate vacancies that repeatedly rise and fall, and commodity prices like crude oil that go up, then back down, and up and down again. Unlike such cycles that rebound from their troughs, however, Easter Island's collapse was marked by the bottoming out of its most critical resource.

In the modern world, understanding systemic effects is essential to avoiding disastrous consequences, because apparently rational behavior does not always work out the way we anticipate. Racial and ethnic segregation, ballooning malpractice insurance, escalating product-liability costs, traffic jams, and even global warming—all of which are affected by the kinds of complex systems dynamics Schelling and other scientists have explored—are just a few of the results in which sensible local decisions create undesirable large-scale outcomes.

In the case of Easter Island, an entire civilization was destroyed by its own hand by continuing to follow practices that had served the society well for a millennium. The Easter Islanders did not simply wake up one morning to find their lives in ruins. The archeological record makes clear that their problems sneaked up on them, as such problems do. Here is one of the most powerful lessons from the study of dynamics: It shifts our focus from the search for simple, close-at-hand causes—and the hope (or pipe dream) of convenient fixes—to the need to fundamentally restructure systems and incentives, preferably early enough to allow for the messy process of change. While it always pays to ponder the costs of completely trusting our biased and imperfect intuition when it comes to matters of risk, when the future of the planet is in the balance, the costs of the greater mistake redefines the meaning of the disaster with which we are flirting.

CHAPTER 9

THE COLLAPSE OF ARTHUR ANDERSEN: THE ROLE OF ORGANIZATIONAL CULTURE

Of all the cases in this book, the collapse of the accounting firm Arthur Andersen in the wake of the Enron scandal is the clearest example of how an organization's very culture can flirt with, and be seduced by, values that lead to disaster. Understanding how an organization recognizes the hazards it faces, as well as how it changes in response to those hazards, is essential to avoiding disaster. The Andersen case, in fact, provides a perfect example of how *not* to handle hazards. Indeed, it provides a veritable picture window view of how these processes can go tragically wrong.

Although the behavior of any complex organization cannot be explained in simple terms, Arthur Andersen—starting in the mid-1990s—began to tolerate an unusually high degree of so-called aggressive accounting practices from some clients. The firm's tolerance appeared to be associated with opportunities to earn large audit and consulting fees. The Enron account was particularly lucrative, with fees expected to reach as high as $100 million per year. By professional accounting standards, that was an exceptionally large amount of money.

To comprehend the temptation Andersen faced, one must recognize that the allegiances of public accounting firms are intrinsically divided. On the one hand, accountants are hired by individual client firms, and thus have the same obligations and opportunities that might exist in any professional–client relationship. Naturally, every service provider seeks to increase the business it does with its customers. On the other hand, the requirement to audit all public companies exists by regulation to assure shareholders that the books and records of the company meet accepted standards and are not violating the law. This latter function supports the needs of the companies, the financial marketplace, and the wider society, but it can be undermined by practices or conflicts of interest that compromise the auditor's independence and judgment.

The main benefit to the client firm of an independent audit is the reduction of its cost of capital—that is, the financial returns to bondholders, bankers, and stockholders. By reducing the risks to the providers of capital associated with deliberate misrepresentations or ambiguities in the reporting of unusual financial transactions, public companies are able to raise money at lower rates than they could otherwise. It is a balancing act, however. Companies do not wish to divulge their secrets to competitors through the complete disclosure of all their books, records, and information, and the recent growth of private equity makes clear that the reporting demands of the public stock market are not always the best route to success for all firms. Since the audit–client relationship is, by definition, one of privileged access to senior management and the board, it offers the accounting company a golden opportunity to sell other services. Unlike an independent consulting firm that might have to work its way into the firm through layers of middle management, the consulting arm of a major auditing firm can often go right to the decision-maker, perhaps even getting an assignment without competitive bidding. In addition, since auditors are consistently present within the firm and have access to proprietary information, they are in an extraordinary position to identify important problems that their consulting arms can then work on.

While the arrangement may seem one-sided in favor of the accounting firm, the client benefits, too. The audit relationship provides quality-control for the client on the auxiliary work, since the auditor has a lot more at stake than just the marginal consulting engagement. With both parties benefiting, it is not surprising that consulting services increased dramatically for all the major accounting firms, in many cases generating fees as great as or greater than the traditional audit. During the 1990s, for example, Andersen Consulting, Andersen's business and information technology consulting organization that had become a separate business in 1989, had several years of over 20 percent annual growth, more than six times the growth of the audit business.

For the accounting firms, however, the growth of consulting services under their own roof came to a crashing halt in the wake of the Enron scandal. That scandal, and Andersen's intimate relationship with the highest levels of Enron management, embroiled the firm in a criminal trial that threatened its right to remain an auditor under the Securities and Exchange Commission's Rule 2(e) that forbids a firm convicted of a felony to audit public companies.

Despite the financial incentives, however, there was no obvious reason for Arthur Andersen to have compromised its ethical standards any more than other firms in the pursuit of additional work. There were other factors involved.

Andersen had pioneered the application of computers to payroll and manufacturing starting in a 1953 project for General Electric. Starting in the 1960s, a largely separate group emerged within Andersen that focused on computer system implementation and services. From its modest beginnings, that group grew in size and prominence under the name of Andersen Consulting (now Accenture). By the mid-1990s, it was equal in size to Andersen's accounting practice, and was growing at a faster rate, generating higher profits for the firm.

The basic economics of professional services firms are relatively simple, though they are often not understood by clients. Essentially, they leverage manpower in the form of junior staff members whose salaries are marked up at substantial multiples. Partners share in the profits (revenues minus costs) according to the number of "units" they hold, units being an equity surrogate awarded through a combination of formula and judgment, often on an annual basis. While partners (and nonpartner senior staff) also bill for their time, in the absence of the economic leverage arising from the manpower pyramid, it is hard to make money on solo partner work because of the firm's high cost structure. As a result, the firm seeks work that involves large numbers of people whose aggregate billing creates greater total gross margin and raises the firm's overall utilization of manpower. In the words of one client of one of the big firms, "They travel in packs. It's pretty much impossible to hire just one of them."

Despite its administrative, operational, and cultural separateness, Andersen Consulting provided substantial revenues to Arthur Andersen, subsidizing each partner's income to the tune of $100,000 per year by the late 1990s as a result of a long-standing agreement between the firms that paid up to 15 percent of the more profitable business to the less profitable one. By that point, Andersen Consulting was effectively an independent business with an excellent brand, strong growth, and high profitability. As a business asset, it was valued at $25 billion, or about $11 million per partner—a lot higher than the rest of Arthur Andersen.

With such a disparity, the relationship between the two sibling firms was far from harmonious. There were bitter struggles over control and money and, as a result, there was considerable acrimony. By the time the firms decided to separate permanently, the relationship had all the earmarks of a nasty divorce, especially the arguments over the settlement Andersen Consulting would pay the accounting firm to gain its freedom after Arthur Andersen moved into consulting areas in direct competition with those of Andersen Consulting.

Consistent with the existing agreement between the two firms, the separation would be arbitrated by a neutral party, the International Chamber of Commerce in Paris. The unlikely selection to perform this arbitration was Guillermo Gamba, a lawyer from Colombia, South America, one of the few places in which neither firm had an office. Gamba's decision—reached in August 2000 after a yearlong review—was not kind to Arthur Andersen. The arbitrator felt that the parent organization, Andersen Worldwide, had violated its obligations under the long-standing agreement to properly coordinate the activities of the two firms. Arthur Andersen was therefore entitled to a separation payment of only $1 billion, a small fraction of AA's asking price of $17.6 billion, and only 4 percent of Andersen Consulting's market value.

Arthur Andersen's partners were thus stripped of current income as well as a big capital payoff. Furthermore, they were now a much smaller firm, the smallest of their accounting peer group. Those factors created acute pressure for fee generation, although it is far from a complete explanation of their role in the Enron debacle, since a number of Andersen's questionable practices appear to predate the Andersen Consulting separation. To understand the activities that ultimately destroyed the firm, a deeper probe is required.

THE ORIGINS OF CULTURE

According to MIT professor emeritus Edgar Schein, all organizations—like countries—have a distinctive culture that reflects their values, beliefs, assumptions about the world, and day-to-day patterns of behavior. Organizational culture emerges as an organic learning process—not unlike natural selection in its reinforcement of that which works and de-emphasis and outright discouragement of that which does not. The evolution of organizational culture is thus path-dependent because the organization's choices strongly determine results, and happenstance can play an important role. One cannot arbitrarily pick and choose a cultural characteristic, as if selecting a tie to go with a shirt. Culture consists of emergent organizational properties that cannot be separated from history, especially the actions taken by company leaders.

Andersen might have gone down another route than the one that led to its demise. As the end of the Andersen Consulting era approached in 2001, it might have merged with another accounting firm, become more specialized, or formulated a different strategy to fill the gap in partner earnings and bolster its prestige. If it had, the story would be different.

Instead, during the 1990s a few partners relaxed the firm's historical ethical standards when their clients implemented accounting transactions that fell into the gray area termed "overly aggressive." While it is difficult to say from available material precisely when those practices began, from the mid-1990s onward a series of accounting-related scandals emerged involving Arthur Andersen. They included Waste Management, Sunbeam, Baptist Foundation of Arizona, McKesson/HBOC, Global Crossing, Qwest Communications, WorldCom, and Enron. As of October 2002, three of the five largest U.S. bankruptcies were Andersen clients with accounting problems.

In keeping with the organizational culture theme, it is important to examine how Andersen's leadership reacted to the various early warning signs of ethical trouble and then, later, in the wake of the scandals when they erupted. In terms of the creation of a corporate culture, it matters greatly whether "engagement partners"—the experienced auditors, such as David Duncan, the senior man on the Enron account, who were in charge of all the business done with a particular client and had the final say on most important matters—confronted their clients. Just as important is how the firm's top management responded to the inevitable conflicts between the firm and its clients when the firm refused to sanction dubious transactions. It also greatly matters whether the firm's top management took aggressive steps to determine and correct the internal conditions that might have contributed to Andersen's scandalously embarrassing and, in many cases, clearly misleading reporting practices.

Overall, Andersen's leadership did not take the bold actions required to return to the values defined by its founder Arthur Andersen and his successor, Leonard Spacek, who, as managing partner, kept the firm together in the wake of its founder's death in 1947, and then held the top job until 1963. Spacek was principled, opinionated, and controversial: His accounting industry colleagues once tried to drive him from the profession when he accused them in a widely attended speech of being lax on accounting ethics, particularly misleading reporting.

Following its founder's and Spacek's principles, years before the 1980s S&L crisis, Andersen walked away from many of its savings and loan clients when its leadership at that time believed that a tax loophole allowed S&Ls to artificially boost their reported earnings by including deferred taxes. Rather than go along with this permitted industrywide practice, Andersen chose to reject work from clients that would not adopt more conservative reporting practices.

Largely as a result of, in effect, telling their savings and loan clients, "We don't want your business"—Andersen avoided the nightmare of the savings and loan crisis that resulted in losses of more than $150 billion. The S&L crisis was largely a regulatory failure similar to the FDA's laxity that contributed to the Vioxx debacle.

During the 1990s, Andersen's leadership abandoned the firm's vigilant watchdog role, choosing instead an overtly client-friendly, self-protective path. They supported their clients, settled lawsuits with big payments, and never admitted any guilt.

Such actions were both precedent-setting and culturally defining. Andersen might have responded with contrition rather than arrogance, even if the firm never acknowledged any wrongdoing. Although Andersen talked a good game in the press, the implications of shutting down clients' misleading practices would have ended the firm's relationships with a number of high-flying companies that wanted precisely the sort of "creative accounting" Andersen provided. Andersen's leadership had apparently decided to transform the firm into a highflier, just like its clients, although whether that was a conscious decision or simply the path of least resistance is unclear.

To be fair to Andersen's middle management, psychological factors doubtless influenced their perceptions of the severity of their clients' violation of accounting standards. Issues of materiality and the violation of rules are sometimes (but not always) ambiguous, and auditors are expected to exercise judgment. Just as in many other cases examined in the book, perceptual distortions of the facts seem likely. Under pressure, such as in the space shuttle accidents and the Black Hawk shoot-down, people often see what they want to see, especially if their bosses push the company and subordinates in a particular direction.

At the very top, however, one must judge by a less forgiving standard. In incident after incident, warning signs were downplayed and aggressive investigatory actions were not taken, even when evidence was presented directly to senior partners, such as the members of the firm's Risk Management Committee. Each incident raised a clear conflict between two strongly valued aspects of the Andersen culture: accounting integrity and growth. Unlike their predecessors, Andersen's 1990s leadership unequivocally chose growth.

Augmenting the firm's slide down the slippery slope that made it permissible to endorse clients' questionable bookkeeping was Andersen's cultural value of allegiance to the engagement partners who ran the work of their clients like separate fiefdoms. Lower-level auditors owed their success to the senior partner who supervised them, and going against the wishes of that partner could severely damage one's career. Andersen was a firm with unusually high discipline, and its staff were selected and trained to know their place. In the early days, recruits were encouraged to dress alike, eat lunch in certain kinds of restaurants, and maintain a certain profile in the community. Junior employees were commonly known as "Androids."

Such conformity was a great strength for much of the company's history. The consistent delivery of an audit anywhere in the world was a historical source of competitive advantage and organizational cohesion. Andersen's St. Charles, Illinois, education center, forty miles west of the firm's Chicago headquarters, employed a full-time staff of five hundred, ran four hundred courses for sixty-eight thousand staff members annually, and was regarded as a model for the industry and a key to the firm's success. Internal discipline thus emerged as part of the culture, one of the many unquestioned "how we do things around here" assumptions that defined the firm. At Andersen, seriously questioning one's seniors was simply not done.

WHAT DOES IT MEAN?

Many of Andersen's partners and staff did nothing wrong, nor were they even involved with clients who did. It also seems likely that many of the partners who went along with the firm's practices felt that they had little option. (While walking out was always a possibility, it was rarely taken.)

For most ordinary people, the erosion of what they know to be the right thing to do occurs at a slow enough rate that it goes unnoticed. We saw analogous erosions at NASA, although the underlying issues were different. We also know that people can be eternal optimists—or simply in denial—both characteristics that blind them to risk with a belief that there will be time to fix things (and sometimes there is, but often not). On the other hand, we have learned that people are not good judges of cumulative risk, and the number of incidents in which Andersen was taking such risks appears to have been growing over time, as was the scale of the deviations they were expected to certify.

At Andersen, a number of people crossed the line of good judgment in pursuit of money and stature. Neither is an uncommon sin. More serious was that the firm's leaders appear to have been tempted by the same sirens' call. Perhaps it was greed, long-standing competitive rivalries between audit and consulting partners, or some other factors we cannot know. Whatever leadership's motives, the infection slowly spread because "crown jewel" clients—as the payers of big fees were called—were highly celebrated, and their engagement partners hailed as local heroes. In Andersen's highly disciplined culture, a call that the emperor has no clothes was likely to be shouted down, so it never came.

Cracks in the Dam

As is usually the case, a series of early warning incidents foreshadowed the firm's eventual collapse. In 1998, when the Waste Management scandal erupted, Andersen did not publicly admit its guilt.

Since an accounting firm's integrity is essential to its role as auditor, an accounting firm has little choice about admitting it has violated key rules. "Plausible deniability" is, literally, a matter of survival, and all settlements involved no admission of serious wrongdoing. To do otherwise would effectively have shut the firm down. In the case of its most valuable crown jewel, Enron, Andersen's luck ran out with a felony conviction.

One cannot know, of course, the degree to which the generous fees earned by Andersen from these clients were in part compensation for their loyal support—hush money, as it were. Certainly, the opposite tack of issuing a qualified opinion or refusing to sign the financial statements would not have been appreciated, and might have ended the relationship. In the case of Waste Management, despite an SEC investigation that resulted in a $7 million fine for Arthur Andersen (at the time the largest ever levied on an accounting firm), the company continued to employ Andersen as its auditors. In 2000, WM paid them an extraordinary $48 million in audit fees and $31 million in consulting fees.

In this light, Andersen's practices with Enron were not significantly different—at least in kind, if not in extent—than those the firm had followed with other high-risk clients. Of course, the Enron context is somewhat different because a number of that company's senior officers were engaged in criminal activity. Any complicity on Andersen's part became far more serious, although they might have escaped disaster if they had been spared a guilty verdict on the obstruction of justice charges brought by the Justice Department in an Enron-related prosecution. (Although it was too late to save the firm, the U.S. Supreme Court unanimously overturned Andersen's conviction in 2005 due to ambiguities in jury instructions.)

Andersen's choice came down to the basic issue of the firm's mission and, in particular, the decision about whom a public accounting firm ultimately serves. Many parties (especially the SEC) expect all the big firms to be public watchdogs, and to operate an early warning system for the financial markets and the public. Instead, Andersen's approach appears to have been client-centered in the extreme. This is a hotly debated and often political issue. After many years of a liberal attitude toward advocacy by audit firms on behalf of their clients, the scales have been rebalanced toward caution in the wake of Enron.

The Arthur Andersen case illustrates that when circumstances shift, a number of elements in the organizational culture may fall out of alignment, perhaps even into opposition. In the early days, a relatively balanced portfolio of clients could allow the occasional sacrifice of one or two as a course correction and values reaffirmation. In the contemporary case, more aggressive changes would have required more courage by Andersen's senior management as well as a viable alternative strategy. With the slow growth of traditional accounting and the potential loss of the Andersen Consulting revenues, success with so-called high-risk clients seemed to be Andersen's special niche, albeit one of dubious ethical standing. It seems likely that no one inside the company wanted to look very closely at what was really going on, nor were they really determined to understand the full implications of their clients' behavior.

BYSTANDERS

A number of Andersen employees reported irregularities in regard to Enron and other Andersen client audits. They and many others up and down the chain of command within Arthur Andersen had serious misgivings about the questionable practices in which the firm was engaging. Yet no one spoke out publicly, even when Carl Bass, a member of Andersen's Professional Standards Group that was supposed to be the last word on audit rule interpretation, was removed from the Enron account under pressure from its CFO Andrew Fastow (now an inmate at the Federal Detention Center in Oakdale, Louisiana, with a projected release date in 2011) after objecting to some of Enron's accounting practices. Even Andersen's managing partner, Joseph Berardino, SEC chairman Arthur Levitt's accounting industry ally in the political fight to create rules ensuring greater auditor independence, caved in when Enron insisted that Bass had to go. As the *New York Times'* Kurt Eichenwald put it in *Conspiracy of Fools*, his comprehensive book on Enron, "Standing up to Enron wasn't considered a plausible option; the deep-pocketed client could shift its consulting business at the drop of a hat, leaving Andersen only the low-paying audit work. That was a risk that the Andersen partners were simply unwilling to take."

While simple greed might be an adequate explanation of why Andersen leadership allowed such permissive accounting to continue, it does not explain why so many thousands of employees simply went along with it without speaking up. Perhaps careerism and greed explain that, too; but the pattern was so pervasive, it seems clear that other organizational and cultural factors must have been at work.

We can see a number of factors related to organizational culture that worked in both the *Columbia* shuttle disaster and the Andersen collapse to create widespread bystander behavior.

"Command and Control" Leadership Style

Bystander behavior is more likely to occur in organizations with strong hierarchies and rigid group boundaries that are populated with leaders lacking the ability to value, foster, and manage dissent. Such organizations are also more likely to be staffed by midlevel managers who lack the motivation or skill to elicit views that differ from those of their bosses. When those in the middle suspect that things are amiss, they tend to ignore their own concerns. Instead, they defer to others in authority, justifying their inaction by attributing greater knowledge and wisdom to their superiors, such as Duncan and Berardino.

Of course, creating a platform for inquiry and dissent requires time and money. Some issues will doubtless lead down blind alleys, thus creating obvious costs. Also, the need for institutional attention to conflicting voices demands a more sophisticated problem-solving process to avoid being mired in a plethora of lesser issues. While those are serious concerns, if we hold a clear image in our minds of the destruction of *Columbia* in the Texas morning sky, picture the thousands of arthritis sufferers who had Vioxx-precipitated heart attacks, consider the workers who lost their retirement funds in the collapse of Enron, or ponder the many at Andersen who largely stayed silent amid widespread knowledge of the firm's questionable practices, we see the overwhelming benefits of organizations with a greater tolerance for conflict.

Failure to Challenge Core Cultural Assumptions

Basic cultural assumptions are deep-level tenets that employees and members of organizations hold to be true, often without realizing it. They can be business assumptions about the marketplace, customers, and competitors; technical assumptions about processes and products; or managerial assumptions about organization structure, efficiency, and critical factors that promote success.

Over time, decisions that may start out as opinions, personal preferences, or practical necessities evolve into internalized truths that become second nature throughout the organization. Such truths influence which problems or opportunities receive attention and which are ignored, as well as the courses of action to be considered and those rejected out of hand. Organization members who "think the unthinkable" find themselves fighting a war on two fronts: the need to prove their case, and the need to establish the legitimacy of the arguments on which their case is based. At Andersen, pleasing the client and growth became the golden rules, while accounting and ethical standards were, at least in the case of certain clients, suspended.

Organizational Tunnel Vision

People within organizations obsessed with maximizing a single metric are especially prone to being blind to other considerations. In this chapter, we've seen the effects of an organizational culture consumed with reeling in bigger and bigger fees. Along the same lines, leading up to the *Columbia* accident, NASA felt great pressure to launch shuttles on time and on budget after many delays and cost overruns.

In fact, Sean O'Keefe, the NASA administrator during that period, had established the completion of Node 2 of the International Space Station as an immovable organizational objective. While providing a clear focus and discipline, the goal also encouraged a production mentality in the Shuttle Program's senior leaders, resulting in their discounting safety concerns and the warnings of safety advocates.

After the *Columbia* accident, investigators noted that to keep to a launch schedule, engineers had to prove that a flight was unsafe rather than to prove that it was safe—NASA's traditional posture and the appropriate conservative attitude when dealing with an unreliable developmental technology such as the space shuttle. This is not to suggest that anyone at NASA deliberately sacrificed safety. Rather, it simply reveals that powerful pressures—what some called "launch fever"— slowly eroded the organization's safety consciousness in a manner quite contrary to people's espoused values and conscious intent.

In a similar manner, "billing fever" up and down the Andersen organization seems likely to have eroded concerns that must have arisen in some partners' minds that the firm's aggressive practices were going to lead to trouble. As a result, the organization unconsciously colluded in one of the most dramatic business meltdowns in history, allowing itself to be completely consumed and obliterated in the process.

CHAPTER 10

WHEN COUNTRIES GO BANKRUPT: THE PRISONER'S DILEMMA WRIT LARGE

Global capital markets pose the same kinds of problems that jet planes do. They are faster, more comfortable, and they get you where you are going better. But the crashes are much more spectacular.

—Lawrence Summers, former deputy secretary of the Treasury, *Time*, February 15, 1999

Corporations are not the only entities subject to financial catastrophe. So, too, are nations. Like people and companies, nations go bankrupt when they run out of money. When a nation fails, massive unemployment and other problems "trickle down" to its citizens, trading partners, and others around the globe with whom they have economic relationships. Make no mistake about it: Economic disasters cause widespread human suffering.

The type of money involved in nation-level bankruptcy is known as "hard currency," and it takes the form of U.S. dollars and a few other currencies such as Japanese yen, euros, and British pounds. The need to rely on hard currency is simple. Since nations can print their own money, they can pay off their debts using local currency at their whim.

However, when debts are paid off to foreigners, unless they are willing to "roll over" those debts or otherwise reinvest in local currency, the money will be exchanged for dollars or pounds or yen when the loans come due. That exchange uses up the debtor's hard currency reserves, which are limited, especially in developing countries.

When things get to the point that a nation can't meet its international obligations for hard currency, it is said to be in "default." Default is not the same as having insufficient assets in total to offset one's obligations, but it is a serious problem nonetheless. It is bad for the nation, its trading partners, and foreign investors and banks, which may think twice about lending in the future.

Like a flu pandemic, a financial crisis in one nation can spread from one to another country via banking, investment, and trade interdependencies. Such a crisis happened in the late 1990s, as trouble spread from Thailand throughout East Asia. The disease almost brought the global economy to its knees.

You may wonder who is to blame for the troubles described in the following pages. Unlike many of the cases presented thus far, there is no consensus about what went wrong, or even how the global economy precisely works, what causes these occasional crises, and what can be done to most effectively resolve them. Furthermore, even if people did agree, it is unclear whether reality could be reconciled with the political and ideological differences that divide the world. Explanations and blame notwithstanding, we all came awfully close to global financial disaster.

GAMES PEOPLE PLAY

Any understanding of nation-engulfing financial disasters has to start with game theory.

Many multinational financial disasters can be traced to some version of the following truth: In every situation, decision-makers base their decisions on the intrinsic rewards of the situation *plus their expectations of what other decision-makers will do*; those other decision-makers, in turn, are doing the same.

We can see how such a situation of mutual interdependence is related to the themes of feedback, delays, and complexity examined in chapter 8. Complexity arises when the results of one process "feed back" to others, whose results contribute to the original, perhaps indirectly. A perfect example is a *bank run*, which will serve as a good metaphor for the cases here, as many of them were essentially bank runs, with an entire nation standing in for the bank.

Say Joe Saver, for whatever reason, gets the idea that Trusty Bank, where he keeps his money, is in trouble and may not have sufficient funds to return the money to all the depositors who might want it. He withdraws his money and starts telling his friends and family to do the same. If a critical mass of people is convinced that Trusty Bank is about to go under, a tipping point may occur in which the *idea* that Trusty Bank is about to go under becomes a self-fulfilling prophecy.

Why do such self-fulfilling prophecies arise? Because rational people base their actions not just on the facts, but on how they *think* others perceive the facts and are therefore likely to behave. This "double vision" creates enormous leverage for ideas to spread contagiously throughout a system of decision-makers. It sometimes creates mountains out of molehills (and sometimes molehills out of mountains when concerns like climate change or other risks are collectively downplayed).

Importantly, not only do the people who believe a certain proposition act in accordance with that belief, but others who don't believe the proposition may also come to act in accordance with it if they think that others will.

The field that examines these phenomena is called game theory. Many people have been introduced to this important field by the vexing problem called the "prisoner's dilemma," a thought experiment attributed to Princeton University's Albert W. Tucker, who prepared it for a seminar in 1950.

We are asked to imagine that two criminals have been appre-hended shortly after a crime they are known to have committed, but without sufficient evidence to convict them. The district attorney would rather have a strong conviction of one perpetrator than take her chances with circumstantial evidence in a trial of both, so she separates the suspects and offers each the chance to inform on the other. The informer will get a very light sentence while the other criminal will get a very harsh one. If each refuses to squeal on the other, the D.A. will charge both with the lesser crime of weapons possession, but one she knows she can win at trial. If they each inform on the other, the D.A. will count herself lucky and seek a sen-tence somewhat less than the harsh extreme but not so light as the weapons charge.

There are many interesting aspects to this problem, and it has been intensely studied both in single-round versions (in which the game is played just once), and in multiple rounds in which participants get to "cooperate" (stay silent) or "defect" (inform) repeatedly. In the latter version, various strategies have been evolved and tested using human subjects as well as with genetic algorithms and other forms of machine learning. The results are an interesting combination of intuition and counterintuition.

For single-round play, the dominant emergent strategy is mutual defection—that is, ratting on each other. While the payoffs in the game clearly reward simultaneous mutual silence, the individual incentives for selling out the other guy encourage a different outcome.

Each party has a clear preference for himself (informing on the other), as well as a preference for the other party (silence). Significantly, these preferences go in *opposite directions*. As a result of these payoffs, and acting from a self-interested perspective in the face of uncertainty about what the other party will do, both parties will defect: They will save their own skins by ratting out the other guy.

What is important is that it is clearly in the interests of both parties to make their *unpreferred* choice of silence (since the rewards are such that they are better off doing what they do not prefer) rather than for either or both to inform. However, this less preferred option only pays off if the decision is mutual, whereas the preferred choice of ratting on the other guy is optimum if you do not know for certain the behavior of the other party. Equally important, it is also optimum if the other party makes its preferred choice to inform.

With rewards structured in this manner, each party has an incentive to try to take advantage of the other by acting without concern for his welfare. It is vital to understand that if both parties try to take advantage of the other, they both lose—but not quite so much as they would if they individually attempt to cooperate but get suckered. These rewards are critical to the outcome and to the exquisitely entangled nature of the problem.

Do all situations with these rewards produce the behavior just described? In extensive single-round experiments structured to prevent the opportunity for collaborative discussion, mutual defection is overwhelmingly the most common outcome. In real life, a lawyer friend pointed out that the choice about whether to hire a divorce lawyer or, equally important, whether to negotiate competitively or to problem-solve with one's spouse, was similar. Acrimony encourages both suspicion and self-interested decision-making, but experience reveals that the outcomes on the issues are not materially different from those obtained through evenhanded negotiation. However, the pursuit of self-interest through tough battling produces legal costs for both parties that significantly reduce their overall net gain. In other words, the pursuit of winning produces a suboptimal result.

A bank run is a *multiparty prisoner's dilemma,* or MPD. The reward structure is much the same as the simpler case just described, except that there is some coalition (a group of a certain size or proportion of the total) for which consistent action improves the outcome for the coalition. The formation and behavioral discipline of this critically sized coalition is the equivalent of "cooperation" in the simple case.

As in the two-party version, the reward structure of the situation makes cooperation unstable, since there is always a temptation to defect—that is, for each party to go its own way in the pursuit of self-interest. Furthermore, even if a successful coalition forms, there is an unavoidable unfair element in the form of "free riding": Those who choose to behave without restraint do better than the coalition, despite the fact that those who act with restraint within the coalition are better off than they would otherwise be. This conflict between self-interest and restraint was precisely the dilemma facing the foreign holders of unhedged East Asian debt, as we will see.

In the case of a national bankruptcy caused by inadequate hard currency reserves, a scramble for the exits will pay off only for those few who make it out the door before a devaluation or involuntary debt restructuring. While cashing in is obviously the universally preferred choice, if a critical mass of the creditors were to cooperate, the country will not default (although downward pressure would likely produce some losses). Unfortunately, in virtually all cases a large percentage of the creditor community would have to restrain themselves, and there is always the temptation to defect in the hope of doing better than one's peers. Just as in the simple case of the two criminals, left to their own devices people will behave selfishly, and their herdlike scramble to save their own skins will backfire. This capacity of individually rational, self-interested behavior to produce economic hardship on a global scale *at the same time as it is likely to fail at the individual level to produce the hoped-for results* is the lesson of this chapter.

MEXICO

With that necessary background, we can turn to Mexico, the first example of a national financial catastrophe we'll discuss.

In May 1994, Mexico was admitted to the Organisation for Economic Co-operation and Development (OECD), an international organization of developed countries that accept the principles of representative democracy and a free market economy and are willing to work cooperatively on a wide variety of economic and social problems. This was celebrated as recognition of Mexico's arrival as a "first-world" nation, the first of the newly industrialized nations to be asked to join the exclusive club of primarily high-income nations that had not had a new member since New Zealand was admitted in 1973. Events reveal, however, that the party was held a tad too early.

Nineteen ninety-four was the last year of President Carlos Salinas de Gortari's administration. Following the pattern of many earlier presidencies, the Salinas government spent money lavishly during the election year, creating a significant national deficit. To finance it, Salinas shifted money-raising from traditional government bonds to *tesobonos*, a debt instrument that was denominated in pesos but indexed to the U.S. dollar. The Mexican government, not the bondholder, took the foreign-exchange risk. That should have had a calming effect on the markets and reduced the outflow of capital, although by indexing the bonds to the dollar, Salinas would ultimately put enormous pressure on Mexico's dollar reserves.

Unfortunately, a rebel insurgency known as the EXLN opened a shooting war with the government, causing grave concern among some investors about Mexico's political stability. A series of high-level political assassinations made matters worse, and in combination with concerns about Mexico's lax banking practices and Salinas's record spending, many investors abandoned their *tesobonos* rather than roll them over. As risk-averse funds left the country, Mexico's scarce reserves became depleted as pesos were exchanged for dollars.

To avoid raising interest rates and choking off prosperity in an election year, Banco de Mexico bought Mexican Treasury Securities to maintain the country's monetary base. This move placed even more pressure on the dwindling reserves, raising the ugly possibility of default and the devaluation of the peso.

On December 1, 1994, after five months of Salinas's foot-dragging on needed economic reforms, Mexico's newly elected president, Ernesto Zedillo, took office. With few options to choose from, Zedillo devalued the peso by 15 percent, although this proved insufficient to satisfy the nervous market. In short order, the peso was allowed to float. In a scenario that has become familiar, a few rich insiders were spared grave losses by advance warning (they had been "consulted" on the planned devaluation), but the impact on the rest of the Mexican economy was severe. The peso crashed, there were massive layoffs, and the economy contracted 7 percent in 1995, the largest reduction ever in a single year.

Many of the adverse economic consequences occurred because of a panic reaction in the credit markets: International lending dried up more than was truly necessary. While Mexico had just $6 billion in reserves to redeem $28 billion in *tesobonos*, that was only about 10 percent of Mexican GDP, and therefore just a "liquidity crunch," not a long-term crisis of economic fundamentals. Mexico had come a long way economically, so there was really no need for alarm.

Salvation came in the form of aggressive open-market peso purchases by the United States and an unprecedented $50 billion loan package led by the U.S. Treasury with the help of the International Monetary Fund (IMF), the Bank for International Settlements, and Canada. Mexico lived up to its promises to mend its ways, the peso stabilized, and the economy rebounded with the help of NAFTA and a buoyant U.S. economy. The U.S. portion of the loans was repaid by Mexico in 1996—ahead of schedule.

Despite the recovery, the speed and severity of the Mexican peso crisis were sobering, especially since they occurred despite a booming U.S. economy and the prospect of NAFTA. Fortunately, those conditions accelerated Mexico's recovery. Michel Camdessus, managing director of the IMF at the time, cautioned in 1995:

> *The increasing international integration of financial markets has brought great benefits by fostering a more efficient allocation of global savings and boosting investment and growth in many countries. But we know there is a downside: vastly increased financial flows across national borders have also made countries more vulnerable to changes in investment portfolios. As we have seen, concerns about economic fundamentals and policy shortcomings can lead to sudden, massive, and destabilizing adjustments in these portfolios. Furthermore, financial globalization has increased the speed with which disturbances in one country can be transmitted to others. So financial globalization, both a product of and a contributor to the economic progress of our time, has heightened the desirability of preventing financial crises, and of resolving them quickly when they occur.*

This was good advice. Unfortunately, Mexico was only the beginning.

THAILAND

After insisting on June 30, 1997, that the Thai baht would not be devalued, Prime Minister Chavalit Yongchaiyudh devalued his country's currency two days later. While Mexico's woes were largely the product of excess consumer spending, in Thailand, property overbuilding using money lent to developers by largely unregulated finance companies created a far more serious problem, the collapse of asset prices.

Beyond that, according to *The Economist*, nonperforming loans in Thailand amounted to 45 percent of GDP, and total financial sector lending soared to a whopping 140 percent of GDP. In comparison, Mexico's nonperforming loans peaked at 15 percent of GDP, and total lending was only 50 percent of GDP.

Thailand had long resisted the rationalization of its banking and financial system, and the government was consistently secretive about the state of its reserves and the capacity of the government to defend the baht. For instance, it evaded questions about the degree to which its reserves were pledged, official records notwithstanding. Many reserves were committed to settle large-scale currency swaps that the government had used to bolster its reserves in the hope that when the swaps needed to be paid off—or "unwound" in finance jargon—the crisis would be over.

Making matters worse, Thailand's weak banking system contributed to vulnerability and slowed recovery. Weak banks meant that there was insufficient credit to take advantage of the devalued currency. Under Chuan Leekpai's government, newly elected in November 1997, half the country's finance companies were shut down, and their assets sold by an Independent Restructuring Authority. The rules were also changed to permit more foreign ownership of financial institutions (although critics have argued that many such purchases were opportunistic rather than long-term investments in the Thai economy).

Still, questions remain about how much of the crisis was due to weak economic fundamentals, how much to mishandling of the crisis by government, how much to inadequately funded yet financially heavy-handed IMF rescues, and how much to the individually rational but collectively reckless behavior of creditors as they rushed to get their money.

SOUTH KOREA

While the Thai crash may have resulted from a massive game of prisoner's dilemma, it turned out to be part of an even larger drama that played out across the globe, spreading through Southeast Asia to Russia, and even to Brazil.

South Korea's crisis was unexpected. The country had excellent fundamentals—high savings rates, near-universal literacy, and an extraordinary work ethic—that had created an economic miracle that was the envy of the world. Modeled closely on Japan, Korea had honed and coddled its large conglomerates, known as *chaebol*, steering large amounts of "policy loans" toward those companies that fit the government's economic objectives. With extraordinary growth, modest inflation, and a consistent current account surplus, South Korea did not appear to be a likely candidate for an international rescue.

Still, similar to Thailand, South Korea's banking system had not been an independent, market-oriented sector, but a policy instrument for the government. Furthermore, not only were Korean *chaebol* massively in debt—at least by Western standards—but Korea's banks had themselves borrowed heavily on the international market, mostly from Japan.

When Thailand started to fail, Japan's banks retrenched their loan positions throughout the region. Korean loans that would ordinarily be rolled over now had to be paid off in hard currency. Further pressure came in the form of the flotation of the New Taiwan dollar in October 1997, a move that unsettled many, since Taiwan held $80 billion in U.S. dollar reserves. People thought that if Taiwan couldn't support its currency, the prospects for others with less staying power were slim.

In short order, the Hong Kong dollar came under great pressure, its stock market crashed, and the Dow Jones tumbled 554 points. In Washington, D.C., by Thanksgiving IMF staffers were on their way to

Seoul to negotiate a rescue package. Several months before, the IMF had assessed Korea's outstanding short-term foreign loans at $70 billion, but that estimate was only a part of the total obligations of $115 billion when Korean firms' overseas obligations were included.

On December 3, the IMF announced a deal with Korea, the largest ever negotiated. But the enthusiasm was premature; within days, Korea was in worse shape than before. Clearly, international lenders were unimpressed by the IMF's efforts, and reserves continued to drain out of Korea's treasury. By December 31, the Bank of Korea predicted that its reserves would be a negative $600 million to $800 million. Obviously, to avoid default, the second act of the solution to Korea's problem had to be quite different if it was to work.

What was needed was no secret: Foreign creditors needed to be convinced to stop withdrawing funds and accept a collective rescheduling of their debt. That required sufficient confidence and trust to put an end to the self-protective defections within the massive prisoner's dilemma being played out. While this classical MPD had the obvious requirement to keep the number of defectors to a minimum, a range of political and logistical constraints complicated the building of the necessary coalition. First, even though most of the lenders were banks, there was no way to impose governmental authority on private institutions. Solutions had to be voluntary, albeit with a certain amount of government-led arm-twisting.

Second, Korea had an election coming up on December 18, and it was essential that the new government and the old one agree to reforms if the markets were to be reassured. Third, negotiations with the foreign bankers were jammed up against the Christmas holidays, a notoriously difficult time to reach key decision-makers as they scatter to country homes, ski resorts, and tropical islands. Finally, even if the plan was to work, there was nothing to stop the banks from pulling their loans from other developing countries to reduce their exposure to similar economies in light of their agreement to remain exposed in Korea. That would merely relocate the crisis rather than solve it. John Reed, chairman of Citicorp, gave the plan no more than a fifty–fifty chance of success.

On Monday morning, December 22, New York Federal Reserve president William McDonough convened a meeting of the top executives of six of America's largest banks. While more of an interventionist than Fed chairman Alan Greenspan, McDonough was careful to tell the banking leaders that his proposal was not U.S. policy—at least not yet. Nevertheless, he was clear that he would recommend to his bosses that no further funds be dispensed unless the banks agreed to a "standstill" on calling in their loans, and to restructuring their Korean loan obligations. Since the alternative was default, and thus widespread losses, the proposal was good for all the parties.

McDonough was acting like a third-party negotiator in a prisoner's dilemma who uses his influence to convince the parties that it is truly in their interests to cooperate, selfish motives notwithstanding. While the assembled bankers agreed—and even wanted to know why it had taken so long to call this meeting—they were not the only ones who had to be convinced. The European and Japanese banks also had to agree not to call in their loans—since free-riding would destroy the essential requirement of fairness and equal treatment—and storming the exits would continue, perhaps with even greater vigor in light of the certainty of Korea's default without collective restraint.

The French and Germans quickly agreed, though officials from both nations resented being called to work during their Christmas holidays, especially to deal with a looming crisis that had been obvious for weeks. The Japanese were more of a problem, however. Overly stretched by nonperforming loans resulting from Japan's real estate and stock market collapse, Japanese banks were panicky, although why they did not hedge their loans against a drop in the won is a mystery.

With a great deal of luck, and at the cost of many spoiled Christmas holidays, Korea's default was averted. Beyond that, despite their complaining and hand-wringing, the international bankers got off virtually scot-free. On January 28, 1998, after a month of negotiations, the banks reached an agreement to exchange $22 billion of short-term loans for an equal amount of one- to three-year bonds with attractive yields fully guaranteed by the Korean government. The Korean people were much less fortunate than the bondholders, however, as their economy crashed and many were forced out of work.

While admitting that fairness demanded that those who lent money to Korea bear the full costs of their actions, U.S. Treasury Secretary Robert E. Rubin put the harsh reality this way as the crisis abated in early 1998:

> *Any action that would force investors and creditors involuntarily to take losses, however appropriate that might seem, would risk serious adverse consequences. It could cause banks to pull money out of the countries involved. It could reduce the ability of these countries to access new sources of private capital. And perhaps most tellingly, it could cause banks to pull back from other emerging markets.*

That brings us to the much-debated concept of "moral hazard." This insurance and economics concept asserts that compensation for distress, such as is provided by various forms of social and economic support, reduces vigilance and self-reliance. In simplistic terms, it means that individuals with burglary insurance are less likely to lock their doors than those who are at risk of financial loss from thieves.

While the idea often has little credibility—for instance, the claim that universal health insurance would somehow make people less conscientious about their physical well-being seems ridiculous—in international economics the notion has greater credibility, especially as it applies to foreign investors. When the loans from massive IMF rescue packages are used to pay off foreign creditors who then have no obligation to reinvest, those investors benefit from high returns without the concomitant risks of default. Such excess returns represent a form of free money, and are clearly a market distortion.

Some members of the international financial community have strong feelings about moral hazard risks, particularly Hans Tietmeyer, former president of the Bundesbank, Germany's central bank, and Alan Greenspan, former chairman of the U.S. Federal Reserve. Whether moral hazard, per se, was a strong factor operating in the East Asia crisis is hard to say, although many believe it was. More obvious were other psychological phenomena such as the race to the exits that seemed to characterize the withdrawal of capital after the crisis hit Thailand and Korea.

In the end, the banks were spared, and to avert the crisis those concerned about moral hazard had to swallow yet another example of "giving credit where blame might be due." In Russia, however, clearly the most important and dramatic part of this entire story, things turned out very differently.

RUSSIA

Russia had been spoiled rotten by the IMF, according to the *Washington Post*'s Paul Blustein in his comprehensive book about the crisis, *The Chastening*. One reason was that there were obvious worries about what might happen to the former Soviet Union's nuclear stockpile and arsenal of lethal technologies if its transformation to capitalism failed. There was also an ideological commitment to transforming the mother ship of Communism and, of course, the opportunities for trade and investment in a country rich in natural resources and a large potential consumer market, about half the population of the United States. So the IMF threw money at Mother Russia, and put up with her shenanigans regarding exploiting every possible loophole in IMF agreements to avoid the collection of taxes, shutting down unprofitable businesses, and other requested reforms.

Throughout its transformation from Communism, and even during the crisis itself, Russian politics continued unabated. In particular, Russia's Duma, the lower parliamentary house, was dominated by hard-line Communists who made it difficult to implement reforms. When President Boris Yeltsin removed Prime Minister Viktor Chernomyrdin in March 1998 as the turmoil escalated, the Duma procrastinated for a month about his replacement, and only confirmed Sergei Kiriyenko's appointment under threat of parliamentary dissolution. Even then, they turned down Kiriyenko's austerity budget.

The real trouble started in April 1998. The Asian recession dampened demand for oil and gas, Russia's most important exports. That caused the price of crude oil to drop by more than 50 percent from $23 per barrel in mid-1997 to $11 a year later, reducing the inflow of hard currency, and shrinking Russia's trade balance in the first half of 1998 by 75 percent from a surplus of $10 or $11 billion during the prior three years to $2.4 billion. The ruble—which President Yeltsin had pledged to support—came under tremendous pressure.

The Asian crisis also depressed the Russian stock market by more than one-third, and the international community began to worry about Russia succumbing to the same disease that had afflicted Thailand, Korea, Malaysia, and Indonesia, and which would soon spread to Brazil: a liquidity crunch arising from a reliance on short-term foreign borrowing.

Unlike Korea's private-sector debt, Russia's government did most of the short-term borrowing, using a high-interest-paying bond called the GKO, a Russian acronym for "state short-term obligations." Foreign investors buying GKOs were accustomed to interest rates of 40 percent or higher, and the Russian Finance Ministry had to borrow more than $1 billion a week just to replace the GKOs that were maturing. This meant that Russia was highly vulnerable to interest rate changes.

Both stock investors and bondholders wanted a *bolshoi paket*, a "big package," from the IMF even though the 1996 IMF program had not yet run its course. What was needed, many claimed, was a Mexico-style bailout in which tens of billions in new money would restore confidence and avoid a meltdown, investors said. It would also save them from frighteningly large losses.

Martin Gilman, the IMF's Moscow representative, and other IMF staff nicknamed the requested program the FIEF, or "Foreign Investor Exit Facility," since they expected that additional IMF funds would enter and leave the country more or less on the same day. The markets might be calmed, but Russia would not necessarily be any better off if new loans could not be found. Besides, the local IMF staffers reasoned, the 50 percent returns that GKO-holders were getting were supposed to be a compensation for risk, and risk means that sometimes you lose. Not everyone saw it that way.

One of those who supported the need for the *bolshoi paket* was President Bill Clinton. Once he weighed in, of course, the debate was over. Well, almost over.

If the IMF staff could not cut off Russia's funding, at least they could make needed reforms stick. On that, they made some progress, but not so much as they'd hoped. Still, some progress was better than none. Then things got worse again.

As in Korea, the logical step for bondholders in the face of likely default was to restructure their debt. Rather than running the risks that Russia would be unable to exchange rubles for dollars at current rates, it was more prudent to accept longer payment terms, and possibly somewhat lower returns. Goldman Sachs, the global investment bank, pitched its help to the Russian government in just such a restructuring deal. The government's side of the deal would be to issue

Eurobonds—dollar-denominated bonds—and Goldman would organize the exchange of existing GKOs for those new investments. The sweetener in the deal was that the risk of currency devaluation was shifted to the Russian government. This turned out to be less of an incentive than expected, and rejecting the deal would turn out to be a big mistake for the GKO-holders.

Encouraged by articles in the *Wall Street Journal* and Merrill Lynch's publication *Emerging Markets Daily*, bondholders figured that with the IMF standing behind the Russians, the high-yielding GKOs were still attractive, and they held on to them. Only a third of the foreign-held bonds were redeemed. Blustein summarized the situation:

> *Thanks to the bailout loan provided courtesy of the world's taxpayers, a bunch of punters in the international money markets decided it was safe for them to continue collecting ruinously high interest payments from the Russian government for a few more weeks or months, instead of accepting a longer-term, lower-interest payback that offered the country at least a chance of getting its economic act together.*

With the tripling of the amount of Russian Eurobonds created by the Goldman deal as well as a few smaller ones, the price of the bonds fell by 50 percent between June and August. Unfortunately, Russian banks had also bought many of these bonds, using money borrowed abroad. They had to quickly sell them to pay off their loans as the value of their collateral fell and the foreign lenders demanded cash to cover the loan exposure. The $4.8 billion that the IMF had disbursed to Russia as part of the new $22 billion rescue package vanished in under two weeks to foreign lenders. By mid-August, legendary speculator George Soros described the situation in a letter to the *Financial Times* as the "terminal phase" of the meltdown of the Russian financial markets.

With market confidence obliterated, virtually no reserves in the Russian treasury, and Russian citizens frantically exchanging rubles for dollars at huge discounts off the posted rates, the situation was becoming desperate. A last-ditch effort to appeal to the G7, the world's wealthy countries, was quickly dashed by Germany's Jürgen Stark, state secretary of the Federal Ministry of Finance and soon to be vice president of the Deutsche Bundesbank. He said that Germany would absolutely not put up any more money. With no chance for another rescue, the Russians were racing the clock to make an announcement before markets opened on Monday, August 17, 1998.

The final Russian plan—hotly debated with the IMF, and announced by Russia with no final agreement from them—was to devalue the ruble by significantly widening the band around which it could float. (This was a fig leaf for Yeltsin on the issue of devaluation.) Next, Russia announced that it would restructure the GKO debt, although the precise terms were left unspecified to accommodate the IMF's desire to involve the bondholders in this decision.

The third element of the Russian announcement was a government-enforced ninety-day moratorium on the repayment of foreign debt by Russian commercial banks. This was agreed to by the IMF, and was necessary because the foreign obligations of the banks combined with the cross-default nature of interbank obligations threatened to destroy the entire Russian banking system.

Although the reaction of the world's markets was initially modest, the news eventually sank in. Germany's market index fell by more than 7 percent, and Latin American markets suffered double-digit losses. At first, surprisingly, neither the U.S. nor U.K. equities markets reacted negatively to the August 17 announcements. In fact, they went up a little. This changed after it became clear that negotiations between existing GKO bondholders and the Russian government had broken down.

The Russians announced their final terms on August 25, and the markets were not pleased. The GKO-holders wanted to exchange their bonds for securities paying 40 to 50 percent. What they got was 30 percent or less. While it can be argued that the bondholders had been offered better deals earlier and should have taken them, in the world of greed and cold-bloodedness that characterizes the professional financial markets, Russia's offer was bad news. The U.K. FTSE 100 fell about 10 percent over the next ten days; the S&P 500 fell 12 percent over the same period. The markets in Brazil, Mexico, Germany, and France were also down significantly.

The real worry was not the equity markets, which are remarkably resilient. What worried the U.S. government financial mandarins were the strange things occurring in the bond market. Unlike equities, which are prone to be affected by all manner of mood swings, the bond markets were usually supremely rational. Bond prices are largely driven by interest rates, and those rates change slowly. Furthermore, differences between bonds of different levels of risk—AAA for the best corporate credits, and then down from there according to risk—were based on careful analysis of financial health by credit rating agencies and little else. Starting in late August 1998, however, the bond market went nuts.

The most disturbing element of Russia's plan was the moratorium on payments related to the currency hedging deals between foreign investors and Russian banks. Unlike many of the foreign lenders to the Asian countries, many GKO-holders were hedged against devaluation of the ruble by agreements with Russian banks. (With GKO returns of more than 40 percent, there was plenty of room to pay the cost of currency risk insurance.) One can imagine the shock when investors found themselves in midair without the parachute they had purchased. It was clearly a game-changing event in global finance.

As the Russian default worked its way through the world's financial system, many reacted with a "flight to quality." Not knowing how much cash they might need, or how easy or difficult it might be to sell various bonds, investors around the world retreated to the most salable of instruments, U.S. government bonds. Highly rated corporate bonds begged for buyers, and even the interest rate spreads between similar U.S. government bonds irrationally widened to unprecedented levels.

During the autumn of 1998, concerns surfaced that the bond market might seize up entirely. This would make it very difficult for corporations to raise money or for bond prices to be maintained in proper relation to one another. When the continuity essential to the market mechanism breaks down, no one knows what the true prices are, and risks skyrocket. Senior-level economic policy-makers worried about systemic risk, a cascade failure that might not be contained, even with government intervention. The fate of one giant hedge fund, in particular, kept many people up at night.

LONG-TERM CAPITAL MANAGEMENT

Like Enron, Long-Term Capital Management (LTCM) was once a corporate star. Started by legendary Wall Street trader and Salomon Brothers vice chairman John Meriwether, LTCM assembled a stellar array of Wall Street highfliers, academic superstars (including Nobel Prize winners Myron Scholes and Robert Merton, who, along with the late Fisher Black, had developed the mathematical options pricing model that had arguably invented modern finance), and even a former Fed vice chairman. Of course, Meriwether and his gang did not engage in illegal activities such as those that scuttled Enron and put CEO Jeffrey Skilling and CFO Andrew Fastow behind bars. And yet, LTCM managed to create gargantuan profits—returns of over 40 percent per annum during its early years—thereby eclipsing the size and earnings of many traditional investment banks and mainstay corporations such as Xerox and Gillette.

This case is the story of how they did it and how the Russian bond default just described brought Long-Term's success juggernaut to a screeching halt in only four months. In that brief time, LTCM lost a staggering $4.6 billion, virtually all of its equity. Out of concern about a systemwide meltdown, and putting moral hazard concerns aside, the New York Fed's McDonough reprised his "bailing-in" rescue skills, this time creating a forum for fourteen of the world's largest banks and investment banks that were involved with LTCM to provide over $3.6 billion to keep the hedge fund afloat so that its complex trades could be unwound in an orderly manner.

To understand the collapse of LTCM, it is necessary to understand the intellectual and ideological foundations on which it was built. In July 2005, E. Gerald Corrigan, former head of the New York Fed and a managing director at Goldman Sachs, issued a committee report about the worrisome state of certain aspects of credit derivatives, one of the fastest-growing aspects of the global derivatives marketplace. Just as the value of stock options—the most well-known derivative product—are based upon (or derived from) the value of another asset, in this case exchange-traded equities, the value of credit derivatives are based on the credit-worthiness of various companies. Credit derivative contracts are bets on whether a company will pay its debts or will default.

Trying to put the recent May 2005 downgrade of General Motors bonds to "junk" status, Corrigan said, "Anyone with half a brain knows that models are models." Presumably, he was making the point that people ought to know that the mathematical models used to value derivative securities are not always perfect—there is always some residual risk. Corrigan's wisdom notwithstanding, many of the decision-makers in this chapter must have been using the "other half" of their brains. That was certainly true at Long-Term, but it didn't appear so early on, and they were far from being the only ones who got caught out by the market madness precipitated by August's Russian crisis.

In his best-selling *Liar's Poker*, Michael Lewis portrayed contemporary Wall Street (at least at Salomon Brothers during Meriwether's rise) as a rough-and-tumble fraternity house of big egos and little sub-tlety. But it was not the only game in town. Starting in the early 1970s—with the advent of such breakthroughs as the Black-Scholes-Merton options pricing model, and the arbitrage pricing insights of Stephen Ross—parts of Wall Street began to look and act a lot like Silicon Valley in their hiring practices and emphasis on technology and innovation. High tech has always been about building businesses around ideas, and in finance applying a similar formula has naturally focused on ideas for making money.

Before the academic breakthroughs, the practice of financial risk-taking rested on the intuition of market practitioners. While derivative products like options have long existed (in fact, some for more than one thousand years), there was no definitive way to price them. This uncertainty made it difficult to use derivatives to manage risk with any precision, or to provide a solid basis for inventing new derivatives (such as the credit derivatives mentioned above) to solve problems. Everything changed with the new financial models and the power of fast desktop computers like Sun workstations to recalculate thousands of trading positions in response to real-time market changes in the prices of stocks, bonds, and currencies.

The approach that Meriwether and his followers pioneered at Salomon and then deployed with a vengeance at LTCM involved four elements. First, they identified an arbitrage opportunity, perhaps involving related bonds that were mispriced relative to one another because of peculiarities in the marketplace. (Arbitrage involves profiting or otherwise taking advantage of a price differential between two or more markets.) Mispricing meant that arbitrage profits could be made by buying the underpriced security and selling the overpriced one in closely coordinated transactions.

Second, they decomposed the risks inherent in the trade that might negate any profits, hedging away those that were undesirable (such as shifts in interest rates or currencies) by using derivatives until all that was left was the sliver of profit inherent in the arbitrage itself.

Third, they developed ways of affordably borrowing hundreds of millions of dollars to leverage each thin arbitrage idea into a fat profit by performing their trades on a grand scale. That typically involved using some portion of the purchased financial instruments, such as bonds, as collateral so that the lender was fully protected against loss. (Loss protection meant that the lender could afford to lend at lower rates.) The protection allowed LTCM to apply enormous financial leverage, thereby creating enough profit to justify the considerable effort required to do its deals.

Fourth, Long-Term covered its tracks by executing the components of its deals with different financial institutions. LTCM's lenders and trading partners never saw the whole picture. This tactic prolonged the life of the arbitrage by slowing competition, since Wall Street firms are quick to copy any profitable idea.

Long-Term's deals were not just complicated, but they were also demanding to execute. It is useful to think of them as vast "money machines," to use Wall Street jargon. Such machines have to be constantly fed with raw material, such as newly issued bonds, and as each deal played out, or as market conditions changed, new purchases and sales had to be executed, payments and receipts from trading partners processed, and the dynamic collateral adjustments among LTCM's myriad trading partners needed to be documented.

Learning to orchestrate all these moving parts had been a slow, trial-and-error process at Salomon Brothers, but Meriwether planted his seeds there and harvested his learning with amazing speed at LTCM. To help, he reassembled many from his original team, including Eric Rosenfeld, his number two at Salomon, and both Merton and Scholes, among the most prestigious and capable members of the world's financial brain trust. It all worked: LTCM made $1.6 billion profit in 1996, just two years after opening its doors. The founders bet their personal fortunes—as well as those of their children in many cases—on the success of the firm. They may have been in it for the money (since profit is the purpose of Wall Street), but they were also true believers in what they were doing.

In the quest for ever-greater profit, LTCM ventured into more ambitious investments, which included mortgage-backed securities, Italian government bonds, and one of Long-Term's most audacious ventures, long-dated volatility options. An option on volatility is a bet on the degree of up-and-down movement in a particular market. Unlike a normal investment that one hopes will rise in value, a volatility bet is not directional; it is concerned only with the degree of the swings in market prices, irrespective of direction.

It certainly sounds like an arcane undertaking, and might be worth skipping over if it were not one of the main areas that eventually scuttled the firm. As the financial world went crazy in August and September 1998, Long-Term's volatility options cost them $1.3 billion of their $4.6 billion in capital.

LTCM had come to be known as the "Central Bank of Volatility," as it was willing to sell large amounts of long-dated volatility options to others, such as French investment bank Paribas, who would then sell them on to retail banks or insurance companies to help them control their risks. Long-Term was willing to do so because of the firm's fervent belief in the long-term reversion of the French, German, and other major markets to typical levels. For instance, the average volatility of the U.S. S&P 500 is about 14 percent since 1950, and the French and German markets are similar, although there have been periods when all these markets have been much more volatile. However, by pricing its options using volatility estimates somewhat higher than the expected levels and taking the long view, Long-Term could make a handsome profit. Of course, as with its other trades, profits would emerge only over time. In the meantime, precious capital—the equivalent of scarce hard currency for developing countries—had to be allocated to the volatility-related money machines if volatility estimates rose. For each point of volatility increase on the French and German stock market indexes, LTCM had to hand over $100 million of its precious capital.

As the emerging markets crisis finally caught up with Russia in the late summer of 1998, the worldwide reaction brought the LTCM juggernaut to an abrupt end. Its vast money machines were built around rationality and statistical principles that were supposed to act like laws of nature. In the end, the firm's demise resulted from the caprice of man. The Russian default set into motion a flight to quality of rare proportions. Slightly more desirable bonds such as recently issued on-the-run treasuries became even more sought after, increasing their price. Less popular off-the-run bonds decreased instead of increasing in price as they should have done—and would have done in a rational world. To its horror, Long-Term found that many of its money machines were running backwards, generating losses instead of gains, and at an alarming rate. During the first three weeks of September 1998, it lost half a billion dollars a week.

To make matters worse, once the wheels started to come off, market conditions were not the only problem. With the market topsy-turvy, traders in New York, London, Frankfurt, Zurich, and Tokyo were pressured by their firms' risk managers to cut their positions as losses mounted. Furthermore, with Long-Term's blood in the water, the firm's trading partners were encouraged to trade against it, adding to the company's losses. As part of their contractual agreement, buyers of volatility options had the right to use judgment to constantly reassess their value—called "marking to market"—and did so with a vengeance that cost Long-Term over a billion dollars as increasingly more capital had to be reserved as collateral.

LTCM's end was fast approaching, but there was always hope for a rescue, although few had the money to bail them out. Warren Buffett, legendary Omaha investor and the world's third richest man, made an offer, but was turned down by Meriwether on the basis that his terms were inconsistent with the LTCM partnership agreement.

In the end, the consortium of fourteen banks with interests in Long Term invested more than $3.6 billion in a negotiated bankruptcy. However, there was to be no bail-out: Long-Term Capital Management was liquidated.

THE COST OF HOT MONEY

Like the other disasters in this book, these economic collapses resulted from human actions that were driven by human nature. Most significant may have been the pressure exerted by the United States to open up the financial systems of developing nations. That "globalization" is generally regarded by its proponents as good for everyone. But Joseph Stiglitz, Nobel laureate and former chief economist for the World Bank, Harvard's Jeffrey Sachs and Davi Rodrik, and others have argued that openness to the global financial markets without adequate controls sometimes does more long-term harm than good, especially to developing countries with immature economies. In fact, anti-globalization critics argue that pressure to rapidly open the world's financial systems may have more to do with catering to U.S. banking interests than to the needs of the developing countries. Experience suggests that countries that took a more moderated approach to opening their financial borders, such as China and Malaysia, were much less affected by the Asian crisis than those that opened their doors to opportunistic "hot money" without putting adequate controls in place.

A second criticism from the same quarters is that the IMF's form of "tough love," requiring fiscal and economic austerity, made recovery more difficult. Even without getting into details, it seems obvious that except for Mexico (which was more of a U.S.-led effort in any case), the financial aspects of the IMF rescues failed to stem the collapse of the vulnerable currencies. It is also arguable that IMF intervention created at least as many economic problems for the rescued countries as it solved.

Perhaps the most pointed criticism is that IMF monies appear to have done more to bail out foreign lenders than to restore faith in the economies of the developing nations. If true, burdening each country's citizens with repaying the bailout loans causes the affected country to pay twice: first by way of high interest rates paid to foreign investors, and then once again to repay the rescue funds used to bail them out when investors storm the exits trying to get their money out.

From a systemic perspective, when one combines insufficiently regulated open financial systems with the IMF's risk-reducing inducements (one investment banking wag called these situations "moral hazard plays") the resulting greed stampede is difficult to stem. That was plain in Russia, where two-thirds of the GKO-holders held on to their bonds rather than take the Goldman deal after the IMF's *bolshoi paket* was announced. Doubtless they thought, How can I lose?

Actually, they could lose because all systems have limits and design vulnerabilities, especially those that have been idealized through mathematical model-building. Much of contemporary finance is founded on a rational model of human behavior and assumptions of frictionless, continuous markets that behave with mathematical certainty. The late Fisher Black, co-inventor with Scholes and Merton of the world-famous options pricing model, was always a stickler for departures from the ideal, but with his passing there was no one of iconic stature to carry forward that particular torch.

The big financial crises of the Great Depression, Black Monday in 1987, and the near crash of 1998 described here are events in which the mathematically orderly financial world and the theories and models that had worked well enough in the past collided with the political, psychological, and technological context in which they were embedded. Globalization of the world's financial markets was supposed to lead to efficient growth. Instead, it has contributed to instability and almost to disaster (although global financial crises have clearly been known in other eras).

Long-Term Capital Management, the perfect manifestation of contemporary financial thinking and advanced technology, should have been able to go on forever. But in the end, the firm became a victim of its own success and the limits of the elegant models that had given it birth. By their very nature, arbitrage trades are self-limiting. Eventually, a trader's own behavior exhausts the opportunity, or others figure out where the free money lies. By 1997, LTCM found it difficult to make exceptional returns, electing to give capital back to investors. It also structured riskier deals farther away from the deep, liquid markets of U.S. treasuries and mortgage-backed securities that aligned almost perfectly with the idealized assumptions that were the foundation for their model-based arbitrage.

In the aftermath of the Russian default, the global trading community reacted with predictable irrationality—like rushing to the exits when someone yells "fire." Ironically, each firm's safety system—a near-universal form of risk management based on mathematical Value at Risk (VAR) calculations—demanded that traders cut their positions to lower their exposure. But the models that made up VAR were not designed to work with everyone doing the same thing at the same time. Essentially, the models said "Rush to the nearest exit," and that's what people did. Like slamming down the control rods in the Chernobyl reactor, the market's emergency shutdown system ended up working in reverse. While coordinating a bail-in of a single conference room full of bankers might have been feasible for Korea, that was simply impossible to orchestrate on a global scale, even if someone had thought of trying. As we saw in the case of the Russian GKOs, most preferred greed over safety.

We cannot know, of course, what would have happened to the world's markets if events had calmed down as 1998 came to a close. But the crisis spread to Brazil in 1999, the U.S. tech bubble burst in 2000, and 9/11 indelibly marked 2001. One important thing to learn from all these events, and from the example of LTCM in particular, is that we might all be better off if we could count on that "half a brain" that *does* understand that models really are just models.

POSTSCRIPT: AN ACCIDENT WAITING TO HAPPEN?

Seattle is not your prototypical city when one thinks of civil protest. Yet this is exactly what happened there in December 1999, as thousands of protesters took to the city's streets, trapping people in hotels and disrupting the opening ceremonies of an important World Trade Organization meeting to be attended by President Clinton and other dignitaries. As a fog of tear gas hung over Seattle's otherwise laid-back downtown and the National Guard mobilized, many wondered why so many ordinary Americans were so distressed by their country's version of globalization that they would resort to such measures.

This is a book about accidents, not about global economic policy. Yet, in the foregoing case, it is difficult to separate the two. The cascade of economic failures in the late 1990s was a function of the poor design of the global financial system, not of the failure of misguided intentions or faulty execution of otherwise good policy. For the most part, the players in the drama—global financial institutions, governments, the IMF, and the U.S. Treasury—acted consistently with the free-market-oriented self-interest that is supposed to bring prosperity and growth instead of a cascade of economic disasters that spread from country to country from East Asia to Russia to Brazil.

Banking and foreign exchange crises are far from rare in the historical record. However, the contemporary version that bails out the banks by restructuring debts that must be borne by developing countries tends to create crises that have greater impact and last longer than the historical crises of developing nations from earlier centuries.

Perhaps the most important idea to take from the above examples is this: Pursuing that which seems logically best for each individual participant does not necessarily produce that which is best for everyone. I'm not arguing for the self-sacrificial egalitarianism of idealized socialism, but something much more hard-nosed: recognizing the inability of the "invisible hand"—the market essence that is supposed to produce the best results for all—to live up to its promise.

Unfortunately, the intrinsic flaws in unconstrained markets fly in the face of the free enterprise and free trade ideology that has become a form of fundamentalism in some quarters. Contrary to traditional economic dogma, we now have a very good understanding of the economic distortions that arise when free market assumptions are not fulfilled. It turns out—like the physical universe and mathematics itself—that things are far messier than we previously understood. The complexity makes both our intuition and much received wisdom not only obsolete but dangerous as well. For the markets to work as we might once have hoped, information and power need to be much more equally distributed than is possible in the real world. Furthermore, like many other lessons from complexity science, modest departures from the ideal sometimes make a disproportionate difference. Reality is often capriciously nonlinear.

Judging from the aftermath of the late 1990s financial crisis, however, everyone seems to have learned some valuable lessons. Today, for instance, developing countries maintain significant hard-currency reserves against the possibility of unforeseen panics. And yet, the structure of the system itself is largely unchanged. Let us close with a few thoughts about a less accident-prone design.

A New Global Financial Architecture

Unlike many other systems discussed in these pages, no single entity or group "owns" the global financial architecture, or has responsibility for its configuration. As a result, each participating party tries to exploit the system to its maximum benefit. We have seen that unrestrained self-interest produces dangerous side effects, so there are compelling reasons to restructure the global financial system, and many proposals have been put forward to do so.

The principal requirements for global finance involve the management of capital flows and foreign exchange rates in a manner that moderates the extremes seen in this chapter. That challenge goes well beyond the obvious desire on behalf of foreign financial institutions to have their loans repaid, and that of the borrowing economies to have a stable, affordable long-term source of investment funds. The current model of double-barreled borrowing and exchange crises burdens the developing countries severely. As Brazil's former economy minister, Luiz Carlos Bresser Pereira, put it when reflecting on Latin America's late-1980s crisis: "There were actually two debt crises, one for the debtors and one for the creditors, and only the latter has been solved. For our countries, the problem is as serious as ever."

In domestic banking, regulators and economists have long agreed that some combination of capital requirements, central banking, and supervision is essential. Unregulated banking leads to economic chaos, as the U.S. savings and loan crisis of the 1980s and many other such incidents have illustrated over the decades. Internationally, even greater care must be devoted to ensuring mindful financial activity. In addition to so-called prudential financial institutional regulation, it is essential that capital inflows be carefully managed through proper incentives and controls while ensuring that loans are fully hedged to avoid panicked withdrawals as risks increase.

The foreign-exchange system needs at least as much attention. Evidence suggests that exchange rates can remain far from equilibrium levels. However, such arrangements suit the needs of the exporting countries, multinational corporations, and global banks that profit from the status quo. At the same time, the non-equilibrium situation serves to hollow out the manufacturing base of importing nations, leading increasingly to economies based upon consumer spending and trade imbalances. In the United States, in particular, the reliance on consumption is further dependent upon consumer credit, as evidenced by the vulnerability of the U.S. economy to the subprime lending crisis that emerged in August 2007. As this book goes to press in early 2008, it is evident the crisis is far from over, and will continue to plague domestic and global financial markets—and the investment portfolios of millions of people—for some time.

The subprime crisis can well be characterized as an avoidable disaster—not purely an accident, as suggested by this book's subtitle—possessing as it does many of the same characteristics of greed, self-interest, denial, and politics as the events described elsewhere in this chapter.)

While some have argued that the current international arrangement is stable, counterarguments insist this spending/credit dependency leads to a structural instability in the U.S. economy. With the United States central to the world economy, a deep and sustained recession could well lead to disastrous global consequences and a protracted recovery. Like all latent conditions, of course, there is no guarantee that a serious accident will come to pass, or, if it does, that the contagion will spread. If we apply the principle of avoiding the greater mistake, and consider that the entire world's economy is in the balance, we'd be wise to pursue long-term prudence rather than short-term greed.

CHAPTER 11

WHAT HAVE WE LEARNED? WHAT CAN WE DO?

In December 2004, a ten-year-old British schoolgirl named Tilly Smith, on vacation with her parents on Maikhao Beach, Thailand, noticed that the ocean waters were frothing and rapidly receding from the shore. Just two weeks earlier, Tilly's geography teacher had taught her class that such phenomena were signs of an impending tsunami.

Tilly alerted her mother, who told Craig Smith, the American manager of the JW Marriott Hotel where Tilly's family was staying. Tilly's mother and the manager had little time to debate the significance of the girl's statement. While tourists elsewhere stood and stared as the disappearing waters left boats and fish stranded in the receding surf, Tilly's mother and Thai hotel staff quickly cleared the beach just minutes before a huge wave crashed ashore. Maikhao was one of the few beaches on the island of Phuket where no one was killed. Tilly's story flashed around the world as one of the few bright spots in an otherwise horrific disaster.

The astuteness of young Tilly, and the foresight shown by her mother and the hotel's management, exemplify the main points of this book and can serve as a useful summary as well as an introduction to the recommendations in our final chapters. As you read the advice, though, you may be struck by how obvious—even trite—much of it is.

Like many of the other characteristics of risk blindness cataloged in chapter 2, violating obvious safety precautions for reasons of convenience, haste, social pressure, and denial is a commonplace phenomenon. Even though the advice may be "obvious," it is nonetheless sound.

Despite its apparent simplicity, the advice offered here is often difficult to implement. Everyday examples include routine hand-washing as a means to slow the spread of colds and infections, wearing seat belts in taxis, and completely avoiding the use of mobile phones while driving. The problem is that people are tempted by short-term gains or coerced by social pressure, and then their risky behavior is strongly reinforced when they repeatedly get away without incident. What is strange, perhaps even bizarre, is that the same social and psychological forces apply whether we are dealing with consequences that affect just us personally or impact the lives of thousands of strangers. (See Dr. Ellsberg's afterword for a further discussion of this phenomenon.)

RULES TO LIVE BY

The first rule of preventing and coping with accidents is *understanding the risks you face.* This is a multipart requirement that involves grasping the statistical risks—what's likely to happen each time you are exposed to a hazard, as well as the cumulative risk that arises over multiple exposures. Just as important, you must come to emotional terms with the fundamental difference between the probability of a mishap and the consequences should an adverse event come to pass. While the likelihood of a major tsunami in Thailand was relatively low, when it happened, its consequences were catastrophic. Probabilities don't matter once any such event occurs: At that point, the probability is 100 percent.

The second rule is to *avoid being in denial.* There is often a gap between our intellectual understanding of a risk and our emotional acceptance of its danger. Perhaps the best example is how casually we treat car journeys without coming to terms with the truly dangerous possibilities that lurk around every corner, freeway on-ramp, and roundabout. (Of course, when your teenager starts to take the car out on her own, the highways are suddenly dangerous places.)

The most unusual aspect of Tilly's story is that there was virtually no denial. Tilly, her mother, and hotel management understood the danger a tsunami posed, and they were willing to accept the possibility that a giant wave might overtake the hotel at any moment. Whatever natural psychological defensiveness there might have been to the possibility of an impending disaster quickly dissolved.

The third rule is *pay attention to weak signals and early warnings*. These are a telegraph warning of possible danger. Contrary to intuition, accidents don't "just happen," and are often not accidental at all. Many complex machines and systems exhibit hints that they are about to fail, and many poorly designed systems experience near misses before the "big one" hits. The people on Maikhao Beach were lucky because not all tsunami waves demonstrate the telltale receding-sea phenomenon that Tilly had learned about at school. Yet even when the sea receded elsewhere, many people did not know the meaning of that sign, or they failed to move quickly enough if they did. Ignoring weak signals is a pervasive temptation you must learn to overcome.

The fourth rule is that it is essential *not to subordinate the chance to avoid catastrophe to other considerations*. It is all too easy to focus on other objectives, whether you are driving too fast so that you don't miss your plane, or trying to avoid "getting into trouble" for going against the edicts of your parents, bosses, or other authorities. With little imagination, it is easy to see what would have happened if Tilly thought she was just being foolish, or her mother was worried about "making a big deal out of nothing," as grown-ups often do. Similarly, the hotel manager might have been concerned that if he cleared the beach and nothing happened, he would get into trouble for "scaring away the tourists."

As we have already seen in all the cases in this book, particularly *Challenger*, *Columbia*, and Chernobyl, flawed responses to intense schedule, financial, and policy pressures often underlie many disasters. Such pressures distort people's thinking and encourage denial, thereby directly contributing to the faulty judgments that lead to catastrophe. If accidents are to be avoided, safety must be the first priority, and not just a slogan unsupported by true commitment.

The final rule: *Don't delay by waiting for absolute proof or permission to act.* What would have happened if Tilly, her mother, or the hotel manager decided to wait before taking action? It would not have been unusual for a manager to want to "think about it" before clearing the beach, especially since tsunami scares were already a big issue with the Thai government. It's likely that managers at other beachfront hotels may have delayed before taking action, or waited for permission from their superiors before doing so. In this case, we know the terrible consequences.

Avoiding the Bigger Mistake

We all have to make judgments regarding risks. Figuring out the right thing to do is usually not that difficult. And yet, we often don't do what we know to be the right thing. The problem is that we must go against our intuition, expend money or time we'd rather use elsewhere, or rub against the grain of the organizations in which we work. None of those choices is easy, since the costs in money and trouble are guaranteed while the benefits are not. That trade-off is in the very nature of uncertainty.

The principle of avoiding the bigger mistake underlies dealing sensibly with all types of risk. For everyday hazards, little more than disciplined common sense is demanded: taking out prudent amounts of insurance; going to the doctor quickly when we have symptoms we can't account for; holding the banister when using the stairs; ensuring that medicines, small objects, and household poisons are out of the reach of children; observing sensible safety precautions when using power saws and other dangerous tools; and having someone hold the ladder when we're pruning the hedge.

The same principle also encourages taking precautions for less common occurrences, such as floods, hurricanes, tornadoes, epidemics, and terrorist attacks. It may not seem that advice about a home mishap can be linked to one's preparations for a terrorist attack. But preparing for either event involves thinking about prevention, developing tactics for rapid response, and managing the aftermath if the worst happens. Furthermore, both sets of events have probabilities that one must understand.

The purpose of this chapter is to provide advice on thinking about and dealing with risk. We will deal with actions in our roles as individuals, parents, and citizens. Since most large-scale accidents take place in institutional settings, this chapter and the next also deal with how professionals, managers, and leaders should act.

THE DISASTER TIME LINE

Disasters can be partitioned into *before*, *during*, and *after*, obvious distinctions that reveal more than meets the eye. In many accidents, the bulk of the damage occurs in the aftermath, not during the event. A tremendous amount of harm can be reduced by early warning systems, defense construction, contingency planning, and rapid response. Even when the incident can't be prevented, as is often the case in natural disasters like the Asian tsunami, anticipation can often mitigate a lot of the harm.

Unfortunately, in Thailand the responsible government authority, the Thai Meteorological Department known colloquially as Thai Met, did not pass on real-time information it had about the earthquake near Sumatra that set the devastating tsunami in motion. It was a matter of government policy that such a warning would frighten the tourists and damage the Thai economy if it proved to be a false alarm. Thai Met employees reported that they were concerned that if they issued an unnecessary warning they would be punished by their bosses. So they withheld the information, and thousands died through their inaction. However, the ultimate responsibility rests with the Thai Met bosses who placed tourist marketing above tourist safety by threatening their employees to make sure the irresponsible government directives were followed.

The same norm of "politics trumps safety" led to the destruction of *Challenger*, delayed the deployment of FEMA resources to New Orleans after Katrina, and turned Chernobyl from a local accident into a large-scale disaster whose consequences spanned national borders and passed radioactive toxins down to succeeding generations.

From studying disaster time lines, it is clear that there is usually ample time before any low-probability hazard breaks loose. The problem, of course, is getting people to pay attention so that the lead time can be used productively. A Thai Met official and expert, Smith Dharmasaroja, had warned of the tsunami threat seven years before it occurred. He was fired. "People called me a lot of names, and criticized me and called me a madman," he reported in a television interview. "Some government officials told me that I destroyed the tourism industry in Thailand."

The earliest references to *Challenger*'s O-ring problems date to 1980, six years before the accident, and engineers like Roger Boisjoly at Morton Thiokol, the makers of the solid rocket motors, as well as officials at NASA's headquarters such as Richard Cook repeatedly warned of the O-ring threat. The same story was true at Merck, since the indications of elevated cardiac risks of Vioxx were suggested by Merck's own studies well before the drug was approved by the FDA. Even after the drug was released, the FDA had data that suggested higher cardiac risks, but it did not release them generally to the public.

Unfortunately, as revealed by the collapse of New Orleans's flood-protection system, even if efforts are made to warn people in advance to minimize the damage from a major threat, the efforts may be too little, too late, or poorly implemented. After the Katrina disaster, studies of New Orleans flood controls indicated that they were barely adequate overall and significantly vulnerable in specific cases. When people "cheat" in the face of known risk, they are in denial that the danger is real. Our advice: *Don't squander your early warnings with delays or half measures.* If you do, don't be surprised if the clock runs out.

Real-Time Responses

Okay now we're into the event. Shit has happened. It might not seem that there's time left to do much of anything, but that is untrue. Such pessimism is known by the rationalizing tagline "There's nothing that could have been done," the passive-voiced consolation offered to Rodney Rocha by his *Columbia* space shuttle colleagues. Contrary to such claims, there is often a lot that can be done in virtually all catastrophes. As in the case of prevention, the key to effective real-time response is preparation.

For example, to prepare for the worst, all commercial airplane pilots are trained extensively in emergency procedures that only a very few will ever use. Pilots train because in an emergency their responses must be the right ones, and performed flawlessly without delay. The 1994 China Airlines Flight 140 crash at Nagoya, Japan, that killed 260 people or the crash of American Airlines Flight 587 in Queens, New York, in 2001 show what happens when emergency training isn't good enough.

The at-home equivalent is to learn—and routinely practice—CPR, emergency first aid, poison protocols, and proper anti-choking procedures. Will these methods ever be needed? Probably not, but in the United States *someone's* baby needs help from life-threatening choking about once an hour, and if it happens to your child, the overall probabilities no longer matter because it's your baby's life in the balance.

It is useful to mention that sometimes the timescales of the actual events vary from seconds, in the case of a car crash and most trips and falls, to minutes in the case of a choking episode, a drowning, the Black Hawk shoot-down, and many medical emergencies or terrorist attacks, to much longer periods in the case of the *Columbia* space shuttle's foam strike (days) and climate change (decades and longer). The important fact to keep in mind is that your response to a real-time threat has to match its onset and timescale. If you are late off the mark or slow in "relative terms"—minutes instead of seconds, hours instead of minutes—then your effectiveness may diminish accordingly. That said, you still may have some options, but real-time intervention is far better than belated efforts to make the best of a bad situation.

Even if real-time intervention during the unfolding event is impossible, keep in mind that a surprisingly large amount of harm occurs in the aftermath of tragedy. Consequently, emergency medical help dispatched by motorcycle can render aid more quickly than ambulances that have to fight their way through traffic in heavily congested cities like London. The shame of Katrina was that FEMA didn't stage its resources to be ready to pounce as soon as the storm had passed. If you have an accident at home, how long will it take you to get to the closest hospital emergency room or to get emergency medical personnel to you? Do you know what to do if that's not soon enough?

It's not our purpose to scare readers with a litany of concerns. The important thing is to think through what's possible and, most of all, what's *most likely*, as well as what we can and should do in each instance, including the worst-case scenario.

Believe the Facts, Not Your Intuition

You may be asking, If many safety precautions are common sense, why do so many "routine" accidents occur? The answers provide the key to the advice in this chapter, and apply to our lives at home and on the job.

Before explaining, though, a personal story may help to illustrate some of these issues. Like most people, I had always thought that serious slips, trips, and falls happened to "other people," and I paid about as much concern to them as I did to political developments in Mongolia. That is, until my son, Jamie, then seven years old, took a fall down his school's concrete staircase.

The knowledge that his fall might have been avoided by the application of nonslip paint and better discipline on the stairs didn't help us, of course, as we took our terrified child to the doctor complaining of a terrible pain in his arm. It was so sensitive that we couldn't even roll up his sleeve to take a look, but our pediatrician had no qualms about quickly taking a pair of scissors to the shirtsleeve. Taking one glance, she reached for the phone and the directory of area specialists. It was not so easy to find any pediatric orthopedists in the office late on a Friday afternoon, but we lucked out with one of the best.

With the aid of a high-tech X-ray system that displayed my son's broken arm on its digital screen, the orthopedic surgeon quickly had all the information he needed to know what to do next. Telling his assistant to call the hospital to schedule an operating room as soon as we could get there, he explained to us that Jamie's break "is about as serious as it gets without the bone poking through the skin." The operation would have to be done immediately because the longer we waited, the greater was the chance that swelling would complicate matters. As it was, Jamie would have to be in the hospital for three days, and it would be months before we would know whether he would regain the full use of his arm.

As traumatic as that situation was, it could have been far worse. Not only the fall itself, which could well have been more severe, but the myriad ways in which either the surgery or Jamie's recovery could have gone badly. Today, years later, always grasping the banister, wearing proper shoes, and an inviolate "no playing on the stairs" rule have become part of the way we do things in our family. However, to my knowledge, the school has not yet fixed the known slippery spots on the stairs, and kids still race up and down when grown-ups aren't around. While Jamie has learned the lesson that stairs are dangerous places, he is still prone to treating them more casually than I'd like. Not surprisingly, those around him have learned almost nothing from his accident, but I, for one, have never looked at staircases the same way.

While any individual exposure to a routine hazard such as a staircase is not very likely to result in a mishap, we are exposed so often to this hazard that accidents are bound to happen eventually to some people. Of course, we never think about them until they happen to us, but that doesn't make them any less likely. The number of flights of stairs people climb each year is incalculably large, so a small accident rate still produces a large number of mishaps. Of these, most slips, trips, and falls are minor, but those involving the old or young, hard or sharp surfaces, and greater heights are likely to result in serious injuries, even deaths. Again, as a result of the large numbers overall, and despite the fact that most slips and falls are minor, many people are seriously injured and killed this way, so ignoring the risks and remedies is both negligent and foolish. To protect yourself and your loved ones, you must understand the risks, and this demands that you put your intuition to one side and focus squarely on the numbers— something I failed to do in the case of trips, slips, and falls until an accident struck my own family.

The second part of the answer about why so many "routine" accidents occur is that people are irrational about danger. They can be disproportionately scared about things that are extremely unlikely to occur, such as anthrax poisoning and avian flu epidemics, and sanguine about more common mishaps, such as automobile crashes and accidents at work and at home. Each type of risk requires a different response, and we discuss a full range of them in this chapter and the next.

Everyone has heard Willie Sutton's famous answer to the question about why he robs banks: "That's where the money is." If you want to save lives and prevent injuries, look first at those activities that kill and harm the most people. While that strategy seems obvious, we might recall from chapter 2 that cognitive biases and the media encourage people to overplay the likelihood of rare risks and underplay more common ones. People's fondness for memorable stories biases their concerns and deflects their attention from the important to the dramatic. We will first deal with more likely risks and return to the low-probability dangers in the next section.

To keep us on the right path, mathematician John Paulos introduced the idea of a "danger index" in his best-seller, *Innumeracy: Mathematical Illiteracy and Its Consequences*. Instead of using probabilities—representations that many people don't understand and generally don't like—Paulos suggested a simpler "Richter scale" for risk.

The only complication with Paulos's approach is that his Danger Index numbers are logarithmic. Like the Richter scale for earthquake intensity, this means that a 6.0 danger index is *ten times* as likely a risk as a 5.0, a difference of two points represents a factor of one hundred, and a 0.5 difference (such as between 6.2 and 6.7) represents a factor of about three. Although that seems horribly mathematical, the good news is that logarithms turn multiplication and division into addition and subtraction (which is why they were invented). What does a difference of 1.5 points mean? Since 1 is a factor of 10 and 0.5 is a factor of 3, and since 1.5 is one plus a half, the answer must be 10 times 3.

Simple, once you get the hang of it. (Not only that, it will help you better understand the intensity and measurement of earthquakes.)

Using Paulos's index, we can rate some common accident risks to see how they relate to one another. (Please note that this table uses primarily U.S. numbers. Other locations will show different results.)

Before considering the numbers in the table, keep a couple of things in mind. First, in addition to the number of actual occurrences of each risk, we have to consider the number of people who might be affected. Population size is important, because if a hazard affects a small community—motorcycle riders, for instance—then we will see a relatively small number of occurrences for what is a relatively dangerous activity.

The table incorporates the subpopulations of U.S. children under the ages of fourteen, ten, and five; babies a year old and younger; motorcycle riders; all soldiers in World War II; as well as the overall population of the United States and that of Wajir District, Kenya. However, it ignores other subpopulations for which information was not readily available. For example, since people who do not fly in airplanes have much less to fear from their crashes, by using the entire population of the U.S. rather than excluding nonfliers, the figures in the table somewhat understate the risk of flying. (The table also does not include a separate entry for those killed on the ground by falling aircraft debris.) Similarly, lightning strikes occur far more frequently in some parts of the United States than in others. If one lives in Florida, one is at much greater risk because this state has many more lightning strikes than other places do. Also, localities in which people tend to spend time a lot of time outdoors have more lightning-related accidents. Neither consideration is included in this table, but a more careful study would reflect those facts.

In calculating your own risks, you don't want to ignore the size of the affected group. For instance, if you were considering climbing Mount

Everest, you'd want to evaluate the risk to the subpopulation of Everest climbers. When flying with a private pilot under low-visibility conditions known as "instrument flight rules" or IFR, you would want to know the size of the subpopulation of general aviation flight pilots and passengers flying under IFR as well as their death and injury rates. Despite these omissions, the table provides a good overview of a variety of risks.

The key figures in the table are in the column headed the Danger Index. It is calculated as 10 minus the logarithm of the column labeled One in How Many. One-in-how-many is a measure of *average safety* in which a bigger number is a smaller risk. Since people tend to think in terms of danger rather than safety, we "reverse" this likelihood measure by subtracting its log from 10 (it could be any number, but 10 is convenient, as you'll see in a moment). When transformed in this way, higher numbers represent a greater risk, which is what we want to know. In particular, zero represents a very low probability (1 in 10 billion—less than one person on earth per year—but not numerically zero because this is a log measure). A score of 10.0 represents certain death, which is very tidy.

You can see, therefore, that being a World War II soldier, with a score of 9.30, was the nearest thing to a death sentence on the chart. The Axis side of the conflict, in particular, was extraordinarily risky— its soldiers suffered at least ten times the casualty and MIA rates as the Allies, although many Axis soldiers deserted near the end of the war, which doubtless biases these numbers upward.

For illustration purposes, the table contains a mix of entries for accidents and fatalities. You can see that the most likely mishaps in the United States are motorcycle accidents and bicycle injuries to children. One in two hundred children (there are about sixty million under-fourteen-year-olds within the total U.S. population of about 290 million) has a bicycle accident each year, a very high percentage. Fortunately, as you can see from lower down in the table, the chances

FIGURE 11.1. RISKS OF VARIOUS ACCIDENTS

Risk Category (Data from Multiple Years and Sources)	Actual Occurrences	One in How Many	Danger Index	Amount More Than One Below
World War II military deaths + missing in action (MIA) and deserters	19,221,261	5	9.30	x 2 times
Malaria epidemic 1998 deaths, Wajir, Kenya	10,545	10	9.00	+ 90 percent
Motorcycle fatalities	200,000	20	8.70	x 10 times
Children's bicycle injuries	300,000	200	7.70	+ 46 percent
Slips, trips, and falls injuries	1,000,000	300	7.52	+ 53 percent
Heart-related deaths	655,000	400	7.40	+ 19 percent
Malignant cancer deaths	550,000	500	7.30	+ 53 percent
Babies nonfatal choking (≤1 year)	9,283	800	7.10	+ 9 percent
Motorcycle fatalities	4,500	900	7.05	+ 10 percent
Smoking-related deaths	300,000	1,000	7.00	x 7 times
Automobile fatalities	42,000	7,000	6.15	x 2 times
Common flu deaths	20,000	14,700	5.83	+ 18 percent
Slips, trips, and falls deaths	17,000	17,000	5.77	+ 13 percent
Murders	15,000	19,500	5.71	x 4 times
Children's drowning (< 10 years)	550	70,100	5.15	+ 39 percent
Residence fire deaths	3,000	100,000	5.00	x 4 times
Children < 5 prescription drug poisonings—no child-resistant packaging	50	340,000	4.47	+ 4 percent
Children's bicycle deaths	168	360,000	4.44	+ 1 percent
Children's choking deaths (<14 years)	160	362,500	4.44	+ 73 percent
Children < 5 yrs. prescription drug poisonings—child-resistant packaging	27	630,000	4.20	x 4 times
Airline crashes (19-year average)	120	2,440,000	3.61	+ 33 percent
Lightning strikes	90	3,260,000	3.49	x 180 times
Shark attack deaths	0.5	586,000,000	1.23	

of a child dying from such accidents is only one in 360,000. That is pretty safe, although it is about seven times more likely than any one of us dying in an airplane crash. Still, in terms of risk of death, it is perfectly sensible to let your kids ride their bikes (but make sure they wear a helmet and stay away from road traffic).

On the other hand, as you can see from the table, allowing young children to swim in a pool is about five times more dangerous than riding their bikes, although it seems likely that lack of supervision is an important factor. Unfenced pools and small children are a lethal combination.

A surprising entry in the table is the number of people in the United States who die from slips, trips, and falls, a hazard that takes one life per year for every seventeen thousand people. However, there are far greater chances of dying in a car crash, which takes one life in seven thousand. The common flu is, surprisingly, 20 percent more dangerous than slips and falls, but smoking, cancer, and heart disease produce the really big numbers. One in four hundred Americans die of heart-related ailments each year, and one in five hundred from cancer. (I've skipped over motorcycle riding, which affects relatively few people but is about as dangerous as smoking, and some might argue just as self-destructive.)

The high heart disease death rate is the reason that Vioxx represented such a public health menace. As a drug used by two million people, many of whom were older and already in cardiac high-risk categories, Vioxx's significantly elevated cardiac risks exacerbated the likelihood of the heart attacks that were already the single greatest taker of life. Taking Vioxx for someone in a cardiac high-risk category is a bit like pouring oil on an icy walk.

Another surprising entry is the number of babies treated at emergency rooms for choking incidents. In terms of frequency, that's about the same as motorcycle deaths. Food is most often the culprit for children in this age group, but coins, marbles, and puzzle pieces are also a serious hazard for toddlers who, as we all know, may put almost anything within reach into their mouths. Fortunately, the risk of death for children from choking is about the same as that from bicycle injuries, but I doubt that this statistic would provide much consolation for anyone racing to the hospital with a child who can't breathe.

The table also shows the result of instituting child-resistant packaging (CRP) on the deaths of children less than five years old from accidental poisoning with prescription drugs. Before the new packaging requirements went into effect in 1974, the risks were about the same as bicycle deaths. They were reduced by about 45 percent by the new packaging from these already low numbers. (Note that the numbers for these statistics are corrected for both the general downward trend in child mortality and the upward trend in prescription drug use.)

The most dramatic statistic in the table is the chance of dying during a major malaria epidemic. In the 1998 epidemic in Wajir District, Kenya, the World Health Organization estimated that about one in ten died, about 40 percent from malaria itself and the rest from other causes. During the Wajir epidemic, the average person was forty times more likely to die than in the United States from heart disease, and seven hundred times more likely than from U.S. car crashes. These are astonishing statistics.

What can we learn from all these numbers?

The most important lesson is that *constant vigilance is required in all high-hazard categories.* If there is a loose carpet or wobbly banister on your stairs, fix it. If your driveway is icy, sand and salt it before someone slips on it; don't wait until afterwards.

At the same time, while you would certainly want to prevent your baby grandchild from putting your loose change and medicines in her mouth by childproofing your home, there are many greater risks, such as the pool in the backyard that is nearly ten times as dangerous.

The mention of babies raises another point. While disease accounts for 97 percent of all deaths, other causes actually account for a significant number of "life years lost." Younger victims mean more family disruption, economic hardship, and loss to society than those who die of natural causes late in life. The most significant group to focus on is fifteen- to thirty-four-year-olds. Using numbers from the United Kingdom in 2000, for example, shows that while this group of younger people accounts for only 2.1 percent of total U.K. deaths, they account for a whopping 26 percent of the total life years lost. Within this group, about 40 percent of the deaths arise from accidents, suicides, and murders, the vast proportion of them occurring to young men. In contrast, among those people over sixty-five years old—where over 80 percent of total deaths occur—only about 1.5 percent are due to causes other than disease.

With over a quarter of U.K. society's lost years concentrated in this key age group, it is the logical focus of major safety initiatives. If you want to save years of life, help keep young men from killing themselves and one another. In the United States, the large number of deaths from murder—most by handguns—exacerbates the problem.

TAKE LOW-PROBABILITY CATASTROPHIC RISKS SERIOUSLY

The subject of danger signals serves as a useful introduction to dealing with low-probability risks. When the signs of a threat show up before an incident occurs—such as the intermittent O-ring damage in the prelude to the *Challenger* disaster—embracing the possibility of danger from the first warning may well provide the time to prevent the catastrophe. We'll get back to this type of advance warning in a moment. In contrast, when signals emerge as the event unfolds—as illustrated by the seismic signature of a possible tsunami—preventing the worst becomes a race against time.

At 10:14 P.M. on Wednesday, November 15, 2006, a massive ocean earthquake (Richter 8.3) four hundred miles northeast of Japan's northern island of Hokkaido caused great concern, especially after the devastating tsunami that killed hundreds of thousands two years earlier. Municipalities at risk issued tsunami warnings and evacuation recommendations, but many citizens did not seek shelter. Investigations showed that there was confusion about the degree of danger, misinformation posted to government Web sites that the threat had passed, uncertainty about the location of shelters, and other problems. Since tsunami waves can travel at over five hundred miles per hour across the deep ocean, residents had less than an hour before the wave traveled from the quake's epicenter near the Kuril Islands to Hokkaido's northeast coast. If you consider the inevitable delays in the human aspects of any government warning system and the logistics of mobilizing the citizenry during the evening hours (the Hokkaido local time was 8:14 P.M.), the need for accurate information and rapid response is obvious.

Fortunately, the tsunami largely subsided before it reached Hokkaido's shore. Japan's sea levels rose only about twenty inches, although six-and-a-half-foot sea-level changes and some damage occurred as far away as California. While tsunami threats are not universal, our recommendations concerning low-probability danger have broad applicability: *Understand each threat, its severity, and timing; decide in advance what you and other family members will do in each case; know where the nearest escape route or shelter is to home, work, and school; keep a go-bag packed and ready; make sure you have access to the money you'll need, including plenty of cash; and avoid the greater mistake—don't delay your actions waiting for perfect information that may never come.*

PAY ATTENTION TO WEAK SIGNALS AND NEAR MISSES

As mentioned above, a particularly important aspect of human irrationality is that we often ignore weak signals of potential danger. We've already seen the many ways in which hazards telegraph their presence, even when the underlying risk has a low probability. The receding sea preceding a tsunami is but one example.

Perhaps the biggest fallacy associated with the signaling of risk is that certainty of an accident is required in order to take action. On the contrary, taking action on the basis of *rational concern* before an adverse event occurs is obviously better than preventing harm from the second such incident. While many prefer to wait to be sure, when it comes to crippling injuries and fatalities, there are no second chances.

Avoiding the greater mistake argues for treating a threat as real whenever there are potentially serious consequences. Unfortunately, that seems to be a difficult lesson for some people to master, even when family safety is involved.

A friend told me an instructive story of how her children were stranded when their class's school bus became lost on the way back from a weekend camping trip. The onboard parent chaperones prudently sought overnight shelter rather than pressing on in the dark, but they were out of range of cell phone service (as unbelievable as this might be in the northeastern United States) and had no way to let others know their plight until they found a place with a wired telephone. Making matters worse, even once a call was made, there was no way to inform the children's parents of events, since there was no one "on duty" at the school on a Sunday evening to field calls or access parents' emergency numbers, nor had anyone organized a "phone chain" for parents to inform one another. Needless to say, some parents imagined the worst until a spontaneously organized phone network was set up late into the evening that let them know what was happening with their long-overdue children.

In the aftermath, my friend—a consummate problem-solver by nature and occupation—developed a set of recommendations for future trips. Despite the wisdom of these recommendations (they dealt primarily with contingency planning and communications), the school administrators insisted that they were unnecessary because "nothing bad had happened." That sentiment was echoed by a number of parents, who expressed the feeling that "it was a one-in-a-million occurrence" that "could never happen again." Arguments that this near miss could have involved a real accident fell on deaf ears.

It is a safety sine qua non that near misses and other forms of weak signals be treated as if they were genuine accidents. They are considered "free tuition"—valuable lessons without much cost. In high-reliability workplace safety, following up weak signals is institutionalized despite the inevitable desire to cheat to save money. In spite of the wisdom of that approach, the temptation to ignore weak signal messages is great; for many, it is irresistible. Our advice: *Always pay attention as if the worst had actually occurred, but develop efficient ways of confirming or disconfirming the actual danger to minimize your time and effort.*

EVERYDAY LIFE'S LOW-PROBABILITY RISKS

Unlike risks with greater likelihood, such as household accidents, low-probability but statistically predictable risks pose special problems for us all. Since an automobile accident or slip, trip, or fall incident to oneself, a family member, or close friend is almost a certainty over the course of a lifetime, it's hard afterwards not to take the risk more seriously than before, even if one has a lucky escape.

On the other hand, low-probability risks do not always manifest themselves in everyday life. This makes them harder to anticipate and plan for.

Of the many conversations I've had with people while writing this book, one best illustrates the cost of faulty thinking regarding such risks. A colleague told me that her daughter and son-in-law had purchased their first "real house" in a semi-urban area that was vulnerable to occasional floods. While no flooding of consequence had occurred for more than fifty years, flood insurance was nevertheless expensive, and the couple's new dream house was already a financial stretch for them, even with each working a full-time job. To make matters worse, when they moved in, money was needed for repairs and upgrades to the kitchen and bathrooms, and their first child was on the way, halving their income for a while, at least.

Unfortunately, less than a year after they bought the house, a major flood from a "freak" rainstorm damaged it severely, destroying their investment, crippling them financially, and forcing the young mother back to work when she would have preferred more time at home with the baby.

With the benefit of hindsight, this young couple appears reckless. But the same critique can be made of virtually all the decision-makers described in these pages. Katrina stands out, both due to the common factor of flooding and because so many people's houses were inadequately insured in the face of known flood risks.

The principle of avoiding the greater mistake provides effective guidance in both situations. Despite what might have felt like the relatively small chances of a catastrophic loss (in the case of New Orleans's risk from severe hurricanes, the risks were greater than one in fifty in any given year, and more than one in six cumulatively over ten years), the severe consequences should have outweighed the inevitable short-term financial pain and sacrifice necessitated by protection. Both sets of decision-makers were in denial about the consequences of flooding.

In the case of Katrina, New Orleans's flood contingency plans were incomplete, communications systems were fragile, pumping systems inadequate and vulnerable, and shelters marginal at best. While New Orleans's flood risks were clear to many and well documented, government officials seemed in denial. Likewise, for our young homeowners, they appear to have been oblivious to the "cumulative risk" of flooding and, consequently, they did not have a viable contingency plan if a major flood were to occur.

These examples illustrate a common mistake when preparing for low-probability risks: *gearing one's protection to the perceived likelihood of occurrence rather than the severity of the consequences*. If the adverse event does occur—no matter how unlikely—one needs a full measure of protection, such as we get with proper insurance. When someone steals your car, you want a new one whether you live in a safe neighborhood or a risky one, or have been paying premiums for one month or twenty-five years. (Note, however, that since about one in two hundred vehicles are stolen in the United States, this is a commonplace rather than a rare occurrence.)

While the *cost* of insurance protection will inevitably be based on the likelihood of the adverse event (you pay less for flood insurance in low-risk areas), it is silly for consumers to base decisions regarding the extent of protection to buy (how much of the cost of the damage you recover if the adverse event occurs) on the probability of the event; if your house floods, you want the house fixed completely, whether the chance of the flood was high or low.

When we "self-insure"—something we have to do for many types of risks—we are always tempted to cheat and, like our young homeowners, we are rewarded for doing so as long as our luck holds. In the short term, New Orleans residents benefited from lower taxes (most flood-control projects are federally cost-shared because they create benefits for local private interests) and the use of private and corporate monies that might otherwise have gone to floodproof their city. Meanwhile, the young homeowners refitted their bathrooms sooner than they would have if their limited funds had been allocated to pay flood insurance premiums.

When the consequences of an adverse event exceed our tolerance—as in the cases above and throughout this book—we must fully acknowledge them, along with the costs of full protection. That is often an unpleasant recognition, and is prone to self-deception—and politics. In Florida's 2006 governor's race, the Republican candidate, Charlie Crist, was elected on the strength of his promise to reduce state homeowners' insurance rates by creating a state-subsidized $28 billion catastrophe insurance pool that would sell insurance for one-sixth market rates. Unfortunately, $28 billion would not cover the damage from even one serious storm. Also, using taxpayers' money in this manner primarily benefits the affluent who live near the ocean at the expense of the majority who do not.

In the end, our decision may be to recognize our unavoidable vulnerability and simply take our chances. This occurs when we can't afford the protection or there simply isn't any. (A great deal of Californians' earthquake risk is unprotected by insurance because it is so expensive.) We may continue to take the subway, tube, or metro to work in spite of its being a terrorist target, ignore the ultimate risks of avian flu (and hope that the government is watching our back), or simply ignore the risk of living in a brush fire zone, on a spit of land near the ocean, or in proximity to a live volcano. In some such cases, we may feel that have no choice but to accept risk, but flirting with disaster out of ignorance or denial rather than rational choice is simply foolish.

While some may counter that ignorance is bliss, in many cases contingency plans and partial protection increase the chances of survival and reduced injury even when complete protection is impossible or unaffordable. A good example is preventing and responding to residential fires, especially those related to cooking. While a lower-likelihood risk than many others in the table above, home cooking is nevertheless responsible for starting over a quarter of the 400,000 residential fires that cause 13,000 injuries and 3,000 deaths in the United States each year. Smoke alarms, fire blankets, and fire extinguishers as well as safe practices for deep-fat frying and other high-risk activities are sensible precautions even if they are not perfect solutions.

For very rare events, such as the outbreak of a devastating flu that occurs on average every fifty years or so, preparations are a balancing act. Many believe that in the case of a highly contagious disease all those who are susceptible will become ill until a vaccine is available. Should such an event occur, the risk shifts from that posed by the risk of infection to the risks and consequences of the collapse of health care facilities and overall infrastructure, especially in densely populated urban areas. Shortages of food and medical supplies are likely, especially as the epidemic peaks. The economic risks arising from the epidemic are also likely to be significant.

As an individual (rather than as an organizational leader), it is wise to be as self-sufficient as possible, although the optimum size of a food, water, and medical supplies inventory is hard to estimate, since there are so many potential scenarios. As with most calamities, contingency planning is essential to ensure that one does not have to do all one's what-if thinking in real time.

In summary, the enemies of effectively dealing with low-probability risks are denial, ignorance, and lack of preparation. Denial prevents our dealing with the risks in the first place; ignorance constrains our choices and distorts our priorities; and lack of preparation forces us to deal with complex problems under emotional pressure and time constraints, vastly increasing the chances of bad judgment and the possibility that we will be overtaken by events.

Our advice: *Examine the cumulative risk of all low-probability threats and make your plans according to the rule of avoiding the greater mistake.* You may not always make the same choice for each risk, or the same choices as other people, but they will be your choices, made with knowledge and forethought. (See our Web site, www.flirtingwithdisaster.net, for more information.)

ENDEAVOR TO BE "RISK-NEUTRAL"

Low-probability but mundane risks, such as flooding, create the inevitable temptation to view the situation in an optimistic light—the "domain of gains." With such a mind-set, one is strongly tempted—as were our young homeowners—to see spending for a new bathroom as a certain benefit while expenditures for flood insurance to be a risky bet—one that requires a flood in order to pay off. Of course, it would be unwise for our homeowners to jump to the other extreme and see a flood as inevitable unless conditions had changed dramatically. (If they had, they might want to sell their house at a loss rather than run the risk of total ruin.)

The third possible perspective is risk neutrality: an objective assessment of the situation based on the probabilities and consequences. Risk neutrality views a fifty–fifty gamble for $100 to be the same as certain gain of $50, and a guaranteed loss of $50 to be the same as a fifty–fifty chance to lose $100. Of course, as we've explained in chapter 2, few people see things that way, which is one reason why decision-making is not rational. To remain risk-neutral, you must place an explicit value on subjective factors such as peace of mind, personal safety, and inconvenience, trading these off against financial costs. While most people attempt to do so intuitively, our advice is to *evaluate such risks explicitly*. If our young homeowners had done so, they might not have bought their house in the first place because its purchase price might have been considerably higher than its "risk-adjusted value" (market value less total insurance cost and additional costs-of-worry).

We can systematize this way of achieving risk neutrality by looking at the entire collection of one's decisions rather than viewing them in isolation. While viewing choices one at a time invites framing bias, looking at all our choices over time encourages a more risk-neutral approach. We will be lucky in some things and unlucky in others, especially as time goes on. Our recommendation: *Develop a rational, long-term "portfolio" approach to life's risks*. Also, while it may seem unnecessary, actually do the math. You might be surprised what you learn.

Be "Safe at Any Speed"

In 1965, consumer advocate Ralph Nader achieved national prominence in the United States by attacking the unsafe design of

American-made cars, particularly GM's Chevrolet Corvair, in his book *Unsafe at Any Speed*. Whether the Corvair was actually as unsafe as Nader claimed was debated then, but he was nevertheless a fearless crusader for taking on the world's biggest corporation, and GM was deeply embarrassed when its heavy-handed tactics to morally entrap Nader with prostitutes in order to discredit his accusations were revealed. GM was forced to apologize to Nader during the same time that he was testifying in U.S. Senate hearings.

While product safety is generally regarded as better today, dangerous and nonperforming products such as the Firestone 500 radial tire, Guidant's implanted defibrillator, and dangerous prescription drugs like Vioxx still make it to market. Fortunately, the Internet has now made it possible to instantly gain access to information that would previously have taken weeks of specialized research. Examples of categories in which one can obtain useful safety information include vehicle crash, rollover, and survival statistics; hotel and cruise ship safety ratings; drug side effects; health and beauty aid evaluations; and children's toy safety ratings.

To illustrate, a 2000 report analyzing the results of the 1986 EU hotel fire safety regulations revealed wide disparities in fire rates, with a disproportionate number occurring in Greece, Spain, and Turkey, according to data from the U.K.'s Federation of Tour Operators from 1999 to 2000. Local hotel management was deemed to have a significant impact on safety, since the provision of basic safety equipment (such as smoke alarms) and emergency fire exits is often a voluntary decision.

It must be said that advice on the Internet is often inconsistent and influenced by self-interest, even as the Web has become many consumers' first choice for looking things up. Nevertheless, by doing your homework, you can avoid many mistakes. The key is to not stop with your first useful Web site but to look for patterns in the ratings, especially those backed up by quantitative research from independent parties. It is also essential to be mindful of the influence of undisclosed sponsors and other sources of bias. If a particular product usually shows up in the middle of most ratings tables, it pays to be suspicious of an outstanding review or a complete condemnation. Like gymnastic scoring at the Olympics, you'd be wise to throw out the highest and lowest ratings.

There's no doubt that all this takes time and effort. The question you must ask yourself is whether the work required helps you avoid the greater mistake. If the consequences of making a mistake are minor, then the research may not be worth it. On the other hand, if you've planned a trip to Turkey, you may want to make sure that management at your hotel doesn't think that chain-locking the fire doors "protects the guests"—as one misguided hotel manager reported in the EU survey.

MOVING FROM BYSTANDER TO WITNESS TO WHISTLE-BLOWER

One of the most important pieces of advice in this book is not to be a bystander. Often unsafe situations (such as *Challenger*'s O-rings or BP's Texas City refinery) or unethical acts (such as Enron's shamelessly misleading financial reporting) persist because people look away or in other ways make it clear that others' danger-producing or immoral actions are none of their business. In one's role as a community or organizational member, reducing risk and achieving moral course corrections often takes very little effort.

Psychologist Petruska Clarkson used to tell a story that makes the point in the day-to-day context. A woman observed two policemen harassing a member of an ethnic minority. Rather than intervene directly, the woman made herself a "conspicuous observer," carefully watching the unfolding events from a safe distance. Realizing they were being observed, the policemen became less aggressive and more respectful of the man they were questioning, eventually letting him go. The policemen then went their way and the observer hers.

Sometimes just "active watching," visibly taking notes, or writing a concerned e-mail is enough to change the course of a situation. I am not advocating recklessness. I am, however, suggesting that being visible and questioning clearly inappropriate actions rather than fading into the background often makes a difference, even if it is not a decisive action. Equally important, when someone else takes a stand-up action, lending visible support matters a great deal. While each single person may be relatively impotent, two or more in mutual support quickly break the spell that the wrongdoers can operate outside the boundaries of ethics and prudence. Doing something is always better than doing nothing, and once you let go of the grandiose notion that your actions must definitively resolve the problem, or the equally erroneous idea that apparently minor actions have no beneficial impact, you have a greater number of choices about how to behave.

One other benefit from becoming engaged in life's dramas involving ethics and risk is that it is likely to make you feel better. Silently colluding with wrongdoing or risk-making is debilitating to the psyche, while taking action activates the sense of heroism in each of us while encouraging other observers' sense of the legitimacy of an oppositional stand.

At work, of course, the situation is always complicated. If a supervisor directs one of his employees to engage in an unsafe practice or to falsify or destroy records in order to meet a production goal or cover up a misdeed, taking any visible action invites the threat of management retaliation or peer-group ostracism if one's co-workers are complicit in the wrongdoing. The key question is whether the boss is acting on his own or is part of a larger pattern, as was the case in most of the examples in this book.

If the work situation is more benign—and many are—the key to taking action is finding allies. Many organizations have formal groups such as safety officers, human resource specialists, and union representatives to whom one can turn for advice and assistance. If two or more people go together when voicing their concerns, it strengthens the argument manyfold. Assuming that the organization is merely blind to its risks rather than deliberately hiding them, opening the door will usually be enough (although you should be prepared to furnish some documented proof of your concerns).

On the other hand, an overly defensive organization engaged in a cover-up will usually block or subvert the channels of complaint. In such cases, simply standing by may do little, even if multiple people get involved. Unfortunately, the transition from simply standing by to organized resistance and whistle-blowing is a big one, and not to be taken lightly. Research reveals that whistle-blowers in hostile organizations encounter severe resistance. They are often subjected to harassment and punishment, sometimes becoming the object of a counterclaim if they don't back down. Most steadfast whistle-blowers lose their jobs or privileges, and many require legal counsel. So why do they do it?

According to research, committed whistle-blowers in hostile organizations tend to be people with strong and unwavering principles. At work, their colleagues are likely to consider them picky about the facts and not prone to convenient memory lapses. Potential whistle-blowers often face up to their responsibilities with deep ambivalence, caught between the need to do the right thing so that they can live with themselves and the certain knowledge that they will be persecuted. Many whistle-blowers in celebrated cases become pariahs in their organizations, forced to transition to new careers as ethical advocates. If they are heroes, they are usually reluctant ones.

The key to successful whistle-blowing is documentation. Unsubstantiated accusations are easily deflected, even if they are true. Unfortunately, that means many potential whistle-blowers are stymied by both corporate and government rules that categorize many documents as proprietary or classified. This may make their external disclosure either a contractual violation or illegal. Expert legal advice is essential. (See our Web site, www.flirtingwithdisaster.net, for resources.)

In light of the likely consequences, despite the moral imperatives, I do not advocate anyone casually becoming a whistle-blower. It is an act of conscience, a personal and family decision involving considerable sacrifice quite separate from benefits to others. On the other hand, I do not condone colluding with any cover-up that may follow the revelations that may come to light by other means. Despite the fact that "There are careers at stake," as one NASA manager said in the wake of the *Challenger* disaster, even passively contributing to a cover-up is an immoral second offense, as tempting as it may be to hope that the storm will blow over without blowing you down with it.

Before the story breaks, cautious legal advisers suggest making one's protests within the chain of command or other legitimate avenues, but then departing the organization on as good terms as possible if one's complaints come to naught. In comparison with remaining as a silent co-conspirator once you know the truth, or running the risks of being a whistle-blower, that is sound advice.

Unfortunately, most people choose silence, for departure has its own costs. In most cases, it seems safer to just keep a low profile. The question is, "Safer for whom?"

CHAPTER 12

ADVICE FOR LEADERS

Virtually all the accidents described in this book occurred in organizational settings. Of course, disasters such as Katrina and the Asian tsunami happened in nature, as it were, but considerable damage and loss of life resulted from organizational inaction or ineptitude and, thus, also qualify as organizational accidents.

Not all organization-centric catastrophes are accidents, however, and it is useful to differentiate those that are not. When Jeffrey Skilling, the CEO of Enron, came before Judge Simeon Lake for sentencing on October 23, 2006, his attorney made a last-minute plea for leniency that would have allowed Skilling to serve his twenty-four-year sentence in a more benign facility than his sentence dictated.

During the sentencing hearing, the court had heard many statements about the lives that had been ruined by the collapse of Enron. "Mr. Skilling has proven to be a liar, a thief, and a drunk," long-term Enron employee Dawn Powers Martin told the court. These were not the only names he was called, many unsuitable for print here.

In light of the showcase nature of the trial, Judge Lake was unmoved by the defense's appeal, and let the sentence stand. Skilling would serve "hard time," a rare white-collar criminal among drug dealers, rapists, and murderers.

But unlike the cases in this book, Enron was not an accident. It was a fraud and high-class con game. The elaborate private partnerships that Enron's CFO Andrew Fastow had set up were bewilderingly complex, designed to deceive investors even though they were ostensibly disclosed in Enron's financial statements. Like any good con, Enron showcased its best assets to make sure people didn't search for the undisclosed guarantees, buried losses, and other skulduggery that had hidden Enron's true condition from view. And it worked—until the very end.

This book, and this chapter in particular, are not about the Enrons of this world, those fraudulent enterprises deeply based upon deceit, if not deliberate harm. For that, CEO Skilling got what many thought he deserved: one of the most severe sentences for white-collar crime in history.

Back in the ordinary world, however, most people are not harmed by malice but by risk blindness, the failure to see potential harm and imminent danger until it is too late.

As doctors, architects, engineers, accountants, managers, or other professionals, we are obligated to prevent harm while also achieving our production and financial objectives. Since the damage done by Chernobyl, Vioxx, or Katrina is at least as great as that done by Enron, despite being "accidental," this chapter is about those responsibilities. We must all take a greater share in preventing unintended consequences.

Beyond the protective actions we might take as individuals, a different set of opportunities arise from our professional and managerial roles. While most hierarchical organizations expect unquestioned loyalty to one's superiors and co-workers, in instances those obligations conflict with safety and ethics. Complicating the matter is that the real-world impediments to lofty safety and ethical principles are rarely discussed. Therefore, conflicts between espoused values and actual practice inevitably draw people into loyalty tests and cover-ups when an apparently sensible shortcut invites a catastrophic outcome.

For instance, NASA's decision to fly the space shuttle *Challenger* "as is" to satisfy the military, the White House, and its public image forced all those with knowledge of the dangerous O-rings to take sides both before the accident and during the investigation. Similarly, all those within Merck and the FDA who were aware of Vioxx's elevated cardiac risks had to decide whether to go along with the company's decisions to delay the public release of this data, collude in deflecting attention from the risks in physician communications and packaging, and condone aggressively silencing Vioxx's critics.

SUGGESTIONS FOR PROFESSIONALS AND MANAGERS

Professionals and managers in many large organizations face many of the same dilemmas as do ordinary employees. They do not set policy, and often have only an arm's-length relationship with high-level decision-makers. Rodney Rocha, the main character in our telling of the *Columbia* space shuttle story, is typical. As a middle-management "everyman," he was emboldened by his desire to do the right thing. At the same time, he was intimidated by his aloof or overly career-protective bosses, and ultimately tempted to take the easy way out in spite of the potentially disastrous consequences.

Our suggestions for those caught in the middle begin with the following list for all employees. These suggestions, like those in the previous chapter, are not easy to implement despite the fact that many seem obvious and commonsensical. It is easy to say that Rodney Rocha should have spoken up more forcefully, but it should be clear that it was truly difficult for him to do so. Many people find themselves in a similar position, and if we are to make things better for them and their peers, we must be sympathetic to the difficulty of change as we read the following suggestions.

First and foremost, we shouldn't be bystanders and shouldn't encourage bystander behavior in those around us. An English friend, a head of practice in a National Health Service hospital, changed the ground rules for the young doctors he supervises and whose careers he strongly controls. Instead of rewarding politeness and "sucking-up" behavior, he now demands that they talk back to him by asking tough questions and critiquing his decisions and surgical technique. It's a lot harder for all concerned, and not all the young doctors seem emotionally capable of criticizing him, but everyone is learning more, and they've detected several pitfalls that might otherwise have compromised patient safety.

Second, we should all do what we can to ensure that dissent is encouraged, not repressed, and that the channels of complaint are open. The best time to nurture such practices is when things are going well. When things get ugly, there will be little appetite for candor. If the systems and norms that support dissent are not firmly in place and stress-tested in advance, the likelihood that they will perform in a crisis is low.

Third, we should do what we can to build viable information and reporting systems that widely disseminate risk-related performance information. The more people know what's going on in detail, and the more widely this information is distributed, the more likely it will be that people will do what they are supposed to do, take timely action, and be less tempted to run away from or cover up the facts if things go wrong. According to research, when people's actions go unrecorded, and are therefore undetectable, the chances of shortcuts under pressure rise by a factor of ten.

Fourth, we should not collude in cover-ups, even minor ones. Protecting our colleagues and our institution from minor errors and embarrassments may appear to be in everyone's interests, but such cover-ups may also lead to increased difficulty when it becomes necessary to reveal embarrassing facts later on. NASA had many opportunities to correct the problems with the space shuttle's O-rings but chose to reclassify them as an "acceptable risk" rather than ground the shuttle fleet so that the solid rocket boosters could be redesigned.

In the case of Vioxx, Merck was trapped by its drug's success. While shutting down a potentially hazardous drug late in clinical trials would have been costly and embarrassing, shutting down a blockbuster making $7 million a day is quite another matter and far more difficult, especially if the risk information had been previously available but had not precipitated timely action.

The Vioxx case also reveals the nasty problem of decision-making delays when it comes to risk. What first appears as sensible prudence may later appear to be a cover-up that has unavoidable adverse consequences for the decision-makers. This ethical downward spiral is visible in most of our cases, and is perhaps the most dangerous pitfall of the failure to take the obvious step of rapid and decisive intervention at the first sign of danger.

Fifth, when there is a likely and documentable unacknowledged risk, each of us should assemble our allies and pursue a complaint with the appropriate institutional body. This will offend the loyalty norms of many organizations, but silence raises serious ethical questions that argue for doing it anyway.

If all else fails, we should consider blowing the whistle (with documents).

Those readers working in institutional settings are probably thinking that some of this advice is unrealistic, if not crazy. It is neither, but it is certainly difficult. Like all the managers in government, the military, and private corporations described in these pages, most of us are prisoners of institutional realities that tolerate unacceptable risk in the name of practicality. The fallacy in most organizations is that lowering risks is unacceptably expensive. In fact, not only is it probably much less expensive than people think, over the long term it will probably save money as well as lives.

Our argument for this position stems from the success of the Total Quality Management movement that started in earnest in Japan after World War II and has transformed manufacturing around the world.

The catchphrase is Philip Crosby's mantra that "quality is free." I believe we can say the same thing about avoiding catastrophe.

Avoiding Catastrophe Is Free

Crosby's tagline is an assertion about the positive return on investment from eliminating mistakes. The argument goes that quality failures result in expensive "costs of nonconformance." The cost includes the consequences of repairs, lost production time and other outlays involved in making things right, increased customer support requirements arising from quality problems, and, ultimately, lost sales due to a company's or a product's damaged reputation.

When applied to safety, the logic is equally compelling, and the false assumption that safety and production are antithetical is just as deeply ingrained—and as equally incorrect—as the beliefs about quality that have been completely overturned over the last fifty years. False assumptions about quality are significant contributors to the failure of Ford and General Motors at the hands of the Japanese, and similar incorrect assumptions about safety seem to be a particular problem of governments.

The abysmal performance of the U.S. federal government and the state of Louisiana during the Katrina disaster also reflect the unmistakable truth that the costs of nonconformance were not borne by those who made the decisions in Washington and Baton Rouge. The burden of the deaths, injuries, business and property damage, and emotional costs of the flooding fell largely on the shoulders of the local citizenry, especially those with the fewest resources. Even promised funds and assistance have been slow in coming in the years since, doubtless complicated by the simultaneously spiraling costs of the Iraq War.

The USSR's behavior relative to Chernobyl, Thai Met's decisions regarding tsunamis, and the conduct of many governments during the Asian financial crisis also appear to be part of the same pattern.

The private sector is somewhat better at redressing harm, but primarily after the fact and largely in those cases in which a visible crisis occurs and harm can be proved in court. Vioxx and the BP Texas City refinery explosion precipitated many lawsuits, although it goes without saying that financial settlements can never compensate for the loss of a loved one or a crippling injury. They do, however, tend to have a corrective—though impermanent—influence on corporate policies.

SUGGESTIONS FOR LEADERS

While I am sympathetic to the constraints of folks at the bottom and in the middle of large organizations, I am much less so to those who knowingly establish policies that sacrifice safety and ethical conduct on the altar of short-term results and political expediency. The key to figuring out what to do is realizing that practicalities and shortcuts have costs that inevitably even out in time, and that one's choice is to either pay now or pay later.

Students of history know that progress is irregular, not steady. While many contemporary organizations have embraced the goal of innovation, they pay much less attention to avoiding setbacks, apparently assuming that things can only get better. The United States started off substantially behind the USSR in the space race, but the Mercury and Apollo programs created by the newly minted NASA organization were among America's finest achievements since World War II.

Despite its success—and some say because of it—the manned space program during the shuttle era has been stalled for forty years, starved for resources, hobbled by bureaucracy, and plagued by embarrassing technical setbacks. In contrast, over the same period of time the less glamorous unmanned programs like the Mars Rover have excelled in both their creativity and results. Clearly, one should not assume the continuity of either success or mediocrity.

Along the same lines, after many years of being one of America's most admired and best-managed companies, Merck and its Vioxx debacle cost the drugmaker's shareholders $30 billion in market capitalization, effectively a decade's worth of growth. It took three years for the stock price to recover since the nadir of the crisis when the drug was withdrawn in September 2004. As in the case of Katrina, how can we really put a price tag on so many injuries and needless deaths?

Unfortunately, unless a crisis erupts, in many organizations traditional organizational performance policies largely ignore safety and ethical risks by focusing on short-term, backwards-looking financial indicators. Such measures often encourage imprudent risk-taking, although it takes exceptional candor to admit it. Building financial value is the raison d'être of corporations, the goal of many institutional investors that hold their stock, and the driver of internal reward systems. Reorienting this guidance system is essential if we are to reduce disasters. After the accidental Texas City refinery explosion that killed fifteen workers in March 2005, the Baker Panel recommended that BP adopt a set of "leading indicators" of process safety to reinforce needed changes to its safety culture. That is sage advice for many organizations, since there is no doubt that the old saying "what gets measured gets managed" is more true today than ever.

Unfortunately, as the BP incident exemplifies, leadership is often the originator of the financial, scheduling, or political pressures, and thus is the ultimate source of a significant increase in risk. Many leaders fail to recognize the dangers of monolithic performance targets and budget cuts. The study of many accidents such as Chernobyl and *Challenger* reveals that imposing nonnegotiable performance objectives combined with severe sanctions for failure encourages the violation of safety rules, reporting distortions, and dangerous shortcuts. As many of this book's cases suggest, putting people in no-win performance situations encourages recklessness and fraud, inevitably increasing the chances of a major catastrophe. Leaders must therefore hold themselves accountable for the inadvertent consequences of their management philosophy and tactics.

Kenneth Lay, who founded Enron and built it into the symbol of a modern global corporation that made its money more in the style of Long-Term Capital Management than that of the traditional pipeline company that was its roots, seems an extreme case of an executive who denied the impact of his policies on the organization. Along with Jeffrey Skilling, a jury found Lay guilty in May 2006 of six counts of conspiracy and fraud, and Judge Lake also found him guilty of four counts of bank fraud in a separate trial. (Lay died six weeks after his conviction, and case law required that his indictment and conviction be dismissed because he could not pursue his appeal.)

Despite his conviction and the extensive evidence that he and Skilling had lied to the public about the company's condition and hidden other critical information, Lay insisted to his death that he had done nothing wrong, and that Enron had been brought down by bad publicity. There seems little doubt that Lay's denials—both verbal and psychological—were very much part of Enron's culture, and they created the foundation for its extensive misdeeds.

A related warning—one that Lay might well have been wise to heed—is to be wary of excessive optimism. That is an extraordinarily difficult challenge, since there is an almost unstoppable temptation to inflate proposals to make them appear more attractive. Excessive optimism puts every proposal—often including the current do-nothing case—in the domain of gains. Like humorist Garrison Keillor's Lake Wobegon, in corporate and government planning no project comes in late or over budget, there are no accidents, and all proposals are "above average." Sometimes, pessimism is necessary: The domain of losses invites more aggressive remedies. Often, as we have seen in this book's many cases, admitting mistakes and accepting the need for radical solutions are essential.

The second major piece of leadership advice is to pay scrupulous attention to design. The likelihood that things will go wrong is closely connected to the design of the organization's equipment, software, training programs, maintenance procedures, and hazard defense systems. While human error plays a role in accidents, its influence can be dramatically reduced by first-class hardware, well-designed systems, and effective training. When design is faulty, accidents happen. *In organizational settings, accidents are never "accidental": They are inevitably the result of faulty management, particularly the management of safety.*

The third piece of advice, therefore, is for leaders to systematize paying attention to near misses, weak signals, and assessments of engineers and safety officials. This vigilance is difficult for those at the top because bureaucracies filter bad news, often letting leaders know of worrisome conditions only when a crisis erupts. People fervently want to believe that the seriousness of the problem is indicated by the intensity of its warning, and that causes and consequences will be visibly linked in space and time. As we have repeatedly seen, clear patterns of causation are often not evident in complex systems, and weak signals may be the only warnings one has.

To compensate, *leaders have to create monitoring systems, systematic review procedures, and independent information channels that do not report through the operational chain of command.* While safety and risk management is perfectly compatible with efficient operations over the long term, it often runs contrary to it in the short term, especially if there have been long periods of neglect. For organizations under performance pressure, getting reliable and unfiltered information through the chain of command can be all but impossible.

The fourth idea is to recognize that while every organization tolerates some dissent, on certain subjects it does not. Only leaders can eliminate these "undiscussables." Without adequate protections for naysayers and internal whistle-blowers, widespread bystander behavior is inevitable. Various whistle-blower protections in government and industry have been enacted, although advocates and research suggest that they are less effective than necessary because they tend to focus on the substance of the accusation rather than on the retaliation against whistle-blowers and the consequent chilling effects on truth-telling. If leaders want to be informed in a timely manner about risks and malfeasance, they have to protect the people who do the telling and severely punish or remove those who would silence them.

The fifth suggestion is to create effective contingency plans for serious but low-probability risks. As revealed by the Katrina disaster, it is in the very nature of large-scale catastrophes to be overtaken by events. Just as in our role as individuals described previously, it is essential to avoid doing all one's thinking in real time, especially in light of the delays when moving information up the line or coordinating separate stovepiped channels within an organization. Research suggests that the combination of situational unfamiliarity, time pressure, and poor information is lethal—it increases the chances of an accident by nearly two thousand times.

When combined with a sensitivity to weak signals, extensive preparation plus on-the-ground debugging can be remarkably effective in reducing adverse consequences. Just weeks before the July 7 bombings, London's emergency services had staged a full-dress rehearsal on city streets. If not for that practice run, it seems likely that emergency response would not have been as rapid or effective, although many problems still remained. When it comes to complex coordination tasks, there is simply no substitute for real-world war games to create familiarity, establish coordination mechanisms, and flush out procedural and technical bugs.

An equally elaborate exercise is going on today at the U.S. Centers for Disease Control and Prevention in Atlanta. The focus is avian flu, although the organizational learning will doubtless be more far-reaching. Since early 2007, the CDC has been engaging in detailed ongoing live-action simulation to train its staff, confront organizational and procedural problems, and come to terms with policy trade-offs. For example, should all inbound flights to the United States from countries with outbreaks and sick passengers be diverted to specialized facilities to be medically screened? While screening all potential disease carriers seems a cautious preventive step to reduce the chances of infection, diverting flights might be premature and would certainly cause public panic and trigger financial market reactions with global economic repercussions.

The simulation focuses on dealing with such complex issues—with scenarios and contingencies—not with finding "right answers," which often don't exist, since each situation is likely to be different.

In planning for climate change, the Netherlands is once again taking the lead preparing for a possible crisis. After a flood that devastated the country in 1953, the Dutch created the Delta Project, the most elaborate flood-control system in the world. Now, in recognition of even greater risks from climate change, they are addressing the nation's vulnerability once again with characteristic zeal and innovation. Of course, the Dutch people's rare enduring awareness of their lowcountry's vulnerability contributes to their willingness to cooperate in this effort despite the extraordinary expense. Nevertheless, others can learn from their ability to think about and respond to long-term risks.

Sixth, every organization requires robust, independent watchdogs. Actions that make watchdogs more "client-centered" and "efficient" run serious risks of reducing their effectiveness. As evidenced by cases such as Andersen, Chernobyl, *Columbia*, and Vioxx, the critical question is this: Which is more important, watchdog efficiency or avoiding low-probability disasters? Watchdogs are not consultants; they are a form of insurance whose benefits may not appear directly in the short-term P&L. While there are certainly ways to effectively utilize watchdog feedback and therefore amortize some of the costs, there is no substitute for regulatory independence. In the long run, we tend to get the protection we pay for.

Finally, and perhaps most important, leadership must subject itself to relentless review and self-criticism. The most difficult challenge for any leadership team is learning from experience without defensiveness and denial. The U.S. Army and many private companies employ a method called the After Action Review that focuses on correct and incorrect actions at every rank. Proponents believe that constancy of the process (rather than conventional postmortems that focus only on reviewing mistakes) combined with critiques at all levels (as opposed to leaving out top management) vastly improves results. When the top is immune from fact-based criticism, there is very little organizational learning.

CONCLUSION: AN OPPORTUNITY, NOT A PROBLEM

Relabeling problems as opportunities has become a cliché in many organizations. Yet, there is wisdom in that semantic legerdemain if the recasting is done with a true shift in our mental framework. Such shifts are never easy, but can have real benefits in organizations that embrace them.

The first big mental shift is accepting the inevitability of accidents and catastrophes without giving in to them. Not even once. Whenever tragedy strikes—a child falls down the stairs at school and is seriously injured, as mine was—people always ask "what if?" The dilemma is that asking what-if after the fact is useful only if it turns into disciplined action. As I can tell you from experience, asking what-if would have been much more valuable before my son's accident. Ironically, while he has learned the hard way always to hold on to the banister and that the stairs are not for games, the free lesson from my son's accident has not been picked up by many of his classmates or their parents, despite my frequent reminders.

As I write this, it appears that at least one organization detailed in this book has learned from experience. The following comes from a *New York Times* article discussing NASA's response to foam hitting the underside of the shuttle *Endeavour*, in comparison with its response to the similar problem with *Columbia*: "Confronted with the same kind of problem that doomed the space shuttle *Columbia*, NASA officials, chastened by years of criticism and upheaval in the agency, took a markedly different approach during the current mission of the *Endeavour*, calling on an array of new tools and procedures to analyze and respond to the problem." It is inspiring to know that organizations can change. Still, we may ask, why wait until after a disaster strikes?

The second big mental shift is appreciating the difference between new ideas and unpracticed old ones. The former is what many people *think* will create the most value for them because "new must be better." The latter, in contrast, is often where the bulk of the value actually lies. One of the guilty secrets of my forty years of organizational consulting is that the most useful advice has often been drawn from classic ideas, not from freshly minted theory. That doesn't mean there is no value in new ideas; it's simply that the accumulated value of the tried and true is far, far greater than that contained in many trendy articles, best-sellers, and consulting sales pitches.

The fact is that just because people have been previously exposed to advice and theory does not mean that they practice it, especially if the advice is counterintuitive, is emotionally difficult to implement, or involves short-term sacrifices in productivity. Sound advice, delivered in context and tailored to the specific situation, is usually all that is needed. Newness, per se, is less often necessary than many people think.

What does that mean for accidents? In modern life, people often look for fast and easy answers to difficulties. Sometimes, their wishes are even fulfilled. Not that long ago, mankind spent the vast majority of its time paying attention just to basic survival. Life was hard and dangerous, and accidents and disease were inevitable and usually meant death or lifelong infirmity. While many people on our planet still have such problems, some of us in the "advanced" societies do not.

For institutional leaders among those more fortunate, the question is simple: Is the safety of one's workforce, customers, and community sufficiently important to mandate significant change? It seems likely that such change can be justified by the prospect of positive return on investment, leave alone other real benefits to people's health and safety. It is true, of course, that to make the numbers work, organizations must acknowledge the costs of low-probability accidents and take some responsibility for wider harm that may exceed their legal liability. Mostly, though, the decision rests on the degree to which we want our institutional legacy to be written in broad or in narrow terms.

What kind of leader do you want to be?

AFTERWORD: WHEN THE LEADERS ARE THE PROBLEM

Daniel Ellsberg

Dr. Gerstein's final chapter has given guidelines for leaders on how they might avert the kinds of catastrophes described in this book. It would be good for society (and all organizations) if more leaders exhibited this kind of concern and followed the suggestions he gives.

However, in my own experience in government, and in my study of national security policy catastrophes in the decades since, I have come to believe that the most dangerous practices in the national security realm reflect priorities, in general, that are set by top officials: getting reelected, avoiding condemnation for past actions, or other political or bureaucratic objectives. Those priorities generally take great precedence over safety or preventing public harm.

The behavior of the people down below in the hierarchy is generally responsive to those priorities, because the way for them to keep their jobs and get ahead is self-evidently to conform to the priorities of their superiors, and especially the top boss. It isn't as though the lower people in the organization themselves profit by adopting those priorities over other priorities, such as safety. But they want to keep their jobs, and they keep them by delivering to their superiors what they want. And what those superiors often want is help in avoiding or concealing documentation of warnings or recommendations that might convict them, on later examination, of self-interest or recklessness in choosing or continuing policies that failed.

Many of the examples in this book involve leaders consciously gambling with other people's lives, on a catastrophic scale. In the case of *Challenger*, there was only a single instance when the engineers from Morton Thiokol, who had to sign off on the launch, tried to stop it. It wasn't as though they were Chicken Littles, always getting in the way and making trouble. Launches were routinely being postponed for a day, but not by the Thiokol engineers. So that was an unprecedented warning by them. Yet the decision-makers went ahead.

You don't have to be especially sympathetic to the decision-makers in these cases to assume that they didn't consciously desire the disastrous outcomes that arose. That's generally obvious. But the public tends to accept as a corollary: "No reasonable, decent person could have consciously *risked* this outcome if they recognized it was a serious possibility."

That is a very plausible assumption. It expresses our deeply ingrained sense of ourselves and other human beings. But it is wrong. It is a widely held misunderstanding of the way we ordinary humans act in organizational settings, either in positions of power and responsibility, or as subordinates. Officials who have a public responsibility to make responsible choices do take reckless, unreasonable risks, more often and on a greater scale than most outsiders can even imagine. That fact is unfamiliar because, to avoid accountability and blame, those same officials conceal it, and direct their subordinates to cover it up; and the subordinates do so, again for understandable (though not admirable) career motives, acting as bystanders while risky gambles are undertaken. Dr. Gerstein focuses especially on the latter behavior, that of subordinates. Let me add some reflections on the behavior of the leaders.

What Dr. Gerstein shows is that reasonable people, who are not malicious, and whose intent is not to kill or injure other people, will nonetheless risk killing vast numbers of people. And they will do it predictably, with awareness. The Merck officials knew they were risking vast numbers of lives with Vioxx. So did the decision-makers responsible for protecting New Orleans. They knew the risks from the beginning, at every stage. In these and other cases, the responsible decision-makers may have underrated the risks in their own minds, but they knowingly took great efforts to conceal evidential data, at the time and later, from those who might judge differently.

In most of the cases in this book—*Challenger*, Katrina, Vioxx, *Columbia*, Chernobyl, Andersen—the leaders chose, in the face of serious warnings, to consciously take chances that risked disaster. What are the circumstances under which leaders take these kinds of gambles? My own experience and research suggests, very often, the following answer: when the potentially disastrous gamble offers the possibility of avoiding loss altogether, coming out even or a little ahead; and when the alternative to taking the gamble assures the certainty of loss in the short run—a loss that impacts the leader personally.

The sure loss that is rejected may appear small or even trivial to an observer, compared with the much greater damage, perhaps societally catastrophic, that is risked and often subsequently experienced. The latter damage, however, may be to "other people," outside the decision-maker's organization or even nation, and inflicted in "the long run": thus, less easily attributed to this decision-maker, who may well have moved on by the time of the disaster. In effect, the decision-maker acts as if a sure, short-term loss to his own position—a perceived failure, risking his job or reelection or his influence—were *comparably* disastrous to a possible social catastrophe that costs many lives: an avoidable war, a widely used drug that proves to have lethal side effects, a dangerous product, the explosion of a nuclear plant or space vehicle.

In the leader's eyes, both of these outcomes are "disasters." One of them, resulting from a particular course of action, is sure to occur. The other is uncertain, a possibility under another course of action, though perhaps very likely—and it is combined with the possibility, not available with the other course, of coming out even or perhaps ahead, winning or at least not losing. In choosing the latter option, he sees himself as accepting the possibility of a loss—in the hope of coming out even—rather than accepting a *certainty* of a failure, defeat. It seems—and it is so presented to him by some advisers—a simple, inescapable decision, "no real choice": the possibility of winning, or at least of avoiding or postponing defeat, versus a "no-win" course of action or, worse, a sure loss in the short run. He and these advisers simply ignore the fact that the scale of the respective losses, and who it is that mainly suffers them, are vastly different in the two courses. (I observed this bureaucratically over and over in Vietnam, and it is evident in current advocacy of occupying Iraq or attacking Iran.)

It was, in fact, the experimental work on choice by Kahneman and Tversky described by Dr. Gerstein that led me to recognize the frequency of the above choice-context, and of the resulting choice of a gamble involving possible catastrophe, as a common precursor to organizational or social disaster. In particular, these researchers' discovery of the special salience given to "sure" outcomes, and of the greater strength of the impulse to avoid any loss—relative to some chosen benchmark—than to increase one's gain, led me to understand in a new way otherwise baffling decisions that have led to major catastrophes in national security.

Applying hypotheses suggested by this research to decisions—including the escalation of the Vietnam War (in which I participated personally, on a staff level), the decision to invade and occupy Iraq, and to serious, secret threats to initiate nuclear war in more than a dozen crises—I have been forced to the following unhappy conclusion (which applies, on a smaller but still tragic scale, to many of the examples in this book): Men in power are willing to risk any number of human lives to avoid an otherwise certain loss to themselves, a sure reversal of their own prospects in the short run.

That grim proposition sounds extreme, I would say, largely because of near-universal and effective efforts to conceal the organizational decision-making data on alternatives and prospects that would reveal such preferences. Failure to conceal these data would point to culpability, recklessness, perhaps criminality on the part of specific decision-makers or a whole organizational team. Results could range from embarrassment, loss of prestige and influence, to expulsion from job or office, the downfall of an administration, even a prison sentence. The cover-up to avoid such accountability is usually successful. Hence, specific disasters—when the gambles are lost—appear to the public as shocking, inexplicable surprises. (And the public mistakenly infers, as it is meant to, that it appears the same way to the decision-makers involved.)

One lesson of this book is that you will not reduce those risks adequately by action within the firm or government agency. The organization has to be monitored by other organizations that are not under the same management, that don't respond to the same boss. You can set up processes within the organization that make truth-telling, realistic assessments, and warnings of danger somewhat more likely. But that isn't close to being an adequate solution. Subordinates who act like bystanders (to keep their jobs) are indeed part of the problem, as Gerstein argues, but the organization's leaders themselves are the major part.

The most promising solution—in the case of government—is going back to the system that our founders set up. It obviously didn't provide any guarantee, but it was an ingenious system of confronting men of power with other men of power within the system. Checks and balances; investigative powers of Congress, with subpoenas; investigators with some degree of independence from the president; an independent judiciary. All of these are things that you don't have in a dictatorship. They are institutions that leaders such as Vice President Richard Cheney, for one, openly disdain.

These are not just luxuries that make us feel more free and privileged. They are vital safety mechanisms. Democratic, republican, constitutional government of the form invented here, revered at least in principle till recently, is less efficient and decisive than unrestrained executive power in what is effectively an absolute monarchy or dictatorship. Things move less fast, and there are constant complaints that nothing gets done, compared with a "unitary executive," a presidency of unlimited "inherent powers" of the sort that Cheney and his special band of legal advisers prefer and proclaim. But the latter leads straight to a succession of Iraqs. As Tom Paine put it, most wars arise from "the pride of kings."

Similar checks to unaccountable power and secrecy are needed, as Gerstein's case studies show, in nongovernmental organizations and corporations. To mention a spectacular case not covered in this book, where cover-up was even more blatant than in most of Gerstein's examples and the lethal effects even greater (comparable to the death tolls in major wars): Tobacco executives didn't need more truth-telling within their organization to reduce vast dangers to the public. (For a recent account, see *The Cigarette Century* by Allan M. Brandt.) They were busily engaged in muffling every subordinate who brought up any warning, and preventing or neutralizing any warning by outsiders. All the major tobacco CEOs perjured themselves when they said in sworn testimony before Congress that "We have no knowledge that our product is carcinogenic, or that we market it to minors, or that it is addictive." That was clear-cut perjury in every case, quite apart from the arguable criminality and certain lethality of their practices. Yet not one of them has been brought up on criminal charges, or even contempt of Congress.

Such indictments would be useful. It would save lives in the future if not only figures such as Jeffrey Skilling of Enron but also, more important, a lot of other leaders who take and conceal risks to the lives of others were to be indicted or impeached and subjected to criminal prosecution, if convicted, prison.

But above all, we need more whistle-blowers from within. Their truth-telling to outside authorities and audiences is essential. And the only way to get it—since dangers to their own careers in their organizations cannot be eliminated—is to somehow encourage them to accept those risks, for the benefit of others.

Is that asking the impossible? Difficult, unusual, unlikely, yes: yet it is humanly possible, and essential. Humans have the capability for great concern, altruism, and even self-sacrifice in the interest of others outside their immediate families and teams, and they very often show it: only not often enough, indeed quite rarely, in their official roles within organizations. Unfortunately, as human beings, we also all have the capability of being selective in our concern, and of being manipulated in our selectivity of concern by our leaders and colleagues in our groups.

A major reason for the occurrence of disasters is that, as humans, we often choose keeping our job, protecting our reputation, getting promoted, maintaining our access to inside information, getting reelected, assuring college education for our children, preserving our marriage, and holding on to our house in a nice neighborhood—all considerations that are neither trivial nor discreditable for any of us— over actions, including truth-telling to the public, that would risk some of these but which could potentially save vast numbers of other people's lives.

I would like readers to realize—and this book has great potential for alerting them—that there may well come times when the amount of harm they could avert by speaking out could well outweigh the personal harm they might suffer by doing so, great though that might be.

When I released the Pentagon Papers in 1971, former senator Wayne Morse told me that if I had given him those documents at the time of the Tonkin Gulf Resolution in 1964 (when I had many of them in my office safe in the Pentagon), "The Resolution would never have gotten out of committee. And if it had been brought to a vote, it would never have passed." That's a heavy burden to bear. But scores of other officials, perhaps a hundred, could have given those documents to the Senate as well as I.

More recently, any one of a hundred people within the government could have averted the Iraq War by telling the public—with documents—what they knew about the lies the president was feeding the public. Yet no one did. A middle manager or even lower-level person could have saved the *Challenger*, or rung the bell on Vioxx. Shouldn't one of them have done it, or more than one? Every one of the stories Dr. Gerstein tells could have had a happier ending if his book, existing earlier, had inspired one person in the respective organization—at the top, bottom, or in between—to act with moral courage.

When confronted with potential looming catastrophes, people within large organizations often think, *Somebody else will take care of this. And surely the top people know more than I do. It's their job to take care of it, and surely they will.* The truth is, there's no likelihood at all that the leaders will take care of it. If readers who find themselves facing organizational disasters realize, perhaps from this book, *It's up to me, and if I don't do it, it's probably not going to get done. The others aren't going to do it. Maybe I'm the one who needs to do it,* some may be more willing to take personal risks to avert catastrophes.

Thus, reading this book could change lives. From the examples given, a reader could recognize two things. First, in the words of a Chinese proverb my wife, Patricia, likes to quote: "If you don't change course, you are likely to end up where you are heading." If the course your team, your organization, or your nation is on looks to you as though it is going over a cliff, heading for a disaster, it may well be doing so.

Second, readers should realize, *If I see this, and lots of other people see it, too, it does not follow that somebody else will take care of it. Disasters occur because leaders often choose crazy or dangerous courses and people like me don't rock the boat.* You, the reader, can choose otherwise.

In the situations Dr. Gerstein describes, the leaders do not lack for subordinates giving warnings within the organizational chain of command. The problem is that the warnings are stifled or overridden; subsequently, those who see the dangers and even see them happening keep their silence. My hope is that people reading this book might decide that averting catastrophe can be worth going outside the organization—warning the public, Congress, investigative bodies—and the media directly with documents to back it up. Many individuals inside government and corporations, from low-level clerks to upper managers and cabinet members, have that power—at the risk of their careers, to be sure—to tell the truth, and perhaps to rescue their own organizations or countries from disaster, as well as rescuing other potential victims.

For the last six years, since the Iraq War first approached (and more recently, equally disastrous prospects of attack on Iran), I have been urging patriotic and conscientious insiders who may be in the situation I once was in—holding secret, official knowledge of lies, crimes, and dangers of impending, wrongful, catastrophic wars or escalations—to do what I wish I had done in 1964 or early 1965, years earlier than I did: Go to Congress and the press and reveal the truth, with documents. The personal risks are real, but a war's-worth of lives might be saved.

Daniel Ellsberg
Berkeley, California
July 2007

ACKNOWLEDGMENTS

While the words on these pages are my own, this book is a team effort, and I have been blessed with extraordinary teammates.

Daniel Ellsberg has been a hero of mine since I was in graduate school when he released the Pentagon Papers to the *New York Times* and the *Washington Post*. It is an enormous honor to be working with him on this project. Dan's input on my work raised it to a much higher level, and I am enormously indebted to him for his inspiration and contribution.

Michael Ellsberg worked magic organizing the material, always finding a better way to tell the story. He also has an unerring nose for boredom, and ruthlessly cut away whatever we could do without or was better suited for the Web site, where readers can go for more detail.

Alan Bisbort was another secret weapon, a writer and editor extraordinaire who polished my prose to a fine luster.

Special thanks to my friend and colleague Martin Lloyd-Elliott, who has been invaluable in helping me to understand the psychological and social factors that give rise to biased decision-making. Such factors loom large in the accidents described in these pages, and are a vital consideration in any remedies.

Robert Shaw, managing principal of Princeton MCG, co-wrote the article version of the *Columbia* space shuttle story that eventually became the first chapter of this book. The discussion here of organizational bystanders is as much his thinking as it is mine.

Edgar H. Schein, professor emeritus at the MIT Sloan School of Management, has also been of enormous encouragement in this project, as well as the source of most of my understanding of organizational culture and the need for open inquiry during any change process.

Lee Jacobson of Lee Jacobson Consultants/Brand Producers helped me understand the design process from the inside out, providing an endless series of illustrations of good and bad design. Lee was also a project booster from its earliest beginnings, and a great friend throughout its long evolution.

Scott Love, CEO of AquaMinds, Inc., and my friend of many years, enthusiastically supported this book from its earliest draft, and like me, he is zealous to avoid disasters and minimize their damage. Scott's firm is also the developer of NoteShare, the superb collaborative software that allowed the manuscript to be written and edited across four continents and, at times, thirteen times zones.

My work on this book would have been impossible without the help of many creators of other technical and analytical software. Thanks to Bradley Harden, Maureen Newman, and Michael Trott at Wolfram Research, makers of Mathematica; John Verzani and other members of the vast international open-source community behind R, the statistics and computing platform; the generous folks at The MathWorks, makers of Matlab; Maplesoft, developers of the Maple computer algebra system; Uri Wilensky and his team at Northwestern University, developers of NetLogo; Craig Loehle, creator of RiskQ; Innova Financial Solutions, makers of Derivatives Expert; Palisade software, developers of the @Risk Monte Carlo modeling system; and Daniel H. Fylstra and Duane Lincoln of Frontline Systems, Inc., makers of sophisticated simulation and optimization software.

My colleagues on the board of the Organization Design Forum played an important role in this book's development. They not only provided the encouragement and emotional support every author needs but, by giving me precious airtime at our annual conferences to present my emerging ideas to a wider audience, they provided an opportunity for invaluable field-testing. Thanks to Billie Alban, Dick Axelrod, Mila Baker, Rollin Burhans, Lynn Ernst, Jay Galbraith, Tracy Gibbons, Terri Hill, Christine Irwin, Thomas Jasinski, Amy Kates, Cathy Kuhnau, E. Craig McGee, Barrie Novak, Brenda Price, Lisa Smallwood, Rob Savan, and Stu Winby.

An important group of people also provided support and feedback on the book's ideas and useful comments on the work in progress: Dr. Bruce Handelman, Stephen Hyman, Dr. Frederick Lukash, Benjamin Monderer, David Rose, Myer Rose, and Graeme Stanway.

Margaret Gee, my agent, deserves my endless thanks for seizing upon the potential value of this book from our very first conversation, and for her patience shepherding me and the project through the world of publishing. To fellow author Tony Walker, my warmest thanks for having the good sense to introduce me to Marg.

Philip Turner and Iris Blasi of Union Square Press blessed me with enthusiastic publishing support that really shows in the final product. Philip was excited about the project from the start, and I can only hope that the results satisfy his demanding expectations.

Finally, to my wife, Judi Rose, and son, Jamie—my thanks not only for your love and support during the years it has taken to bring this book to fruition, but also for your enduring faith that it will make the world a safer place for all of us.

NOTES

1. The Bystanders Among Us

page 13 "'If it's not safe, say so'? Yes, it's that serious": *Columbia* Accident Investigation Board Report, vol. 1, p. 157.

page 14 "The shuttle would reenter the earth's atmosphere as scheduled in a little over a week": See *Columbia* Mission Management Team Minutes, January 24, 2003.

Similar stories can be found on large-scale accounting frauds (Barings, Arthur Andersen, and Enron): Andersen was the auditor in several of the largest U.S. bankruptcies and accounting scandals. See chapter 9.

page 18 "'My actions wouldn't have made any difference'": Clarkson, 1996.

page 19 "'I was too low down here in the organization and she's way up here'": ABC News *Prime Time Live*, July 7, 2003.

page 19 "'Oh, Rodney, . . . there's probably nothing we could have done'": *New York Times*, September 26, 2003.

page 19 "certain specific characteristics of the situation . . . strongly affect whether or not people will take action": See Latane and Darley, 1970.

page 21 "insiders may cause dissent to evaporate before it is even expressed": The term *groupthink* was coined by William H. Whyte in 1952. See Irving Janis, 1972, for a full discussion of the concept.

page 21 "accused the Bush administration of manipulating intelligence": See the *New York Times*, July 6, 2003, and Waas, 2007.

2. Human Biases and Distortions

page 23 "A famous psychological experiment . . . based on a description": The material in this chapter is drawn largely from Hastie and Dawes, 2001; Kahneman and Tversky, 2000; Paulos, 1990; and Sutherland, 1992.

page 29 "Juries are often not swayed . . . notorious and well-documented unreliability": See Liptak, *New York Times*, July 23, 2007. Original study reference: Brandon L. Garrett, *Columbia Law Review*, in press.

page 35 "No apparent danger": See Bruce, 2001.

page 40 "Other estimates by statisticians using a different but equally plausible set of assumptions place the estimate even higher": See Good, 1995, and Merz and Caulkins, 1995.

page 41 "a phenomenon recognized by Daniel Ellsberg in 1961": The phenomenon is known as the Ellsberg Paradox because it shows that people are irrationally but consistently willing to violate the laws of traditional utility theory. See Ellsberg, 1961. John Maynard Keynes discussed the same phenomenon forty years earlier. See Keynes, 1962.

page 42 "In fact, people far prefer to bet on their own skills . . . with the same likelihood of success": See Fox and Tversky, 1995.

page 42 "when the performance of experts forms a basis for comparison even though the objective situation is the same": See Howell, 1971.

page 44 "The problem is named after Monty Hall . . . *Let's Make a Deal* for fifteen years": See Stewart, 1997; Gillman, 1992; and *New York Times*, July 21, 1991.

page 46 "'Our brains are just not wired . . . so I'm not surprised there were mistakes'": *New York Times*, July 21, 1991.

page 46 "Humans as 'Paranoid Optimists'": Haselton and Nettle, 2005.

3. Understanding Uncertainty

page 52 "'We, unfortunately, have had that 0.5 percent activity here'": Strock, 2005.

page 53 "as well as any slow-moving Category 3 storm, capable of more damage than a storm of equal intensity that sweeps through quickly": The damage done by hurricanes arises from their ferocious winds, rain, and from the storm surge—the greater sea heights—that overrun the land and, in the case of New Orleans, breach its levees. In addition, flooding may clog or destroy pumping stations and turn floating objects like uprooted trees into battering rams.

page 53 "The key problem with his conclusion originates in the meaning of the interval between storm events used by Strock to define 'flood protection'": The term used in the professional literature is *return period*. It corresponds to the average interval between events of a particular or greater intensity—the same definition we use in the text for a Category 4 or 5 storm.

page 54 "the most frequent intervals between hurricanes . . . do not cluster around a common value but spread out from very small intervals to very large ones": The mathematical model used here (although it does not include long-term hurricane cycles and near-term weather conditions) is a simple geometric distribution that assumes that each hurricane event is independent and has the same likelihood of occurring. The actual hurricane history conforms well to this model, although the less common Category 4 and 5 storms provide little data from which to discern a clear pattern. Hurricane experts use a more complex method to assess return periods for wind, rainfall, and storm surge. See the referenced papers by M. E. Johnson and C. C. Watson Jr. for details.

page 55 "For precisely that reason, our experience can often lead us astray": The underpinnings of these averages are discussed in chapter 5 under the heading "Challenges at the 'Critical Point.'" See also Taleb, 2007.

page 56 "Combining those averages to predict a Category 4 or 5 storm results in . . . four times the frequency Strock quoted": Using their detailed methodology, Johnson and Watson quote a seventy-nine-year return period for ten-and-a-half-foot surges at the Seventeenth Street Canal. This was the height the levee was believed to be breached. (See Johnson and Watson, 2006.) This expansion of the return period from the fifty years used in my model, or the Category 3 SPH storm used by the Corps of Engineers in its own planning, make no difference to the final conclusions presented in the text.

page 58 "for any low-probability disaster . . . there is more than a 60 percent chance that one or more adverse events will occur and only about a 30 percent chance that no adverse events will occur in that period": When using a model based upon the geometric distribution, when the number of periods is the "average interval," the likelihood of the event occurring is always greater than 63 percent, starting from 0.75 with a two-period average. As the probability gets smaller (and the average interval between events gets longer), the probability of one or more events declines, approaching 0.632121..., $1-1/e$. For a probability of 1/50, the probability we have been using for Category 4 or 5 storms in New Orleans based on public data, the likelihood of one or more such storms over fifty years is approximately 0.64.

page 58 "Standard financial discounting creates a 'present value' of the cost of fixing the levee system of about $1.5 billion": Discounting allows you to calculate how expensive a house you can afford to buy today based upon how much you can pay each time period and the prevailing interest rates. The present value is the value of the house. In this case, the yearly payment is $200 million and interest is 5.5 percent, so the starting effective value of the "house"—the flood-control system—is $1.5 billion. It is smaller than the full expenditure of $2 billion because payments made in the future are "discounted" by the effect of interest. Consult any basic finance textbook, such as David G. Luenberger (1998), Stephen A. Ross, et al. (1999), or a reliable Internet source such as MIT's Open Courseware, 15.414 Financial Management, Summer 2003.

page 59 "We can use that number as a single period stand-in . . . were it built all at once at the start": Note that the ratio of the present values are the same as the ratio of the total cash expenditures. This will always be true if the interest rates, time frames, and spending percentages over time are the same for the two sets of cash flows.

4. *Space Shuttle* Challenger

page 71 "in a 1980 NASA report that requested 'additional verification at temperature extremes'": Cook, 2007, p. 396.

page 73 "Clearly, President Reagan and his handlers took public relations and the space shuttle *very* seriously": See Cook, p. 171, in reference to Jane's Spaceflight reporting.

page 76 "An impromptu three-city telephone conference . . . to discuss the issue": See Vaughan, 1996, p. 287.

page 79 "Only one had taken place under relatively cold O-ring conditions": Flight 51C in January 1985 took place under relatively cold conditions at 53 degrees F, while flight 61A in October 1985 was launched at 75 degrees F.

page 85 "there has been considerable criticism in the years since the accident that more evidence could have been mustered than was made available": See Tufte, 1997, pp. 38–53.

page 88 "'Mulloy repeatedly asserted . . . would be proven so when retested'": Cook, p. 42.

page 89 "NASA Public Affairs Director Shirley Green, a political appointee with White House connections": See Cook, p. 465.

page 90 "a relationship the White House stated did not exist": See Cook, p. 469.

5. Chernobyl

page 93 "Beyond the immediate explosion . . . the behavior of governmental authorities compounded the damage done by the accident": The Soviet government forbade taking pictures and videos of the accident and its immediate aftermath, confiscating cameras and film as they discovered them. As a result, there is only a very spotty journalistic record of events.

page 93 "According to the World Health Organization . . . radiation exposure resulting from the Chernobyl accident": There is a voluminous amount of information about the Chernobyl accident. The World Health Organization Web site, for example, contains over 1,300 references. Unfortunately, statistics on health effects vary widely and are highly controversial. Inflation of claims may be related to requests for aid. Equally, there are reasons why governments would try to demonstrate smaller numbers.

page 93 "In particular, nearly five thousand cases of thyroid cancer in children have been reported, according to WHO": See World Health Organization, April 2006.

page 105 "'What this really means . . . hardware and software that operate these systems'": When taken to extremes, of course, pilots can become mere passengers with little to do except look out the window. The original *Mercury 7* astronauts resented being "Spam in a can," reduced to little more than Ham, the space monkey who had preceded Alan Shepard's first flight in May 1961. Unlike Ham and Russian cosmonaut Yuri Gagarin, Shepard was in control of his spacecraft for the entire flight. He is also famous among aviators for a statement known as Shepard's Prayer. Shortly before the launch, he said, "Please, dear God, don't let me fuck up."

page 112 "effectively cut the satellite's life in half": See *Pittsburgh Post-Gazette*, April 24, 1999. This also applies to disasters: Phenomena manifesting power laws also display the type of unusual averages we saw in the Katrina case.

page 115 "Similar monitoring and control failures . . . BP's Texas City refinery calamity of 2005": See BP U.S. Refineries Independent Safety Review Panel report, 2007.

6. The Vioxx Disaster and BP

page 126 "However, company documents produced in court . . . possibly as early as 1996": See Krumholz, et al., 2007, and references therein.

page 127 "Surprisingly, Merck's safety board for the study . . . owned $70,000 worth of Merck stock": See Krumholz, et al.

page 128 "The study also dramatically underscored the elevated risks of Vioxx in comparison with . . . Pfizer's Celebrex": See Graham memo to Paul Seligman, September 30, 2004.

page 129 "'Taken together, these inaccuracies and deletions call into question the integrity of the data on adverse cardiovascular events in this article'": A secondary controversy has erupted as a result of the publication of the VIGOR study. How did the methodological weaknesses in the study fail to attract the attention of the *NEJM*'s peer reviewers?

page 130 "A Spanish court ruled in Laporte's favor": See Laporte, *Butlletí Groc*, juliol–setembre 2003 (in Spanish).

page 130 "Two days after a deposition by Merck critic Dr. Eric Topol, his position of chief academic officer of its medical school had been abolished": Topol is now chief academic officer and chief of genomic medicine and translational science for Scripps Health in California.

page 131 "That is precisely the group about whom Merck's own scientists had been worried": See Topol, 2004.

page 132 "the company has faced legal claims from nearly twenty-seven thousand people": See Krumholz.

page 132 "'Clinical trials prove that Vioxx raises the risk of heart attacks . . . especially when the person had other risk factors like smoking'": Berenson, Alex, "Analysts See Merck Victory in Vioxx Deal," *New York Times*, November 10, 2007, p. A1.

page 137 "In 1992, the agency spent 53 percent of its drug center budget on new drug approvals; by 2003, that had risen to 79 percent": See *New York Times*, December 6, 2004.

page 139 "within the current FDA, the expression of scientific opinions is repressed, reports are censored, and recommendations are ignored": See Wolfe, 2006.

page 140 "Pfizer's Celebrex . . . increasing Merck's marketing urgency": The final story about COX-2 drugs such as Vioxx and Celebrex is still being investigated. In a March 1, 2007 editorial, the *New York Times* stated, "The evidence has gotten even stronger that the COX-2 inhibitors—Celebrex is the only one left on the market in this country—increase the risk of heart attacks and strokes." The American Heart Association recommends a hierarchy of pain medicines, with the COX-2 drugs at the least desirable end of the list. In April 2007, Pfizer was criticized by Dr. Sydney Wolfe, a regular critic of the drug industry, for TV advertising that falsely suggested that its drug Celebrex provided effective pain relief plus the benefits of fewer gastrointestinal side effects, but without any more cardiovascular risk than older NSAID painkillers. Pfizer claimed that Wolfe's criticisms were factually incorrect.

page 142 "The British Petroleum Texas City Refinery Fire": An excellent retrospective look at BP's deteriorating safety record appears in the *Financial Times*, December 18–19, 2006. The *Houston*

Chronicle covered the story on an almost daily basis throughout 2005. "The Report of the BP U.S. Refineries Independent Safety Review Panel," January 1, 2007, provides an excellent and detailed summary of the U.S. government investigation, and the U.S. Chemical Safety and Hazard Investigation Board provided various reports and Webcasts regarding the explosion on its Web site www.chemsafety.gov.

page 144 "'nor any independent means of understanding the deteriorating standards in the plant'": *Daily Telegraph* (London), December 10, 2005.

7. When All the Backups Failed

page 146 "killing all twenty-six people aboard": See Andrus, 1994 and U.S. House of Representatives Subcommittee on Immigration and Claims, Committee on the Judiciary, 1998.

page 165 "Evidence suggests that this AWACS crew had inconsistent performance records": See Piper, 2000.

8. Butterfly Wings and Stone Heads

page 171 "Rather, the second computer run diverged . . . different starting conditions": See Gleick, 1988.

page 172 "Lorenz's weather model . . . the actual starting point appears totally irrelevant": In Lorenz's model, and in deterministic chaos in general, all the results are completely predictable since they are based on a sequential series of mathematical calculations that always come out the same. The issue is that small changes to a given starting point cause the sequence of values that is generated by the model to diverge markedly from those of nearby starting points. After a time (that depends on the formula being used), the starting point appears to be irrelevant, although it is not, of course, since the starting point exactly determines every subsequent value in the series.

page 172 "One of the greatest innovations of the last three hundred years is the mathematics of differential equations": Differential equations express deterministic relationships involving some continuously changing quantities and their rates of change. For example, in classical physics the motion of a body is described by its position and its velocity over time. Newton's Laws relate the position, velocity, acceleration, and forces acting on the body through a differential equation whose solution describes the body's motion over time.

page 172 "the type of phenomena that Lorenz and other chaos-hunters would soon discover": Lorenz did not discover sensitive dependence on initial conditions. It was articulated by Hadamard, Durhem, and Poincaré around the turn of the nineteenth century, and Poincaré even articulated the specific case of meteorology. Such gaps in the continuity of scientific thinking are fairly common, especially across disciplines—as Lorenz's own discoveries exemplify.

page 174 "has been extending the simulation work by Mitchell Resnick of the MIT Media Lab": See Wilensky, 1998, and Resnick, 1998.

page 182 "Here's how Robin Hood worked": *New York Times*, October 7, 2004. For more detail see Hoxby and Kuziemko, 2004.

page 183 "Over the decade that Robin Hood was in effect, $81 billion in property wealth eroded": The GAO estimate of the cost of the S&L crisis was $160 billion, not including interest. This makes Robin Hood about half the cost—very high in the ranking of financial mismanagements. See *Washington Post*, July 13, 1996.

page 183 "Texas's lawmakers managed to destroy as much value as they might ever have hoped to create": Of course, in some ways this is an unfair criticism, since a great deal of the capital loss may be unrealized. Like the fall of stock market values during a recession, only those who actually sell their assets for cash (or exchange them for assets uncorrelated with market values) will actually lose value. Nevertheless, the depression of property values cannot be a good outcome for property owners, and we must assume that many Texans are unhappy about what Robin Hood has done to their net worth. They will be even more upset if property values do not recover, or take an unusually long time to do so.

9. The Collapse of Arthur Andersen

page 192 "The Andersen case . . . provides a veritable picture window of how these processes can go tragically wrong": The facts of the Andersen case are drawn from Toffler, 2003; Eichenwald, 2005; and other sources.

page 193 "Companies do not wish to divulge their secrets . . . the reporting demands of the public stock market are not always the best route to success for all firms": Sometimes making changes out of public view and absent the pressures of quarterly financial reporting can be more effective, especially if a period of poor and unpredictable results—both anathema in the public markets—are likely.

page 194 "came to a crashing halt . . . under the Securities and Exchange Commission's Rule 2(e)": See Lyke, 2002.

page 195 " 'They travel in packs. It's pretty much impossible to hire just one of them' ": Confidential communication with the author during a consulting engagement.

page 202 "Although it was too late to save the firm, the U.S. Supreme Court unanimously overturned Andersen's conviction in 2005 due to ambiguities in jury instructions": The reversal rests on the interpretation of the phrase in the law relating to "knowingly . . . corruptly persuad[ing]" a person to withhold documents from the government. The Court ruled that it was necessary for the jury to determine that there was knowledge of wrongdoing on the part of Andersen, a requirement that was not specified in the jury instructions.

page 203 "Carl Bass . . . after objecting to some of Enron's accounting practices": See Toffler, p. 212, and *New York Times*, June 17, 2002.

page 204 " 'That was a risk that the Andersen partners were simply unwilling to take' ": Eichenwald, 2005, p. 426.

10. When Countries Go Bankrupt

page 210 "Albert W. Tucker, who prepared it for a seminar in 1950": Tucker's work was based on work done by Merril Flood and Melvin Dresher in the late 1940s.

page 211 "the pursuit of self-interest . . . significantly reduce their overall net gain": The mutual defection in the single-round non-cooperative version of the game is known as a Nash equilibrium, named after mathematician John Nash; he won a Nobel Prize for it. While not optimum by any means, the Nash equilibrium solution is the best that either party can do when they act independently and simultaneously in recognition of what the other party can do.

page 212 "A bank run is *multiparty prisoner's dilemma*, or MPD": See Schelling, 1978.

page 212 "This conflict between self-interest and restraint was precisely the dilemma facing the foreign holders of unhedged East Asian debt, as we will see": Debt obligations can be hedged against currency devaluations through bank agreements or financial market transactions such as currency forward contracts or swaps. There is always a cost to such insurance.

page 215 "'So financial globalization . . . resolving them quickly when they occur'": Camdessus, October 6, 1995.

page 216 "Beyond that, according to *The Economist*": See *Economist*, March 7, 1998.

page 216 "when the swaps needed to be paid off . . . the crisis would be over": Swaps are a form of derivative contract. In this case, they were used by the Thai government to exchange baht for dollars over a particular time period. As a contract, they did not have to be officially reported—a form of so-called off-balance-sheet transaction.

page 221 "'giving credit where blame might be due'": Robert Rubin's quote appears in Norris, *New York Times*, January 25, 1998.

page 224 "'at least a chance of getting its economic act together'": Blustein, 2001, p. 263.

page 227 "even the interest rate spreads between similar U.S. government bonds irrationally widened to unprecedented levels": A newly issued thirty-year U.S. Treasury bond might trade at a slight premium—five to six basis points (a basis point is one one-hundredth of a percentage point)—to a similar bond issued two years before. During the crisis, these spreads widened to thirty basis points or more.

page 233 "opened their doors to opportunistic 'hot money' without putting adequate controls in place": See Hellman, et al., 2000, and Stiglitz, 2003.

page 237 "last longer than the historical crises of developing nations": See Bordo and Eichengreen, 1999.

page 238 "We have seen that unrestrained self-interest . . . and many proposals have been put forward to do so": See Radelet et al., 1998; Furman, et al., 1998; Palley, 2006; Stiglitz, 2003.

page 238 "'For our countries, the problem is as serious as ever'": *Los Angeles Times*, August 17, 1992.

page 238 "Unregulated banking leads to economic chaos . . . over the decades": See Bernstein, 1994.

page 239 "Evidence suggests that exchange rates can remain far from equilibrium levels": See Palley, 2006, p. 18.

page 239 "spending/credit dependency leads to a structural instability in the U.S. economy": See Palley for the argument that a deep and sustained recession in the United States could well lead to serious global consequences and a protracted recovery.

11. What Have We Learned? What Can We Do?

page 245 "'Some government officials told me that I destroyed the tourism industry in Thailand'": See transcript of *PBS Newshour with Jim Lehrer*, November 21, 2005.

page 252 "The Axis side . . . at least ten times the casualty and MIA rates as the Allies": These are problematic statistics because of the many German deserters who abandoned their posts when the war was lost, and over 250,000 POWs that died in the hands of the Russians.

page 261 "Also, using taxpayers' money in this manner primarily benefits the affluent who live near the ocean at the expense of the majority who do not": See Lewis, 2007.

12. Advice for Leaders

page 280 "it increases the chances of an accident by nearly two thousand times": See Reason, 1997, p. 142.

page 281 "addressing the nation's vulnerability once again with characteristic zeal and innovation": See Talbot, 2007.

page 282 "the After Action Review that focuses on correct and incorrect actions at every rank": See Gerstein, 1997.

SOURCES

Government Reports and Government-Sponsored Studies

Andrus, James G. "AFR 110-14 Aircraft Accident Investigation Board Report of Investigation: U.S. Army Black Hawk Helicopters 87-26000 and 88-26060." U.S. Air Force, 1994.

Bern, Linda. "Frances Oldham Kelsey: FDA Medical Reviewer Leaves Her Mark on History." U.S. Food and Drug Administration, FDA consumer magazine, March–April 2001.

BP U.S. Refineries Independent Safety Review Panel. The Report of the BP U.S. Refineries Independent Safety Review Panel, January 1, 2007.

Camdessus, Michel. Remarks at a Conference on Banking Crises in Latin America Organized by the Inter-American Development Bank and the Group of 30, Washington, D.C., October 6, 1995, www.imf.org.

Columbia Accident Investigation Board. "Columbia Accident Investigation Board, Report Volume 1," August 2003.

"The Failure of the New Orleans Levee System During Hurricane Katrina." Team Louisiana Forensic Levee Investigation, March 2007, www.publichealth.hurricane.lsu.edu/TeamLA.htm.

Fisher, Louis. "National Security Whistleblowers." Congressional Research Service, Library of Congress, Order Code RL33215, December 30, 2005.

Graham, David J. "Risk of Acute Myocardial Infarction and Sudden Cardiac Death in Patients Treated with COX-2 Selective and Non-Selective NSAIDs." U.S. Food and Drug Administration, FDA internal memorandum to Paul Seligman, acting director, Office of Drug Safety, September 30, 2004.

Johnson, Mark E., and Charles C. Watson Jr. "Return Period Estimation of Hurricane Perils in the Caribbean." USAID-OAS Caribbean Disaster Mitigation Project, April 1999.

Kaliatka, Algirdas, and Eugenijus Uspuras. "Ignalina RBMK-1500. A Source Book." Ignalina Safety Analysis Group, Lithuanian Energy Institute, 1998, www.lei.lt/insc/sourcebook/introext.html.

Little, Richard G. "Controlling Cascading Failure: Understanding the Vulnerabilities of Interconnected Infrastructures." National Research Council Board on Infrastructure and the Constructed Environment, December 7, 2006.

Lyke, Bob. "Auditing and Its Regulators: Reforms After Enron." Congressional Research Service, CRS Web Order Code RS21120, September 3, 2002.

NASA. "Columbia Mission Management Team Minutes, 1/24/03." Mission Management Team Transcripts, July 22, 2003, www.nasa.gov/columbia/foia/index.html.

"Performance Evaluation of the New Orleans and Southeast Louisiana Hurricane Protection System." Final Report of the Interagency Performance Evaluation Task Force (IPET), Interim Final, U.S. Army Corps of Engineers, March 26, 2007, https://ipet.wes.army.mil.

Relyea, Harold C. "Security Classified and Controlled Information: History, Status, and Emerging Management Issues." Congressional Research Service, Report for Congress RL33494, June 26, 2006.

Research Triangle Institute. "Consequences of Whistleblowing for the Whistleblower in Misconduct in Science Cases." Research Triangle Institute, Contract No. 282-92-0045, October 30, 1995.

Seed, R. B., et al. "Investigation of the Performance of the New Orleans Flood Protection Systems in Hurricane Katrina on August 29, 2005." U.S. Geological Survey, July 31, 2006, http://walrus.wr.usgs.gov/geotech/katrina.

Snell, V. G., and J. Q. Howieson. "Chernobyl—A Canadian Perspective." Atomic Energy of Canada Limited, August 1991.

Strock, Lt. Gen. Carl. "Defense Department Special Briefing on Efforts to Mitigate Infrastructure Damage from Hurricane Katrina (transcript)." U.S. Department of Defense, September 2, 2005, www.defenselink.mil/transcripts/transcript.aspx?transcriptid=2070.

U.S. Chemical Safety and Hazard Investigation Board. Various reports and Webcasts regarding BP America Refinery Explosion Texas City, TX, March 23, 2005, www.chemsafety.gov.

U.S. Congress House Government Reform Committee Subcommittee on National Security. Hearing on "Emerging Threats and

International Relations." Testimony of William G. Weaver representing the National Security Whistleblowers Coalition, February 14, 2006.

U.S. Congress, Office of Technology Assessment. "Who Goes There: Friend or Foe?" U.S. Government Printing Office, OTA-ISC-537, June 1, 1993.

U.S. Congress, Senate Committee on Finance. Hearing on "FDA, Merck and Vioxx: Putting Patient Safety First?" Testimony of Gurkirpal Singh, M.D., November 18, 2004.

————. Hearing on "FDA, Merck and Vioxx: Putting Patient Safety First?" Testimony of David J. Graham, M.D., November 18, 2004.

U.S. Fire Administration, FEMA, Department of Homeland Security. A Profile of Fire in the United States 1992–2001. October 2004.

U.S. Food and Drug Administration. "Taste of Raspberries, Taste of Death: The 1937 Elixir Sulfanilamide Incident." FDA consumer magazine, June 1, 1981.

————. "Food and Drug Administration Effect of User Fees on Drug Approval Times, Withdrawals, and Other Agency Activities." Government Accounting Office, GAO-02-958, September 1, 2002.

————. Improvement Needed in FDA's Postmarket Decision-Making and Oversight Process. Government Accountability Office, GAO-06-402, March 1, 2006.

U.S. Government Centers for Disease Control. "Nonfatal Choking-Related Episodes Among Children—United States, 2001." CDC 51(42), October 25, 2002.

U.S. House of Representatives Subcommittee on Immigration and Claims, Committee on the Judiciary. "Operation Provide Comfort: Review of U.S. Air Force Investigation of Black Hawk Fratricide Incident." June 18, 1998.

U.S. Nuclear Regulatory Commission. "Fact Sheet: The Accident at Three Mile Island." NRC, www.nrc.gov/reading-rm/doc-collections/fact-sheets/3mile-isle.pdf.

World Health Organization. "Health Effects of the Chernobyl Accident: An Overview." World Health Organization, Fact Sheet No. 303, April 2006.

Books, Journals, and Magazines

Amram, Martha, and Nalin Kulatilaka, *Real Options: Managing Strategic Investment in an Uncertain World.* Cambridge, Mass.: Harvard Business School Press, 1999.

Anderson, Philip, and Michael Tushman. "Technological Discontinuities and Dominant Designs: A Cyclical Model of Technological Change." *Administrative Science Quarterly* (December 1990).

Arthur, W. Brian. *Increasing Returns and Path Dependence in the Economy.* Ann Arbor: University of Michigan Press, 2000.

Baciu, Alina, Kathleen Stratton, and Sheila P. Burke. "The Future of Drug Safety: Promoting and Protecting the Health of the Public." Advance copy. *Institute of Medicine* (September 26, 2006).

Baker, Tom. "On the Genealogy of Moral Hazard." *Texas Law Review* (December 1996).

Barry, John M. *Rising Tide: The Great Mississippi Flood of 1927 and How It Changed America.* New York: Simon and Schuster, 1998.

BBC. "The Mystery of Easter Island [transcript]." *BBC Horizon,* January 3, 2003, www.bbc.co.uk/science/horizon/2003/easterislandtrans.shtml.

Beckhard, Richard, and Wendy Pritchard. *Changing the Essence: The Art of Creating and Leading Fundamental Change in Organizations.* San Francisco: Jossey-Bass, 1992.

Bernstein, Michael A. "The Contemporary American Banking Crisis in Historical Perspective." *Journal of American History* 80, no. 4 (March 1994).

Bernstein, Peter L. *Against the Gods: The Remarkable Story of Risk.* New York: John Wiley and Sons, 1998.

Blustein, Paul. *The Chastening: Inside the Crisis That Rocked the Global Financial System and Humbled the IMF.* New York: PublicAffairs, 2001.

Bombardier, Claire, et al. "Comparison of Upper Gastrointestinal Toxicity of Rofecoxib and Naproxen in Patients with Rheumatoid Arthritis." *New England Journal of Medicine* 343, no. 21 (November 23, 2000).

Bordo, Michael, and Barry Eichengreen. "Is Our Current International Economic Environment Unusually Crisis Prone?" Reserve Bank of Australia Conference on Private Capital Flows, August 1999.

Brams, Steven J. *Game Theory and Politics*. Mineola, N.Y.: Dover, 2004.

Bruce, Victoria. *No Apparent Danger*. New York: HarperCollins, 2001.

Calvo, Guillermo A., and Carmen M. Reinhart. "Capital Flow Reversals, the Exchange Rate Debate, and Dollarization." *Finance & Development* 36, no. 3 (September 1, 1999).

Carroll, John S., Jenny W. Rudolph, and Sachi Hatakenaka. "Organizational Learning from Experience in High-Hazard Industries: Problem Investigations as Off-Line Reflective Practice." MIT Sloan School of Management, Working Paper 4359, (March 2002).

Casti, John L. *Five Golden Rules: Great Theories of 20th Century Mathematics—and Why They Matter*. New York: John Wiley and Sons, 1996.

Cherrington, David Jack. "Book Review: *Whistleblowers: Broken Lives and Organizational Power* by C. Fred Alford." *Administrative Science Quarterly* (June 1, 2002).

Cohen, Jack, and Ian Stewart. *The Collapse of Chaos: Discovering Simplicity in a Complex World*. New York: Penguin, 1995.

Cook, Richard C. Challenger *Revealed: An Insider's Account of How the Reagan Administration Caused the Greatest Tragedy of the Space Age*. New York: Thunder's Mouth Press, 2007.

Cooper, Christopher, and Robert Block. *Disaster: Hurricane Katrina and the Failure of Homeland Security*. New York: Times Books, 2006.

Copeland, Tom, and Vladimir Antikarov. *Real Options: A Practitioner's Guide*. New York: Texere, 2003.

Coy, Peter, and Suzanne Woolley. "Failed Wizards of Wall Street." *BusinessWeek*, September 21, 1998.

Curfman, Gregory D., Stephen Morrissey, and Jeffrey M. Drazen. "Expression of Concern: Bombardier et al., 'Comparison of Upper Gastrointestinal Toxicity of Rofecoxib and Naproxen in Patients with Rheumatoid Arthritis.'" *New England Journal of Medicine* 353, no. 26 (December 29, 2005).

Desai, Padma. "Why Did the Ruble Collapse in August 1998?" *American Economic Review* 90, no. 2 (2000).

Devine, Tom. "Courage Without Martyrdom: The Whistleblower's Survival Guide." Government Accountability Project, www.whistleblower.org, undated.

Diamond, Jared. *Collapse: How Societies Choose to Fail or Succeed.* New York: Penguin, 2005.

Dixon, Norman F. *On the Psychology of Military Incompetence.* London: Pimlico, 1994.

Dong, Bong-Chan Kho, and Rene M. Lee. "U.S. Banks, Crises, and Bailouts: From Mexico to LTCM." *American Economic Review* 90, no. 2 (2000).

Duffy, Michael. "The Rubin Rrescue." *Time,* January 12, 1998.

Dunbar, Nicholas. *Inventing Money: The Story of Long-Term Capital Management and the Legends Behind It.* Chichester, U.K.: John Wiley and Sons, 2000.

Edwards, Franklin R. "Hedge Funds and the Collapse of Long-Term Capital Management." *Journal of Economic Perspectives* 13, no. 2 (1999).

Eichenwald, Kurt. *Conspiracy of Fools: A True Story.* New York: Broadway Books, 2005.

Ellsberg, Daniel. "Risk, Ambiguity, and the Savage Axioms." *Quarterly Journal of Economics* (November 1961).

—————. *Secrets: A Memoir of Vietnam and the Pentagon Papers.* New York: Viking, 2002.

Feynman, Richard P., and Ralph Leighton. *What Do You Care What Other People Think?: Further Adventures of a Curious Character.* New York: Bantam, 1989.

Fox, Craig R., and Amos Tversky. "Ambiguity Aversion and Comparative Ignorance." *Quarterly Journal of Economics* (August 1, 1995).

Friedman, Benjamin M. "Globalization: Stiglitz's Case." *New York Review of Books,* August 15, 2002.

Furman, Jason, et al. "Economic Crises: Evidence and Insights from East Asia." *Brookings Papers on Economic Activity* 1998, no. 2 (1998).

Gerstner, Louis V. *Who Says Elephants Can't Dance: Inside IBM's Historic Turnaround.* New York: Harper Business, 2002.

Gillman, Leonard. "The Car and the Goats." *American Mathematical Monthly* 99, no. 1 (January 1992).

Gladwell, Malcolm. *The Tipping Point: How Little Things Can Make a Big Difference.* Boston: Little, Brown and Co., 2000.

————. "Open Secrets: Dept. of Public Policy." *New Yorker* January 8, 2007.

Gleick, James. *Chaos: Making a New Science.* New York: Penguin, 1988.

Good, I. J. "When Batterer Turns Murderer." *Nature* 375, no. 6532 (1995): 541.

Groopman, Jerome. "What's the Trouble? How Doctors Think." *The New Yorker*, January 29, 2007.

Halberstam, David. *The Reckoning.* New York: William Morrow and Company, 1986.

Haselton, Martie G., and Daniel Nettle. "The Paranoid Optimist: An Integrative Evolutionary Model of Cognitive Biases." Working paper. University of California–Los Angeles and University of Newcastle, April 28, 2005.

Hastie, Reid, and Robyn M. Dawes. *Rational Choice in an Uncertain World: The Psychology of Judgment and Decision Making.* Thousand Oaks, Calif.: Sage, 2001.

Hellmann, Thomas F., Kevin C. Murdock, and Joseph E. Stiglitz. "Liberalization, Moral Hazard in Banking, and Prudential Regulation: Are Capital Requirements Enough?" *American Economic Review* 90, no. 1 (March 1, 2000).

Horton, Richard C. "Vioxx: An Unequal Partnership Between Safety and Efficacy." *Lancet* 364 (October 9, 2004).

————. "Vioxx, the implosion of Merck, and aftershocks at the FDA." *Lancet* 364 (2004).

Howell, William C. "Uncertainty from Internal and External Sources: A Clear Case of Overconfidence." *Journal of Experimental Psychology* (1971).

"How the Bug Can Spread—Emerging Markets." *Economist* 360, no. 8231 (July 21, 2001).

Hoxby, Caroline M., and Ilyana Kuziemko. "Robin Hood and His Not-So-Merry Plan: Capitalization and the Self-Destruction of Texas'

School Finance Equalization Plan." Working paper. Harvard University, Department of Economics, July 1, 2004.

Hull, John C. *Options, Futures, and Other Derivatives.* 5th ed. Upper Saddle River, N.J.: Prentice Hall, 2003.

Janis, Irving. *Victims of Groupthink: A Psychological Study of Foreign-Policy Decisions and Fiascoes.* Boston: Houghton Mifflin, 1972.

Jervis, Robert. *System Effects: Complexity in Political and Social Life.* Princeton, N.J.: Princeton University Press, 1997.

Johnson, Mark E., and Charles C. Watson Jr. "Hurricane Return Period Estimation." Preprint from 10th Symposium on Global Change Studies, American Meteorological Society, April 1999.

—————. "Fitting Statistical Distributions to Data in Hurricane Modeling." Peer-reviewed paper from Auburn University Symposium on Fitting Statistical Distributions to Data, March 5–11, 2006.

Jos, Philip H., Mark E. Tompkins, and Steven W. Hays. "In Praise of Difficult People: A Portrait of the Committed Whistleblower." *Public Administration Review* 49, no. 6 (November 1989).

Kahneman, Daniel, and Amos Tversky, eds. *Choices, Values, and Frames.* Cambridge: Cambridge University Press, 2000.

Keeney, Ralph L. *Value-Focused Thinking: A Path to Creative Decisionmaking.* Cambridge, Mass.: Harvard University Press, 1992.

Keynes, John Maynard. *A Treatise on Probability.* New York: Harper and Row, 1962.

Kreps, David M. *Game Theory and Economic Modeling.* Oxford: Clarendon Press, 1990.

Krumholz, Harlan M., et al. "What Have We Learnt from Vioxx?" *BMJ* 334 (January 2007): 120–23.

Kuhn, Thomas S. *The Structure of Scientific Revolutions.* 3rd ed. Chicago: University of Chicago Press, 1996.

Ladkin, Peter B. "The Crash of AA587: A Guide." RVS Group, University of Bielefeld, Report RVS-RR-04-03, November 18, 2004, www.rvs.uni-bielefeld.de/publications/Reports/CrashOfAA587.pdf.

Langer, Ellen. *Mindfulness.* Cambridge, Mass.: Da Capo Press, 1989.

Laporte, Joan-Ramon. "Els Suposats Avantatges de Celecoxib i Rofecoxib: Frau Científic." *Butlletí Groc* (juliol–setembre 2003).

Latane, Bibb, and John Darley. *The Unresponsive Bystander: Why Doesn't He Help.* New York: Appleton-Century-Crofts, 1970.

Leakey, Richard, and Roger Lewin. *The Sixth Extinction: Biodiversity and Its Survival.* London: Phoenix, 1995.

Lethal, Carol J., William J. Beaker, and Charles M. Brown. Preventing Injuries from Slips, Trips and Falls. University of Florida, Circular 869, 2001.

Levy, Matthys, and Mario Salvadori. *Why Buildings Fall Down: How Structures Fail.* New York: W. W. Norton, 1992.

Lewis, Michael. *Liar's Poker: Rising Through the Wreckage on Wall Street.* New York: W. W. Norton, 1989.

————. *Moneyball: The Art of Winning an Unfair Game.* New York: W. W. Norton, 2003.

————. "In Nature's Casino." *New York Times Magazine*, August 26, 2007.

Loehle, Craig. *Thinking Strategically.* Cambridge: Cambridge University Press, 1996.

Losey, Stephen. "Air Marshal's Firing Prompts Whistleblower Suit." *Federal Times*, November 7, 2006, www.pogo.org/p/x/2004 governmentsecrecy.html#.

Lowenstein, Roger. *When Genius Failed: The Rise and Fall of Long-Term Capital Management.* New York: Random House, 2000.

Luce, R. Duncan, and Howard Raiffa. *Games and Decisions: Introduction and Critical Survey.* New York: Dover, 1957.

Luenberger, David G. *Investment Science.* New York: Oxford University Press, 1998.

Magnuson, Ed. "The Questions Get Tougher." *Time*, March 3, 1986.

Marples, Donald R. *The Social Impact of the Chernobyl Disaster.* New York: St. Martin's Press, 1988.

Martin, Mitchell. "Arbitrator's Ruling Goes Against Accounting Arm: Consultants Win Battle of Andersen." *International Herald Tribune*, August 8, 2000, www.iht.com/articles/2000/08/08/ consult.2.t.php.

Merz, Jon F., and Jonathan P. Caulkins. "Propensity to Abuse—Propensity to Murder?" *Chance* 8, no. 2 (1995).

Mishkin, Barbara. "Whistleblowing in Biomedical Research: Report from a Workshop." *IRB: Ethics and Human Research* 4, no. 2 (February 1982).

Montaigne, Fen, and Stanley Williams. *Surviving Galeras.* Boston: Houghton Mifflin, 2001.

Mun, Johnathan. *Real Options Analysis: Tools and Techniques for Valuing Strategic Investments and Decisions.* Hoboken, N.J.: John Wiley and Sons, 2002.

Palley, Thomas I. "The Fallacy of the Revised Bretton Woods Hypothesis: Why Today's International Financial System Is Unsustainable." *The Levy Economics Institute of Bard College*, Public Policy Brief No. 85, 2006.

Paulos, John A. *Innumeracy: Mathematical Illiteracy and Its Consequences.* New York: Vintage, 1990.

Perrow, Charles. *Normal Accidents: Living with High-Risk Technologies.* Princeton, N.J.: Princeton University Press, 1999.

—————. *The Next Catastrophe: Reducing Our Vulnerabilities to Natural, Industrial, and Terrorist Disasters.* Princeton, N.J.: Princeton University Press, 2007.

Piper, Joan L. *A Chain of Events: The Government Cover-Up of the Black Hawk Incident and the Friendly-Fire Death of Lt. Laura Piper.* Washington, D.C.: Brassey's, 2000.

Radelet, Steven, et al. "The East Asian Financial Crisis: Diagnosis, Remedies, Prospects." *Brookings Papers on Economic Activity* 1998, no. 1 (1998).

Read, Donald. *The Power of News: The History of Reuters.* New York: Oxford University Press, 1992.

Reason, James T. *Managing the Risks of Organizational Accidents.* Aldershot, U.K.: Ashgate, 1997.

Reinhart, Carmen M., Kenneth S. Rogoff, and Miguel A. Savastano. "Addicted to Dollars." *National Bureau of Economic Research*, Working Paper 10015, 2003.

Resnick, Mitchel. *Turtles, Termites, and Traffic Jams: Explorations in Massively Parallel Microworlds.* Cambridge, Mass.: MIT Press, 1998.

Ross, Stephen A., Randolph W. Westerfield, and Jeffrey Jaffe. *Corporate Finance.* 5th ed. Boston: Irwin/McGraw-Hill, 1999.

"Rumpus in Hong Kong," *Economist* 344, no. 8036 (September 27, 1997).

Ruskeepää, Heikki. *Mathematica Navigator: Graphics and Methods of Applied Mathematics.* San Diego: Academic Press, 1999.

Sagan, Scott D. *The Limits of Safety: Organizations, Accidents, and Nuclear Weapons.* Princeton, N.J.: Princeton University Press, 1993.

Salge, Markus, and Peter M. Milling. "Who Is to Blame, the Operator or the Designer? Two Stages of Human Failure in the Chernobyl Accident." *System Dynamics Review* 22, no. 2 (2006).

Schein, Edgar H. *The Corporate Culture Survival Guide.* San Francisco: Jossey-Bass, 1999.

————. *DEC Is Dead, Long Live DEC: The Lasting Legacy of Digital Equipment Corporation.* San Francisco: Berrett-Koehler Publishers, 2003.

————. *Organizational Culture and Leadership.* San Francisco: Jossey-Bass, 2004.

Schelling, Thomas C. *Micromotives and Macrobehavior.* New York: W. W. Norton, 1978.

Scholes, Myron S. "Crisis and Risk Management." *American Economic Review* 90, no. 2 (2000).

Schrage, Michael. *Serious Play: How the World's Best Companies Simulate to Innovate.* Cambridge, Mass.: Harvard Business School Press, 2000.

Senser, Robert A. "The New Global Economy and Developing Countries: Making Openness Work." *Monthly Labor Review* (November 1999).

Slovic, Paul. *The Perception of Risk.* London: Earthscan, 2000.

Snook, Scott A. *Friendly Fire: The Accidental Shootdown of U.S. Black Hawks Over Northern Iraq.* Princeton, N.J.: Princeton University Press, 2000.

"Special Report: At the Risky End of Finance—Credit Derivatives." *Economist* 383, no. 8525 (April 21, 2007).

Starbuck, William H., and Moshe Farjoun, eds. *Organization at the Limit: Lessons from the Columbia Disaster.* Malden, Mass.: Blackwell, 2005.

Sterman, John D. *Business Dynamics: Systems Thinking and Modeling for a Complex World.* Boston: Irwin McGraw-Hill, 2000.

Stewart, Ian. *The Magical Maze: Seeing the World Through Mathematical Eyes.* London: Phoenix, 1997.

Stiglitz, Joseph E. *The Roaring Nineties: A New History of the World's Most Prosperous Decade.* New York: W. W. Norton, 2003.

Sutherland, Stuart. *Irrationality: The Enemy Within.* London: Penguin, 1992.

Talbot, David. "Saving Holland." *Technology Review* (July–August 2007).

Taleb, Nassim N. *Fooled by Randomness: The Hidden Role of Chance in Life and in the Markets.* New York: Thomson/Texere, 2004.

————. *The Black Swan: The Impact of the Highly Improbable.* New York: Random House, 2007.

Texas A&M University. "Negligence and the Professional 'Debate' Over Responsibility for Design: The Kansas City Hyatt Regency Walkways Collapse." Department of Philosophy and Department of Mechanical Engineering, NSF Grant Number DIR-9012252, http://ethics.tamu.edu/ethics/hyatt/hyatt1.htm.

Thomas, W. John. "The Vioxx Story: Would It Have Ended Differently in the European Union?" *American Journal of Law and Medicine* 32, nos. 2–3 (April 1, 2006).

Toffler, Barbara L., and Jennifer Reingold. *Final Accounting: Ambition, Greed, and the Fall of Arthur Andersen.* New York: Broadway Books, 2003.

Topol, Eric J. "Failing the Public Health—Rofecoxib, Merck, and the FDA." *New England Journal of Medicine* 351, no. 17 (October 21, 2004).

Trainor, Joseph. "Satellite Failure Causes Communications Chaos." *UFO RoundUp* 3, no. 21 (May 24, 1998), www.ufoinfo.com/roundup/v03/rnd03_21.shtml.

Trigeorgis, Lenos. *Real Options: Managerial Flexibility and Strategy in Resource Allocation.* Cambridge, Mass.: MIT Press, 1996.

Trott, Michael. *The Mathematica Guidebooks.* 4 vols. New York: Springer, 2004, 2006.

Tufte, Edward R. *Visual Explanations: Images and Quantities, Evidence and Narrative.* Cheshire, Conn.: Graphics Press, 1997.

————. *The Cognitive Style of Powerpoint.* Cheshire, Conn.: Graphics Press, 2003.

Tversky, Amos, and Daniel Kahneman. "Extensional Versus Intuitive Reasoning: The Conjunction Fallacy in Probability Judgment." *Psychological Review* 90, no. 4 (October 1983).

Vaughan, Diane. *The* Challenger *Launch Decision: Risky Technology, Culture, and Deviance at NASA.* Chicago: University of Chicago Press, 1996.

Verzani, John. *Using R for Introductory Statistics.* Boca Raton, Fla.: Chapman and Hall/CRC, 2005.

Waas, Murray. *United States v. I. Lewis Libby.* New York: Sterling Publishing, 2007.

Waldrop, M. M. *Complexity.* New York: Touchstone, 1992.

Weick, Karl E., and Kathleen M. Sutcliffe. *Managing the Unexpected: Assuring High Performance in an Age of Complexity.* San Francisco: Jossey-Bass, 2001.

Wilensky, Uri. "NetLogo Segregation Model." Center for Connected Learning and Computer-Based Modeling, Northwestern University, Evanston, Ill., http://ccl.northwestern.edu/netlogo/models/Segregation, 1998.

Wink, Diane M. "The 'Catch 22' of Whistleblowing." *American Journal of Nursing* 84, no. 1 (January 1984).

Wolfe, Sidney M. "Statement Before the Institute of Medicine Committee Assessing the U.S. Drug Safety System." HRG Publication #1759, January 19, 2006, www.citizen.org.

————. "The 100th Anniversary of the FDA: The Sleeping Watchdog Whose Master Is Increasingly the Regulated Industries." June 27, 2006, http://cspinet.org/new/pdf/statement_of_sidney_wolfe__md.pdf.

Zeisel, Hans. *Say It with Figures.* 6th ed. New York: Springer-Verlag, 1985.

Zeisel, Hans, and David Kaye. *Prove It with Figures: Empirical Methods in Law and Litigation.* New York: Springer-Verlag, 1997.

Selected Newspaper Articles

Atlas, Riva D. "Trying to Put Some Reins on Derivatives." *New York Times*, September 16, 2005.

Belli, Anne. "Panel Criticizes BP Safety Efforts." *Houston Chronicle*, January 16, 2007.

Berenson, Alex. "For Merck Chief, Credibility at the Capitol." *New York Times*, November 19, 2004.

————. "Analysts See Merck Victory in Vioxx Deal. *New York Times*, November 10, 2007.

Bowman, Lee. "Blame Man, Not Sun, for Pager Satellite Failure." *Pittsburgh Post-Gazette*, April 24, 1999.

Cockburn, Alexander. "Crisis Is Over and the Banks Won Big." *Los Angeles Times*, August 17, 1992.

Eaton, Leslie. "Gulf Hits Snags in Rebuilding Public Works." *New York Times*, March 31, 2007.

"Editorial: Reliable Info Key to Escaping Tsunami." *Daily Yomiuri*, November 17, 2006, www.yomiuri.co.jp.

Eichenwald, Kurt. "Enron's Many Strands: The Overview—Andersen Trial Yields Evidence in Enron's Fall." *New York Times*, June 17, 2002.

"Few Heed Order to Flee After Tsunami Warning." *Daily Yomiuri*, November 17, 2006, www.yomiuri.co.jp.

"46 Killed in Hyatt Collapse as Tea Dance Turns to Terror." *Kansas City Times*, July 18, 1981.

Glanz, James, and John Schwartz. "Dogged Engineers' Effort to Assess Shuttle Damage." *New York Times*, September 26, 2003.

Harris, Gardiner. "Drug-Safety Reviewer Says F.D.A. Delayed Vioxx Study." *New York Times*, November 4, 2004.

————. "At FDA, Strong Drug Ties and Less Monitoring." *New York Times*, December 6, 2004.

————. "Drug Regulators Are Trying to Quash Study, Senator Says." *New York Times*, February 12, 2005.

Hope, Christopher. "BP Blames Death Blast on Its Own Procedures." *Daily Telegraph* (London), December 10, 2005.

Kramer, Andrew E., and Heather Timmons. "After Setbacks, BP May Be Forced to Give Up Some Control of Joint Venture in Russia." *New York Times*, January 16, 2007.

Krugman, Paul. "Drugs, Devices and Doctors." *New York Times*, December 16, 2005.

Liptak, Adam. "Study of Wrongful Convictions Raises Questions Beyond DNA." *New York Times*, July 23, 2007.

McNeil, Donald G. Jr. "In a Daylong Drill, an Agency Tries to Prepare for a Real Outbreak of Avian Flu." *New York Times*, February 1, 2007.

McNulty, Sheila. "A Corroded Culture? How Accidents in Alaska Forced BP on to the Defensive." *Financial Times*, December 18, 2006.

————. "Blowdown: How Faults at BP Led to One of America's Worst Industrial Disasters." *Financial Times*, December 19, 2006.

Mydans, Seth. "After String of Disasters, Indonesians Ask: Why Us?" *New York Times*, February 11, 2007.

Norris, Floyd. "Giving Credit Where Blame Might Be Due." *New York Times*, January 25, 1998.

Postrel, Virginia. "A Texas Experiment That Shifts Money from Rich to Poor School Districts Is Turning into a Major Policy Disaster." *New York Times*, October 7, 2004.

Rashbaum, William K., and William Neuman. "PATH Tunnels Seen as Fragile in Bomb Attack." *New York Times*, December 22, 2006.

Revkin, Andrew C. "World Briefing Asia: Japan: Tiny Tsunamis After Big Quake." *New York Times*, November 16, 2006.

Smith, R. Jeffrey, and Jeffrey H. Birnbaum. "Drug Bill Demonstrates Lobby's Pull: Democrats Feared Industry Would Stall Bigger Changes." *Washington Post*, January 12, 2007.

Timmons, Heather. "Chief's Departure Ignites Criticism of BP's Structure and Environmental Policies." *New York Times*, January 16, 2007.

————. "Report Faults BP for Safety Procedures." *New York Times*, January 16, 2007.

Verhovek, Sam Howe, and Steven Greenhouse. "National Guard Is Called to Quell Trade-Talk Protests." *New York Times*, December 1, 1999.

Von Zielbauer, Paul. "Soldier Who Testified on Killings Says He Feared for His Life." *New York Times*, August 8, 2006.

Radio and Television Programs

ABC News *Prime Time Live* [transcript], American Broadcasting Company, July 7, 2003.

BBC Horizon, "Volcano Hell," 2001, www.bbc.co.uk/science/horizon/2001/volcanohell.shtml.

Gerstein, Marc S. "Mojavia: In Pursuit of Agility." MGA Media, 1997.

PBS Frontline. "The Storm." 2006, www.pbs.org/wgbh/pages/frontline/storm/view.

PBS Newshour with Jim Lehrer. "Thailand Rebuilds After the Tsunami." Transcript, November 21, 2005, www.pbs.org/newshour/bb/asia/july-dec05/tsunami_11-21.html.

PBS NOVA. "Volcano's Deadly Warning." November 12, 2002, www.pbs.org/wgbh/nova/volcano/chouet.html.

Prakash, Snigdha. "Documents Suggest Merck Tried to Censor Vioxx Critics." NPR: *All Things Considered*, June 9, 2005.

————. "Merck Attempted to Quash Vioxx Criticism." NPR: *Morning Edition*, June 10, 2005.

Prakash, Snigdha, and Vikki Valentine. "Timeline: The Rise and Fall of Vioxx." National Public Radio, www.npr.org/templates/story/story.php?storyId=5470430.

ABOUT THE AUTHORS

Marc Gerstein holds a master's degree and Ph.D. in Management from the Sloan School of Management, MIT. He has held positions as an adjunct full professor of management at the Columbia Business School and as a visiting scholar at Sloan. He currently heads Marc Gerstein Associates, Ltd. (mgalimited.net), a management consulting firm, and he is president of The Organization Design Forum, a professional organization. Gerstein is the author of *The Technology Connection: Strategy and Change in the Information Age* (Addison-Wesley, 1987), and co-author of *Organizational Architecture: Designs for Changing Organizations* (Jossey-Bass, 1992). His writing on strategy and organizational dynamics has been published by the *Sloan Management Review*, the *Journal of Business Strategy, Stanford University*, and others.

Michael Ellsberg is a professional developmental editor who did extensive work on the national best-seller *Secrets: A Memoir of Vietnam and the Pentagon Papers* (Viking, 2002), by his father, Daniel Ellsberg.

Daniel Ellsberg received his Ph.D. in economics from Harvard in 1962. His research leading up to his doctoral dissertation, *Risk, Ambiguity and Decision*, is considered a landmark in the development of decision theory. In 1959, he became a strategic analyst at the RAND Corporation, and consultant to the Defense Department and the White House, specializing in problems of the command and control of nuclear weapons, nuclear war plans, and crisis decision-making. He joined the Defense Department in 1964 as special assistant to Assistant Secretary of Defense (International Security Affairs) John McNaughton, working on Vietnam. He transferred to the State Department in 1965 to serve two years at the U.S. embassy in Saigon, evaluating pacification on the front lines.

On return to the RAND Corporation in 1967, he worked on the Top Secret McNamara study of U.S. decision-making in Vietnam, 1945–68, which later came to be known as the Pentagon Papers. In 1969, he photocopied the seven-thousand-page study and gave it to the Senate Foreign Relations Committee; in 1971 he gave it to the *New York Times*, the *Washington Post,* and seventeen other newspapers. His trial, on twelve felony counts posing a possible sentence of 115 years, was dismissed in 1973 on grounds of governmental misconduct against him, which led to the convictions of several White House aides and figured in the impeachment proceedings against President Nixon.

Since the end of the Vietnam War, he has been a lecturer, writer, and activist on the dangers of the nuclear era, government wrong-doing, and the need for patriotic whistle-blowing.

INDEX

Index

Index

Index

Index

Index